CRANFORD PUBLIC LIBRARY N.J.

3 9520 00076 9242

blic Library
. J. 07016

W9-ABX-657

CALL ME ROGER

CALL ME ROGER

ALBERT LEE

CB
CONTEMPORARY
BOOKS
CHICAGO · NEW YORK

Library of Congress Cataloging-in-Publication Data

Lee, Albert, 1942–
    Call me Roger : the story of how Roger Smith, chairman of General
Motors, transformed the industry leader into a fallen giant / Albert
Lee.
        p.   cm.
    ISBN 0-8092-4630-9 : $19.95
    1. Smith, Roger B., 1925–   . 2. Businessmen—United States—
Biography. 3. General Motors Corporation—History. 4. Automobile
industry and trade—United States—History. I. Title.
HD9710.U52S5455   1988
338.7′6292′0924—dc19
    [B]   87-35223
                                                        CIP

An excerpt originally appeared in *Playboy* magazine.

Copyright © 1988 by Albert Lee
All rights reserved
Published by Contemporary Books, Inc.
180 North Michigan Avenue, Chicago, Illinois 60601
Manufactured in the United States of America
Library of Congress Catalog Card Number: 87-35223
International Standard Book Number: 0-8092-4630-9

Published simultaneously in Canada by Beaverbooks, Ltd.
195 Allstate Parkway, Valleywood Business Park
Markham, Ontario L3R 4T8 Canada

This book is dedicated to the real General Motors—the people in the plants, offices, and dealerships, and the suppliers who are GM's extended family.

Contents

Acknowledgments

S pecial thanks go to Robert L. Fenton, literary agent, lawyer, and friend; and to Harvey Plotnick and Bernard Shir-Cliff of Contemporary Books, two of the most professional men I have had the honor to work with in twenty-two years of publishing. Douglas Fraser, former UAW president and one of the true statesmen of labor in America, contributed his firsthand experience and depth of insights. David Cole, director of the Office for the Study of Automotive Transportation, was a great help in his balanced appraisal of the industry.

I also would like to acknowledge the major contributions of dozens of individuals inside of General Motors and recent retirees (forced and otherwise) who contributed to this book. Discretion does not allow me to name them here, but I appreciate their candid insights and owe them a great debt.

CALL ME
ROGER

Introduction

D on't write the book on me until I've been gone at least ten years," Roger Smith often has said. "It's too early. You've got to wait and see." In a way, he is right. The scope of this man's vision is so all-encompassing, the magnitude of his changes of such a monumental scale, that it will probably take several years beyond his retirement in 1990 before the full impact of this GM chairman's ten-year tenure can be finally assessed. To dismantle every tradition of the largest and most tradition-bound of corporations, and to replace every process, plant, and product, is far too grandiose an effort to complete in one decade. Roger's goal has been nothing short of creating a new corporation, the first 21st-century corporation, as he—and sometimes he alone—has envisioned it.

Yet America can't wait. American industry—and the high standard of living inspired by it—has little time left to become world competitive. Already dozens of fundamental industries have fallen to high-quality, low-cost foreign manufacturers. The very best thinking is that the U.S. manufacturers have from three to five years to either become world competitive or accept second-class industrial citizenship. As Roger puts it, "There are no longer any sheltered waters, safe from the gunboats of world competition."

The challenge is clearly one of leadership. Foreign manufacturers have proven that they can produce the highest-quality goods, ship them thousands of miles, and excluding the artificial exchange rates, still sell them for from 25 to 30 percent below U.S. costs. And many foreign manufacturers have established plants in North America—utilizing American union workers and suppliers—and still outperform most homegrown companies. The difference is leadership alone.

Roger Smith's story is a tragedy of leadership. It is an American tragedy about a man gifted with intelligence, determination, and energy, who had at his disposal the deepest pockets of wealth and human resources of any industrialist in world history, yet was unable—or unwilling—to make the transition to new ways of managing people. Far from motivating and inspiring his more than three-quarters of a million employees, Roger polarized factions within his vast empire and supplanted newfound cooperation with confrontation. As one of his senior executives told me, "The tragedy is that Roger might be right. He is without any doubt the boldest strategist and planner in General Motors history, yet, without the ability to lead, execution is impossible."

There is a story about a little boy who was frightened coming aboard the *Queen Mary*. He asked the first sailor he saw, "Sir, do ships this big sink very often?" "No," the sailor said, "only once." General Motors is the largest corporate vessel in the world—the lifeboat for some three million employees, dealers, and suppliers. Because of the actions of a single man, this massive corporation will either sink into mediocrity during the next few years or, as Roger envisions it, be the icebreaker for a new form of world industry. His actions seem so final that there can be no in between.

On a personal note, when an executive speech writer gives up the ghost to do an unauthorized biography about the boss, you can expect the resulting purple prose to taste of sour grapes. Or if the story cloys, you can bet there is a plum of a payoff involved. Neither applies here.

The truth is that after 20-plus years of book and magazine writing, I became a GM speech writer by chance. I had no intention at the time of writing an exposé. Freelance speech writing had always been a quick, and incredibly effortless, way of picking up pocket money while I labored on headier stuff. When I joined GM, first as science writer in the campuslike GM Research Laboratories and shortly thereafter moving to executive speech writer at GM's world headquarters, I became caught up in what was, as I wrote at the time, "the greatest renaissance of any corporation in peacetime history." From the factory floor to the immaculate laboratories to the field sales office, there was a dynamic tension developing, a readiness to change and meet the challenges of world competition. It was like the excitement, the contagious hype, that develops in the locker room just before the big game. Yet in the actual game the coach made so many decisions that confused and contradicted the avowed goals that he has literally taken the heart out of most of the players and thrown the outcome into question.

For 20 years, since I wrote a book about Henry Ford, I have been a student of management styles (as you'll see in this book, Peter Drucker, the founder of the science of management, is my guru). I also wrote motivational materials for Sandy Corporation, the GM supplier that recently was awarded all of GM's dealer training business. At GM, I became fascinated with the entrepreneurial spirit that Roger expounded yet was unable to infuse into the vast GM empire. The failure, I am fundamentally convinced, is due almost exclusively to his personal management style. If style is the man, as Seneca said, it was abundantly clear that GM's renaissance was in trouble.

For nearly three years I was an outside observer inside the corporation. From my first day at GM, no one with any sense expected me to stay. I simply wasn't a corporate type. I had a predilection for colored shirts, wore academic elbow-patched jackets, and smoked a corncob pipe. I had unconventional habits, writing sans shoes and tie and at odd hours, all of which put me in political limbo or, in the GM vernacular, marked me as a (heaven forbid) "non-team player." Yet GM treated me well. In less than three years with the company I received four raises and promotions, and my boss was rummaging about for yet another raise when I departed. While pressure to conform is present in any institutional setting, my experience with GM revealed a tolerance for nonconformity as long as it was attached to a modicum of talent, and the individual accepted a lunatic fringe status. I found bold, innovative people on virtually every staff. Far from the consistent smokestack grey expected, I encountered a rich tapestry of colorful characters and varied perspectives.

It is precisely because of my tremendous respect for GM people that I felt compelled to tell Roger's story. Of the hundreds of people I met within General Motors, there was not a single man or woman who did not want to do an outstanding job. All of them wanted to point to their contributions with pride, to show the products of their labors to their children and friends. Instead, they have been largely frustrated by leadership that they do not trust and that does not trust them. The difference—*all* of the difference—lies in respect for equality of sacrifice and trust in general and participative leadership. As Walt Whitman said, "There is to me something profoundly affecting in large masses of men following the lead of those who do not believe in men."

One question should be answered at the outset. Did Roger Smith and General Motors cooperate in this book's development? The answer is "no" and "yes" and "sort of." Or, to paraphrase from Chevy Chase, "They did, but they didn't enjoy it."

The initial response, when I told my boss, GM vice president of public relations Jack McNulty, that I was going to write a book about Roger, was "No way are we going to cooperate on this." Jack said he had already agreed to cooperate with the well-known and highly respected financial analyst Maryann Keller, who planned to do a history of General Motors in the 1980s. Maryann's book, Jack said, would be "responsible." Responsible, in his lexicon, meaning that she had agreed to submit a 75-page outline for GM public relations' approval before any interviews would be arranged. I knew enough about Maryann, and had enough respect for her integrity, to know that Jack was probably operating under a misconception about how gentle the lady would be. In fact, I had interviewed some of the same people she had, and they told me Maryann was not in GM's pocket, as Jack implied. Still, Jack was convinced that she was "a friend," while I, on the other hand, was breaking the rules.

A good speech writer, like a good politician, once bought, is supposed to stay bought. As speech writer for GM's president, for the vice chairman, for several executive committee members, and occasionally for the chairman himself, I simply knew too much. That much was true. I had complete and ready access to every department and operation in General Motors. I had only to drop the name of the person I was writing for to receive the candid story on any issue or event. An executive in any other position, say a vice president of personnel or purchasing, would have a much narrower view of the corporation and more limited entrée to top executives. Jack considered me such a threat, in fact, that he did the expected and had the door locks changed the day after I left and sent a note to security guards telling them I was "terminated" and access was to be barred. Next he had a director call everyone he thought I might know in General Motors to warn them against any cooperation with me. But the gate was barred after the horse had bolted.

At this point, I could have used my extensive notes and recollections to write the book, but I chose to go further to broaden the perspective. I had some strong opinions based on my experience, and I needed them validated or challenged. So I wrote to more than 300 people I had met in General Motors—from executives to union leaders and clerks in plants. To open the door wider, I placed ads in the major Detroit and southeastern Michigan newspapers. The business and personal column ads simply read: "ROGER B. SMITH. GM Chairman is the subject of major book. Seek firsthand recollections about the man and his decisions. Write in absolute confidence. Box . . . ."

The letters and ads got Roger's attention. Tom Adams, retired chairman of Campbell Ewald, GM's largest and longest standing advertising agency, explained, "You have to understand that GM has never had public relations. They simply have a corporate defense mechanism. They are not out to get good news, but to avoid the bad." Yet the letters and ads made it clear that I wasn't going to go away. So Roger, through his agent Jack McNulty, offered to cooperate on the book. Jack assigned his right-hand director and heir apparent Bill Quigley to "assist me." The morning I met with Quigley I learned what "assist" meant. I presented him with a list of individuals known for their candor whom I wanted to interview (some of them, reinterview). Quigley presented me with his list, containing mostly Roger's family and lifelong friends. He agreed to contact the people on my list but later came up with a plethora of excuses for not setting up appointments with the more outspoken individuals from my list. He was, however, able to contact every person on his list without difficulty.

Still, I conducted many of the "arranged" interviews from Quigley's (read Roger's) testimonial list. I'm glad I did, for I was able to see more of the private side of Roger that is off-limits to even his closest corporate associates. And I had the opportunity to interview Roger specifically on the issues of greatest concern about his management.

With nearly three years of inside experience, numerous off-the-record responses and interviews from my letters and ads, and Roger's arranged testimonials, this book is thoroughly grounded in personal insights from individuals directly involved and critically concerned with Roger Smith's chairmanship. Since many GM insiders spoke only on condition that their names not appear in print, I will identify them generically—a vice president, a board member, a plant manager, a secretary, etc.—which is as far as confidentiality allows. I have no desire to cut short the careers of GM professionals who were courageous enough to speak the truth as they saw it. They spoke out of concern for the survival of one of the oldest and most respected corporate institutions in America. This book shares that concern.

1
Would-Be Prophet

"I'm sailing our own ship."

Roger Smith

C
all me Roger," the slight man with the squeaky voice said, extending his hand.

I was astonished. Not astonished that the most powerful industrialist in the world would speak to me at a press reception. Not even astounded that he would suggest I use his first name. Detroit, after all, is a factory town—a town with grease under its fingernails and the distinct smell of machine oil on its breath. Most auto executives (Roger not among them) are proud of the fact that they are only one generation beyond wielding rivet guns and punching time clocks. It's a shirt-sleeve town with executives named Don and Lee and Roger. It's the common touch.

No, what astonished me was that Roger obviously did not know who I was—even though I had written the speech he would soon deliver and several other speeches for him before this one, even though I'd met him many times before and attended numerous meetings where he had been present, even though I had shared an eight-passenger corporate jet with him for thousands of miles. So here I was holding his hand, wondering how I might tell him diplomatically that I was on his staff.

"Roger, I've checked the microphone height, and I have an extra copy of your speech here if you need it," I said. His near-albino skin flushed, and he let go of my hand as if it contained a joy buzzer. Roger quickly turned and was off to meet people who mattered.

Perhaps I shouldn't have been astonished. After all, the chief executive of a mammoth corporation has more important things to do than to remember what his speech writer looks like. The power of the position was awe-inspiring. General Motors is the largest corporation in the world—with more people than the U.S. Navy and Marine Corps combined and with more assets than all but two dozen of the largest nations of the world. GM has three hundred plants or facilities from Australia to Zaire and makes products from microchips to guided missiles. One of every five cars on the planet was built by General Motors, and so was the only car parked on the surface of the moon. Domestically, GM's closest competitor had less than half its assets. Besides more than three-quarters of a million direct employees, there were another one-half million dealership people and a million and a half or so supplier employees who owed their livelihoods to "Mother Motors," the nickname for the giant. In a typical year GM consumed about 25 percent of all the steel made in America, 22 percent of all the synthetic rubber, and around 10 percent of all the aluminum. Besides cars, the GM empire produced the vast majority of all diesel locomotives and more computers than anyone else on earth and had the largest financial operation outside of the U.S. government. With revenues exceeding $100 billion in a good year, GM had the deepest pockets in industry. And it had an unequaled history of fiscal respectability. Since 1918, for example, GM has never missed paying a dividend—272 consecutive cash dividends, a performance unmatched in the turbulent auto industry. As the chairman of the board *and* chief executive officer of all of this, Roger might not be expected to remember details like who wrote the speech he was about to deliver.

And perhaps I shouldn't have been surprised that he didn't recognize me, since on none of the occasions when I had met him previously had he ever allowed direct eye contact. I re-

membered the first time we met in his 14th-floor office. Ben
Thompson, my boss and Roger's former regular speech writer,
felt compelled to warn me. "If Roger is rude or cold, don't
take it personally," Ben said. "He's like that with everyone."

Ben, a professional Irishman and storyteller of some repute,
underscored his warning by recounting the first time he'd
written for Roger:

"I went up to see Roger along with Jack," he said, referring
to our mutual boss, public relations vice president John
McNulty. "I sat directly in front of Roger's desk, and Jack sat
off to one side. Even though the only subject was my speech
draft, Roger turned sideways in his chair to face Jack. Never
once did that man address me directly. It was 'Tell Ben I don't
like this paragraph' and 'Ask Ben to redo this part' and 'Can
Ben get me a revised copy tonight?' And me sitting right in
front of him as big as life."

I laughed at Ben's story; then he and I went up to the 14th
floor. Around the company, people refer to the massive GM
world headquarters building simply as "The Building" and automatically know when you say "14th floor" you mean the
very pinnacle of executive row. You have to go through two
bulletproof glass doors, the first with an armed security guard,
the second protected by a sweet British lady named Hilda,
who could probably be every bit as fierce as the guard if an
unfamiliar face tried to get past her. But she knew us both and
buzzed us through. Considering that the average executive on
the 14th floor pulls down anywhere from several hundred
thousand to two million dollars a year, the environment is
clearly underwhelming. The walnut-paneled halls are dotted
with paintings, conservative seascapes and pastoral scenes
sans people, purchased as much for investment as aesthetics.
Roger's outer office is about the size of a three-car garage and
holds two secretaries whose desks would make most chief
executives swoon. These ladies, like the guard and Hilda, are
as protective as the three-headed dog at the gates of hell. Mary
Kiloustian, Roger's top secretary, thinks nothing of scowling
at a vice president for being a few minutes early and sending
him back to the outer waiting area to cool his heels and kibitz
clumsily with Hilda.

Ben and I arrived on time. We entered. The inner office was large but as unimpressive as the hallway. Roger was hunched over papers on his desk. He looked even smaller than his five-feet, eight-inches behind the acre of mahogany. His hair was the color of pink champagne and wavy. (It never had been carrot red as the papers reported.) I particularly remember his hair because Roger kept his head down and his nose in the papers for some time after we were seated. Why waste time with amenities?

I sat in front of Roger's desk, Ben to one side. Roger eventually looked up. His skin was clearer than usual. Roger's nearly pigmentless skin varied from a deathly pallor on good days to bright swatches of red rash on bad days. Roger turned sideways in his leather chair and addressed Ben about my speech draft: "Tell Al Lee to check his numbers on this production point. . . . Ask Al Lee to redo that graph. . . . Can Al Lee find a different joke here, or maybe leave it out?"

As they say, it was *déjà vu* all over again.

I finally broke in by handing him a memo: "Roger, the news department says you don't want to see any more press on Saturn. They say you said it was getting too much visibility." Roger exploded, crumpled the paper, and hurled it to the floor. "That's what's wrong with this place," he yelled at Ben. "No communication. I didn't say that. You tell Al Lee to include the reference to Saturn." In an instant, his rage was gone, and his eyes returned to the papers on his desk as if we were no longer present, which, I was later to learn, was his quaint way of saying "good day" to underlings.

This is the Roger Smith whom a *Detroit News* reporter once aptly described as "brilliance unimpeded by humanity." Roger is brilliant, if not a genius, in the financial arena, a grand master at strategic planning. Blessed with boundless energy, he puts more effort into his 7:00 A.M. to 6:00 P.M. day than any three executives by budgeting every second as if each precious moment were the difference between profit and loss. Says one vice president: "I've never met a man who is more task oriented and more indifferent to the human side of the job. He long ago lost 'please' and 'thank you' from his active vocabulary." Roger allows himself temper tantrums, absolutely devastating the uninitiated, and he has been known to stomp out of important committee meetings when the facts did not please him or were not presented in rapid enough order. He speaks in half sentences, assuming full background knowledge by everyone on every subject. He is uncomfortable in public settings, nervously yanking on an ear or adjusting his glasses. At the podium he reads his script without hesitation and without emphasis. If he does stress a multisyllabic word, the emphasis is often on the wrong syllable. Roger is impervious to his audiences, never giving them a chance to gasp at a good line or laugh at a light one. Always onward.

In his office, Roger dispatches notes with the same machine-gun rapidity, so rushed that he occasionally leaves out words or misspells obvious ones, such as spelling *sure* "shur." Roger likes to slip in his own bits of dry humor but will not tolerate anyone else's kidding around. When he removes his glasses, a nervous habit, holding eye contact is nearly impossible, as he has a weak eye that wanders—oddly appropriate, since the windows to this man's soul seem always to be open to more than one horizon at any given moment. One eye wanders ahead to the next item on his agenda. Roger is a man intent on getting on with it, no matter what the "it" on the agenda happens to be.

Within the business press and among industry watchers there is general confusion about who the man actually is. He has been called "visionary" and "the innovator of the age" and has been credited as the one man intent on saving jobs for America. Some of the same journalists have at other times called him "a bumbler" and "a tragic figure." The *Gallagher Report*, for example, rated him among the nation's Ten Worst Executives in America one year, then among the Ten Best Executives the next, then back to the Ten Worst Executives the year after. Roger becomes annoyed with these machinations, yet seems generally impervious to both praise and criticism. "He's not a brooder," his wife, Barbara, says. "He's a doer." Roger simply doesn't have the time to fret for long about public opinion.

Employee morale receives even less consideration. Developed as he was in the rarefied environment of an elite corps of self-motivated men, Roger sees no reason to encourage, cajole, mollify, or motivate. He mandates events that disrupt hundreds of thousands of lives, then appears genuinely surprised when these people do not readily march on command. Douglas Fraser, former United Auto Workers president and currently a university professor, says: "Roger thinks that everyone behaves, or should behave, like him. If that were true, he'd get everything he wanted done. But it isn't true. He's an unusual man who just doesn't understand people."

The endless string of actions and pronouncements during his long tenure at the top has given him the image among hourly and salaried ranks alike of being insensitive and unfeeling. He has made such amazing public relations blunders as giving himself and his top executives massive bonuses at the same time he announced no profit sharing, no merit pay, and demanded that the rest of his employees make major concessions to keep their jobs. Then there was the time he announced outsourcing work to Mexico days before his greatest labor ally came up for union election. Then there was the corporate reorganization that turned GM into a Chinese fire drill to "push authority down in the ranks," but he later took the decision-making authorizations back and scolded his executives like children, saying, "When you can show me you can handle the responsibility you've been given, then I might give you more." And there is more, much more. Even one of his closest and most loyal work associates says: "If Roger had purposely set out to destroy all morale in what once was the most confident and secure company going, he couldn't have done a better job."

Perhaps the most devastating chapter of Roger's chairmanship, and the one most revealing about the man's limitations in understanding the nature of leadership, is the Ross Perot affair. Roger anxiously sought to buy Ross's Texas-based computer services company, Electronic Data Systems (EDS) even though his own financial people were initially against it. He was enamored with the entrepreneurial spirit Perot had infused into EDS and equally infatuated with the folk hero founder. Perot became a legend when he rescued two of his employees from an Iranian jail while President Carter's own attempt at a rescue mission was a dismal failure. He built his company through charismatic leadership, giving his employees low wages, long hours, herculean assignments, and only the unwritten promise that Ross would reward them. While the two men had much in common, the difference in their styles was apparent—Ross demonstrative and philanthropic, Roger private and parsimonious. Roger's ancestor signed the Magna Carta. Ross bought an original copy of the Magna Carta and loaned the historic document to the National Archives.

The much publicized—and mostly misunderstood—EDS debacle reveals the shallowness of Roger's perception of human nature. He bought EDS at an inflated price and with a stock plan that provided the Texas company with an incentive to overcharge General Motors. He took 13,800 EDS people and merged them with a culture of 800,000 and fully expected the smaller culture to pervade GM. He reneged on contractual promises and was surprised when Perot began tearing GM apart in public. Then, at a low point in GM fortunes, he bought out Ross at twice his stock's market value and with a ridiculous buyout agreement that left loopholes large enough for the majority of EDS people to walk through and back to Ross in mid-1988. When EDS's most dynamic people leave, as they probably will, the value of the $2.55 billion EDS purchase will vaporize. During the entire episode, what was more incredible is that Ross, from his distant Dallas base, inspired greater admiration and enthusiasm than Roger did in GM and in Detroit.

Traditionally, there has been a clear reverence for the chief executive officer at General Motors, a quiet respect for authority in this semimilitary hierarchy. Not with Roger in the chair. "People just can't relate to him," a public relations director admits. "No one believes he gives a damn about anyone but himself and his bonus buddies," a Flint foreman says. In every corridor and locker room throughout the vast GM empire, jokes about Roger abound. Just prior to my departure an all-occasion card was passed to me on the 14th floor. It said,

When things go wrong as they usually will,
and your daily road seems all uphill,

when funds are low and debts are high,
when you try to smile but can only cry,
and you really feel you'd like to quit—
don't come to me, I don't give a shit!

and it was signed Roger Smith. An even sicker card was circulated within the public relations staff. It was a picture of Roger and had "AIDS" in large letters, then, in smaller type, "Acquired Income Deficiency Syndrome. If you work at GM, you've been screwed by this man [picture of Roger] and probably have the disease."

Jerk, right? Not really—at least, not completely. For the great irony of the man is that Roger is more than capable of expressing great warmth and sensitivity in his private life or when he chooses to impress someone who matters to him. In these cases it's like watching a master switch thrown, and the light comes on in his eyes. "Sometimes, it's like watching a wife beater at home be 'mister nice guy' in public—only in reverse," a public relations man said.

"Roger is a gentle, unassuming, boyish man who always puts people at ease and never throws his weight around," says Eppie Lederer, better known by her syndicated column name, Ann Landers. Eppie considers herself a close friend of Roger and his family and has made her fortune making quick appraisals of character. "Some people have a veneer that makes it hard to know them," she says. "Not Roger. He's open to everyone." Eppie recounts the story of how she mentioned to Roger that she was frustrated, having shopped for a very specific model and color Cadillac. She knew what she wanted, but couldn't find the car at any Chicago dealership. Roger interrupted his work and took down the details. "He called all over the country and found me the car I wanted that same day," she says [an $80,000-a-year PR person did the calling]. "Roger is a very thoughtful guy."

Another friend of 30-plus years says: "I've never known Roger to as much as raise his voice or say an unkind word about anyone." For another friend, Roger interrupted a business trip to Germany with a 12-hour flight to New York and back, just to spend half an hour at the wedding of his friend's daughter. He is also a prime candidate for family man of the year. "I've never seen a more devoted husband or father," another friend says. "You should see the way he relates to his four kids. I know it sounds corny in this day and age, but I've got to tell you, it's a genuinely touching family scene."

A typical story of Roger's personal life comes from a neighbor: "I was out one morning in my bathrobe, carrying a garbage bag out to the street. It broke open, spewing the contents all over the lawn," she says. "A Cadillac limousine stopped in the street, and a well-dressed man got out and helped me pick up the garbage. He seemed embarrassed when I thanked him. He didn't say who he was, but I knew he lived up the street and that he was the chairman of General Motors, probably on his way to some important meeting."

Even inside of GM Roger occasionally shows sensitivity. Recently, he paused in the hallway to speak to Judy Ferguson. Judy is the secretary for the public relations vice president and therefore an important person (secretaries in industry have the same status as their bosses, much as corporate wives do). Roger asked if she still was "throwing pots." "That had to come from a brief conversation I had with Mr. Smith 10 years ago when he was on the 12th floor," she says. "I couldn't believe that he had actually remembered." Such anecdotes from his work life, however, are rare enough to be precious gems. For the two Rogers are normally mutually exclusive. Those who know him personally are not permitted access to his professional life, and the many who work with him rarely are allowed to glimpse his personal side. When you describe the Mr. Hyde to a friend of Dr. Jekyll, you get a response like that of Allen Parrish, retired vice president of TRW, Inc., and a longtime family friend: "I can't believe anything negative about Roger. He's a real gentleman all of the time. He's too big to be small." And, as Lederer says, "There's nothing hidden. What you see is what you get with Roger."

When I asked Roger why there appear to be two of him, he simply said: "There is nothing surprising about it. There are two different things I do. I work and I play. When I work, I work."

It may not seem that it should matter a great deal how one

businessman relates to people. In another time and place Roger's persona might simply be accepted as nonfunctional secondary success characteristics. Not now. Not at General Motors in the 1980s. Never has a man needed the ability to inspire and motivate people more. For Roger is betting the corporation on his ability to lead millions of employees, dealers, suppliers, and shareholders in a direction they did not choose and do not necessarily agree with. Roger is making the most daring gamble in U.S. industrial history. If the gamble pays off, General Motors will help American industry back to prosperity and lead the world into the 21st century. If the gamble fails, U.S. industrial stability, and the standard of living of every American, could be affected. Roger is anteing up the chips and playing all of the cards. As Walter Winchell said, "The less you bet, the more you lose when you win." Roger is betting it all.

Roger's gamble is to create an entirely new kind of corporation in the decade of the 1980s (which coincides with his ten-year tenure as chief executive). His quest, which is truly visionary, is to establish what he calls "the world's first 21st-century corporation"—the first all-electronic manufacturing corporation with a high-tech elite, paperless processes, and peopleless plants. To accomplish this, Roger went on a buying binge not seen in General Motors since the flamboyant days when Billy Durant purchased everything in sight to establish the corporation originally. Only Roger's buying was far more strategically aimed. He has committed nearly $80 billion—more than the assets of any Fortune 100 company—for high-technology equipment and acquisitions of or investments in computer and electronic talent trusts. He has committed the total human resources and resourcefulness of the corporation's people. When he is through, not a single feature of the 75-year success structure of General Motors will remain unchanged. Even the carefully crafted ascension ladder that Roger was guided up to get to the top has been broken into kindling to feed the fires of his New General Motors. Nothing in what was once the most stable, if not staid, of all corporations will escape his redirection.

The motivation for his plan can be summarized in two

words: world competition. GM, along with all of American industry, was in trouble when Roger was named chairman-elect in 1980. The United States was in the midst of the greatest recession since the Great Depression. Imports were washing onto our shores at flood-tide levels. Imports had more than doubled in a single decade. Fully 70 percent of all goods sold in the U.S. by 1980 had direct import competition on the shelves. The import products, particularly those from Japan, were of outstanding quality and carried price tags well below those of American-made products. Japan had effectively turned the tables on our mercantile system, making the U.S. into its colony. The top U.S. exports to Japan, for example, were soybeans, corn, wood, coal, and wheat—all non-value-added commodities. The top Japanese exports to the U.S. were motorcycles, steel, televisions, and electronics, with cars and trucks at the top of the list.

Two oil crises—the Arab oil embargo in 1973 and the Iranian-triggered embargo in 1979—had turned the American market on its head. They threw the advantage directly to the fuel-efficient econo-boxes from Japan and the gas-stingy luxury cars from Europe. Detroit found its market squeezed from the bottom up by Toyota, Honda, and Datsun (now Nissan) and from the top of the market down by Mercedes, BMW, and Volvo. With quality ratings from both the Japanese and the Europeans coming in from six to ten times better on external appearance items like fits and finishes—the things shoppers notice—it was clear Detroit was in trouble.

The Japanese were a triple threat, with aggressive marketing, high quality, and low prices. The Japanese would have eventually taken over the small-car market anyway. It was simply a matter of time. But the shock of overnight success traumatized the U.S. automakers. Nineteen-eighty was the pivotal year, the year Japan, Inc., became a larger-volume car producer than Detroit.

Ford reported a $1.5 billion loss for 1980, and at Chrysler federal loan guarantees had little impact on losses of $1.7 billion. GM lost money, too. Not a big loss considering the size of General Motors—just $762.5 million. (GM was even able to continue paying quarterly dividends.) But it was a year of loss, the first since 1921, and it sent a shudder of disbelief throughout the organization.

Publicly, Roger was saying that the problem was high American labor costs and cheap energy policies of the past. "If someone found a way of turning seawater into gasoline tomorrow," he said, "the Japanese would be out of business." But his glib dismissal did not square with the depth of the challenge. Japan was a formidable competitor. The shoestring-sized country with few natural resources had a uniform culture and a low birthrate, emphasized primacy of education, saved twice as much money as Americans, had no military overhead, and had a government that was decidedly paternal to industry. The Japanese out-Calvined the American Calvinists. Living in crowded cities with only paper walls between them, they had learned how to cooperate out of necessity. And they had plenty of motivation of their own, since most of their industrial leaders could remember what it meant when, after the war, Occupation general Douglas MacArthur wired the Pentagon to "send me bread or send me bullets."

From 1960 through 1980 Japanese manufacturing productivity grew sixfold, while U.S. productivity only doubled. A confidential report circulated through GM in October 1980 showed the full extent of the competitive situation. The Japanese could build an assembly plant and a stamping facility for about half as much as it cost GM. The Japanese could keep their machinery up and running from 85 to 90 percent of the time, while GM's uptime average was more typically 55 to 60 percent. And they did all this with only five levels of management, compared to 14 levels within General Motors. Early in 1981 another GM study showed that the Japanese could build a small car for $1,800 less than it cost GM to build an identical model—and that was after the cost penalty of shipping the vehicle halfway around the globe and duties were deducted.

The media were already writing the auto industry's obituary, taking GM's measurements publicly, and planning to bury those "smokestack industries" in the same grave in which they had already interred other basic U.S. industries such as steel, televisions, electronics, and shoes. They were saying that America had only two choices—"throw in the towel or throw out the Japanese." Roger decided that GM would take neither course.

To his credit, Roger kept GM aloof from Ford, Chrysler, and others who whined to Washington, D.C., pleading for protective tariffs or outright embargoes. And while he did not reject the Japanese's own voluntary restraints in 1981, Roger predicted they would do little good. As it turned out, he was correct; voluntarily limiting the number of cars Japan would ship to the U.S. for four years served only to redirect that industry's efforts into penetrating the U.S. auto components market and going upscale on its vehicle lines to draw more profits per sale. During the four years of Japan's voluntary restraints on imports to the U.S., the dollar value of cars and components more than tripled. Roger was steadfast in his commitment to open and competitive trade. "The answer is to become competitive," he said. "At best, protectionism can only delay the inevitable. If not now, when?"

Roger recognized that nearly every aspect of the corporation that sired him was in some serious way noncompetitive. In a corporation where the traditional role of chairman was to protect the status quo, he demonstrated unprecedented courage to face the need for fundamental change and to act decisively. As corporate financial wizard, Roger knew the depth of GM's pockets perhaps better than any other man in the organization, and he decided to dig deeply to finance the most extensive renovation ever attempted.

In a sense, Roger's plate was already full when he took on his quest in 1981. His predecessors had committed the corporation to redesigning the vast majority of the company's car lines with the more space- and fuel-efficient front-wheel-drive configuration. This meant that everything had to be new— new transverse-mounted engines and transmissions, new unitized body construction, new suspension and brake systems. It also meant that every assembly plant would have to be redesigned for the radically different products. Traditionally in the auto industry, modernization of facilities is yoked to new product introductions. It simply is not cost-effective to modernize factories with ongoing products. Roger's immediate predecessor, Tom Murphy, made the commitment in the mid-

1970s to renovate facilities along with the vehicles themselves. The transition to front-wheel drive was a monumental ten-year undertaking that would have strained GM's engineering talents without any additional tasks. Already in 1981 it was clear that the transition was not going well. The company was plagued with transmission and engine problems with the new designs. In 1981 and 1982, GM actually recalled more cars than it produced.

Yet Roger was determined to utilize the transition to advance the most fundamental knowledge of manufacturing technologies. Instead of modernizing plants with proven state-of-the-art technologies, he ordered his manufacturing people to "take risks" and leap to the leading edge of computer-based technology and, whenever possible, to push beyond the edge to pioneer advanced equipment and processes. He would even set aside the moving assembly line—Henry Ford's basic approach to production for more than three-quarters of a century—to replace it with modular systems and totally flexible automation. With modular build, entire assemblies—say a complete door with wiring and trim—were built off the assembly line. And the assembly line itself would be composed of individual work stations unhurried by a moving conveyor belt. There would be no standardization among plants. Each new plant would build on, and be more technically advanced than, the one completed just a few months before. As his director of manufacturing engineering, Joe Spielman, put it, "Each plant is our institute of technology. Each one offers all-new lessons for us to master."

At the same time, Roger ordered the complete restructuring of all vehicle operations. Patterned after the German Opel organizational restructuring of the late 1970s, Roger first created a worldwide truck and bus group, then quickly went on to break up the traditional five car divisions into two groups—Chevrolet-Pontiac-Canada for lower-priced cars and Buick-Oldsmobile-Cadillac for the expensive models. In the process, he did away with two of the largest and most powerful divisions, Fisher Body and GM Assembly. Reorganization would move tens of thousands of people around, more than the equivalent of breaking up an AT&T.

While this was going on, Roger took even bolder initiatives. He created a joint venture to build Japanese cars in a GM plant, the New United Motors Manufacturing Inc. (NUMMI) project. And he put together the largest robotics company in the world with another Japanese joint venture. He challenged imaginations with research projects like Trilby, a carefully guarded Manhattan Project-style effort to formulate the ultimate electronic car. And Roger's most publicized visionary experiment of all, a new $5-billion corporation called Saturn, was a *tabula rasa* approach to developing a new family of small, world-competitive cars.

And there is more, much more. Roger bought Electronic Data Systems and announced that it would take over all of GM's computing and communications management. He spent another $5.2 billion to acquire Hughes Aircraft, one of the world leaders in Space Age technology and satellite communications. More billions went into buying out two major mortgage companies that, overnight, turned GM's financial wing into the country's biggest home mortgage holder. A few incidental millions of dollars also went into buying equity interests in a half-dozen machine intelligence and machine vision companies. Almost as an afterthought, he purchased Britain's Lotus, the world-famous sports car company, for its performance engineering expertise. Just to add a bit of spice, Roger authorized the development of another new subsidiary to take a powerful magnetic material developed in the GM Research Labs and make it the essence of a new industry.

With all of this, it is safe to say that no General Motors chairman since the company's free-wheeling founder had ever spent so much so rapidly. One journalist called it "the greatest renaissance of any company in peacetime history." More than a renaissance, Roger's quest was a radical redirection of the empire. His vision of the future was far-reaching. He committed to going further and faster than anyone else, to rush into the next century and be waiting when all of the others caught up.

Roger's 21st-century corporation concept evolved as he moved forward, but Roger says that much of it had already been thought through well before he took office. In a 1985

speech, unusual in that Roger devoted a great deal of his time
to rewriting and refining it, he tells of how his 21st-century
office, factory, and dealership will look:

The office will bear little resemblance to the office of
today. It will consist very simply of two things: a personal
computer and a microphone, or some other method of input.
The computer will respond to voice commands to place
phone calls, to take dictation for electronic mail, and to
process such standard items as accounts payable. The
computer will be our data base, taking all information we
give it, processing the data, and storing it electronically for
future use. Very, very little will have to be written down,
and, because paper will have been virtually eliminated, there
will be no filing cabinets, no in-and-out baskets. For all
intents and purposes, our office will be paperless.

Computers will continue to be great work and time savers
in our design and engineering facilities. But there the savings
in time and effort will accelerate at a rapid pace. In fact, we
believe that future computer applications we're working on
right now will soon allow our designers and engineers to
achieve a twelvefold increase in productivity on some
assignments. This will be a huge breakthrough—and it will
virtually eliminate the chance for human error on those
assignments.

Engineers and other office workers will be tied to the
manufacturing plants by a computer-integrated
communications network. All the computers in the offices
and factories will finally be able to "talk" to each other. It
will be as if the whole world simultaneously spoke the same
language.

With improved communications will come vastly increased
understanding and incredible efficiencies. Each activity in
the offices and plants will have a clearer view of how it fits
into the total operation. And the support systems for the
factory will be directly driven by the assembly process, as
they should be. The assembly line itself will tell suppliers
how many parts to produce, in what sequence, and when
they are needed.

Suppliers will also be paid electronically, based not on
invoices but on actual plant production figures. This might
be the first real opportunity to eliminate purchase orders,

shipping documents, receiving slips, and invoices since Italian merchants introduced double-entry bookkeeping in the 14th century!

Out on the factory floor the network of automated processes will be computer controlled and checked by machine vision technology. Some robots will be programmed to respond to voice commands. . . .

At the dealership, the electronic revolution will reach full swing. . . . Customers will be able to spec and order cars through a computer terminal on-line with the factory. Their orders will generate the actual build orders for the assembly lines and the releases for suppliers to start just-in-time bar-coded shipments. . . . Service itself will be greatly simplified through such diagnostic tools as artificial intelligence, which will also receive constant updates from the factory. . . .

In other speeches he added a vision of the 21st-century car, an all-electronic car in which every major component—engine, transmission, steering, suspension, braking, everything—would be controlled by a central on-board computer. And the owner would never lose touch with the car, as a communications satellite could give its precise geographic location at all times. "That might also be useful in tracking stolen vehicles—and in ending sleepless nights for parents when a young son or daughter is out with the car," Roger added.

The new General Motors would be an electronic brain trust and would spin off an endless array of high-tech satellite business ventures for the corporation. "GM invented and gave away antifreeze," Roger says. "We're not going to miss opportunities like that again just because it isn't cars. We're going to stick with things that have potential, and it doesn't necessarily have to go on a car." And those things, he would add, are going to be high-tech. "I'm a firm believer that we haven't even scratched the surface of technology yet," he has frequently told reporters anxiously taking notes as he rambles off vision after vision.

While this may sound like sci-fi fantasy, Roger clearly saw it as both attainable and imminent. Roger, the accountant who had never once been a plant manager or overseen the development of a single product of any kind, concluded that GM's *deus ex machina* answer to world competition would be robotics—salvation through the machine. Only his machine would have artificial intelligence and articulated mechanical hands. "Roger is fascinated with anything new and high-tech," one of GM's leading engineers and scientists says. "He really doesn't understand, or want to hear about, the limitations of technology, especially leading-edge technology." As Bob Eaton, head of GM's Advanced Engineering Activities, said, "When you told Roger about new technology, he'd get excited and ask, 'Where do I sign?'"

Once Roger almost lost his composure for days over a raw egg. He witnessed a demonstration of a new, touch-sensitive robot. The robot picked up an egg with its mechanical fingers and handed it to Roger without cracking the brittle shell. Roger became almost giddy with excitement and for days waxed eloquent about the technological miracle to anyone who would listen. In the egg was clearly the embryo of Roger's corporate phoenix.

Another extremely revealing aspect of Roger's 21st-century corporation speech is that it contained only one paragraph, tucked in near the end, about the importance of people in the scenario. The head of employee communications expressed some concern to me about this lopsided vision. After all, our official company posture was that we were going to achieve our goals through a balance of technology *and* teamwork. Where was the teamwork? So the next time I had the opportunity to write a speech for Roger, I proposed one I called "21st-Century People." I wrote and submitted it to him based on my own research and feelings and on insights borrowed from the people-oriented president of General Motors, Jim McDonald. When it was drafted and submitted, Roger gave the speech cursory attention, changed only two phrases into his own grammatical style, and read it at a keynote event without comment. In fact, he changed the subject during the question-and-answer session afterward, going into a tirade about the federal government not having the courage of its convictions to deal with the deficit and trade imbalances. The people issue was quickly forgotten.

From the very beginning of his chairmanship, the human side of the equation has eluded Roger. Humanware was simply not as interesting to him as hardware. He tried for a short period at the outset to bully the unions into submitting to his direction, but when that failed he looked more and more to technology. "Every time you ask for another dollar in wages," he told the UAW, "a thousand more robots start looking more practical."

In fact, Roger's quiet scenario was to eliminate the vast majority of the workers and to become competitive almost exclusively through advanced computer-based automation. Roger's mandate was to replace people—who, after all, were not very productive, had bad attitudes, and often belonged to belligerent unions. Roger told the press: "They say 'wait,' we don't have the technology for this. So instead of putting a man in there to do that, we're going to get the technology."

The ultimate example of Roger's end goal is what he called "the lights-out factory of the future." The prototype plant, officially Saginaw Division Vanguard Plant Number Eight, is scheduled to go into daily operation in the spring of 1988. It will produce 1,450 complex front-wheel-drive transmissions and axle combinations a day and can operate around the clock with fewer than 30 regular employees. "What does the plant of the future look like?" an auto writer asked. "It would look like our Saginaw factory of the future," Roger said. "Highly flexible automation of everything." Roger called it "the lights-out factory" because the day shifts could program all of the robots to work the evening shift without supervision—in fact, with just three maintenance people there to shut things down should the machinery go berserk. So, in theory, you could turn off the lights and go home at night, leaving the plant to pump out parts and profits like a palsied slot machine—all without people.

From its inception Roger's high-tech fixation fostered a major rift in the corporation. On the operations side, experienced engineers and researchers warned that *leading edge* meant rough-edged, that going beyond state-of-the-art meant trouble. The management experts had already toured the most successful Japanese plants and reported that the low cost of labor was not the most important advantage the Japanese had—participatory management was. They warned that management systems that guaranteed continuous improvement needed to be in place *before* technology would work. Even Roger's financial experts were guarded in their comments, saying that cost reduction, not costly devices, was the route to lowering the breakeven point and upping profitability. Roger, however, turned a deaf ear to all of this. He continued to say that Japan's advantage was low labor costs, first and foremost. "We have got to have high-tech because we are a high-cost company for labor," he told the press. "Factory lights are going out all over America," Roger said. "They are being extinguished by high labor costs."

Beyond labor costs, the Japanese had more technology, he argued. "Part of the reason for their [Japan's] success," he told a conference of financial executives in 1981, "is the use of highly automated and efficient plants. There are 10,000 robots in use in Japanese industry—most of them in the auto industry. The U.S., by contrast, has only about 4,300 robots." Roger determined that GM would have more robots than anyone else in the world. So, despite major polarization within General Motors over the high-tech thrust, Roger's will prevailed.

For those who have studied General Motors as the textbook example of management by committee, it may seem unlikely that one man could have the power to launch such an all-pervasive effort over reservations from within. Yet under Roger's leadership the traditional committee structure no longer makes the decisions. As Roger told me, "The guy who said a camel is a horse designed by a committee was right. Committees are where you get the facts together, but it's an individual who must decide." And the decisions that count are made by Roger. It is much like a smorgasbord where committees develop and serve up the dishes and Roger decides what goes on the plate. Most executives individually agreed that Roger, more than most of his predecessors, is a one-man show. Says Tom Adams, former chairman of Campbell Ewald, GM's largest advertising supplier, and a 20-year associate of Roger's, "He listens, but you get the impression quickly that what he knows is more important than what you know. So when you talk about General Motors today, you have to talk about Roger Smith. He *is* the corporation."

The board of directors, of course, has the fiduciary responsibility to represent the millions of GM shareholders—to be, in effect, Roger's boss. According to two outside and two inside board members, all of whom preferred not to be quoted, the GM Board of Directors is not directing the corporation. Roger is. Meetings are formal, with little give-and-take discussion. Directors receive copious amounts of information before every meeting and are expected to run through the agenda with track shoes on. Inside board members, Roger's own top executives, are not expected to speak unless Roger either asks them a question or has requested input in advance. Because the union is so critical to the future success of the corporation, there has been for some time a push to have a union representative on the GM board. Roger has steadfastly rejected the notion. "Directors have to represent all of the shareholders," Roger insists. Yet far from encouraging broad-based responsibility for governance, Roger has gone before the American Law Institute to oppose its efforts to mandate regulations requiring board members to be responsible for their actions. Just the opposite, Roger pushed through a proxy at the last shareholders' meeting that exempted directors from liability—effectively lessening the threat of the board's being held accountable for its actions.

"Unanimity on this board is assumed," a recently retired member says. "I don't have to tell you what happened to the only director who voted against one of Roger's proposals." He was referring, of course, to Ross Perot, who, while on the GM board, cast the lone vote against the purchase of Hughes Aircraft Company.

"I'd done some research on my own," Perot said, "and I discovered that 65 percent of Hughes's income came from less than one-half of 1 percent of its total business—and that dominant ½ percent was with contracts that had less than two years to go. It didn't look like it was worth $5 billion to me, so I voted against buying it."

Soon after that vote Perot was informed that there was an undercurrent (the inference being from Roger) to vote Perot off the board. "I told them to try it. I had more shares than all the others combined, so go ahead and try. I love a good fight." The effort was dropped, but eventually Perot's outspoken opposition to Roger's concepts proved to be too much. Perot was bought out for $700 million, and a significant clause in the buyout contract was that Perot must agree to resign from the board.

When I asked Perot about the GM board, he said: "There's very little ownership among outside board members. No one on the board's got more than a couple of hundred shares of stock. One guy's got more, but it's other people's shares he's representing. They've got nothing at stake in the future success of General Motors." Of the non-GM board members, most have surprisingly little stock in the corporation they oversee. Five had only 500 shares each in 1987, three others had only 200 shares apiece, and one board member owned only 100 shares of GM stock. Roger alone has more voting stock in General Motors than all of the outside board members combined.

How important is having significant board member equity? Former Treasury Secretary William Simon thinks it is fundamental to good decision making. "You run the business differently when you think of it as your own money, not somebody else's," Simon has repeatedly argued. Having major stock holdings as a prerequisite would rule out such outstanding GM board members as Rev. Leon Sullivan, the founder of the Sullivan Principles, which established equal standards for companies operating inside of apartheid-torn South Africa. Yet it seems equally true that to pack your board with people who have no major stock holdings is an indication that governance is not your goal.

And, in fact, there is financial motivation not to rock the boat. The average GM board member receives around $42,500 a year plus the use of a new car every three months. That's well over $50,000 a year in pay and perks for attending a once-a-month meeting and an occasional subcommittee session. And it can be even sweeter. A board member who attends every meeting and serves on four subcommittees, chairing one of them, gets $68,000 a year plus the free car—not bad for three or four days a month. Besides the remuneration, being on the board of the largest corporation in the world carries a great deal of status in the business world as a significant intangible benefit. There are a lot of reasons to go along with Roger's program, and without significant stock holdings represented, few reasons to express governance.

Yet another reason the board tends to be ineffectual is that it is packed with GM insiders who take their orders—and depend for their futures—on the chairman. Of the 19 GM directors 7 are insiders. Besides Roger's own board vote, he can count on 6 others who wear 2 hats: one as a board member theoretically speaking for the shareholders and the other hat as a full-time GM employee.

These seven men, Roger included, comprise the ruling GM Executive Committee—the chairman, vice chairman, president, chief financial executive, passenger car and truck executive, truck and overseas executive, and executive over electronics and components. All report directly to the chairman. The inside directors have some very compelling reasons to toe the line. For one, most of them are competing for the ultimate step up to either chairman or president. While the heir to the chair traditionally has come from the financial ranks, Roger has made it clear he will not feel bound by any past practices in defining his 1990 replacement. And those who may not have as clear a shot at the top chair are dependent on Roger for their final retirement package. The chairman has a great deal of latitude in how well a retiring senior executive will be compensated. And even into retirement, there is continuing influence on compensation. As one recently retired executive told me, "If what I tell you gets back to Roger, it could cost me a couple hundred thousand dollars."

Then there is one board seat reserved for the former chairman of the board, currently Tom Murphy. By the bylaws, a retired chairman can serve five years on the board beyond his own retirement. Roger, however, has made an exception to the rule to keep Murphy, his corporate mentor, on the board for three years past his 70th birthday. Murphy is a committed traditionalist who believes in the authority of the chair and is yoked to Roger by having chosen him. He has yet to vote against any Roger Smith proposal.

Recently, three board members retired and one more insider was added. This means that of the total board, 40 percent are GMers—a significant voting block that Roger can assume he has in his hip pocket. And with all the financial motivation of outside board members to stay inside, it is clear why the phrase "rubber stamp board" has been so frequently applied to Roger's governors.

Yet even with all of this, there is an undercurrent of dissatisfaction on the current GM Board of Directors. "There is a great deal of grumbling about Roger on the GM board right now," Doug Fraser says. "I have that on the best authority. But they probably won't do anything about it." The way the GM board is now set up, to muster enough votes to override the chairman would be nearly impossible. Roger is in command.

The two chairmen before Roger were committee men who felt the awesome size of their jobs. Chairman Richard Gerstenberg, an intelligent and thoughtful man who headed GM in the turbulent early 1970s, said: "I am like an ant on the front of a log heading downstream toward a treacherous bend, and all I can do is stick my foot in the water to try to steer us clear and yell, 'Whoa, you S.O.B., whoa.'" Chairman Thomas Aquinas Murphy, Roger's predecessor and mentor, is a Lincolnesque man who was always aware of the great contributions of those around him and saw his role more as one of coordinator and spokesperson. Just before retirement, Murphy said: "The job controls me and not vice versa." Roger doesn't see it that way. Roger assumes authority and, when challenged, has said: "I'm sailing our own ship."

The end result is that without management by committee, or decisive board governance, Roger has no one who can effectively impede his singular will. No one, that is, but the three million people—employees, suppliers, and dealers—who must follow through on his many projects. Roger is asking a great deal of them:

- Asking that an industry with the vast majority of its knowledge and people in mechanical engineering immediately learn to use the most advanced computer-based technologies, shifting from servomechanics to laser electronics overnight.

- Asking hundreds of thousands of people who were attracted to General Motors because of its stability and security to become entrepreneurs and risk takers.
- Asking them to uproot in reorganization, giving up functional contacts in the largest of all "good ol' boy" systems and give up identification and the lifelong pride that came with saying "I'm a Chevy man" or "I'm a Fisher Body man."
- Asking them to send their most talented people away to man Roger's special projects—3,500 to Saturn, 100 to Trilby, dozens more to GMF Robotics, to Saginaw's factory of the future, to an endless array of experiments at the very time they were most needed to deal with the other pressing changes.
- Asking that they assimilate the Electronic Data Systems culture into all of their operations, that they treat these Texas-style electronic commandos with respect, even though these outsiders come to them with only limited experience in their manufacturing field.

While Roger is asking millions to do all of this, he might mention that the vision comes with a price tag: the understanding that they will not receive significant income, or even merit, increases for several years; the reality that one out of every four of their co-workers will be laid off permanently in the process; and that the more aggressively they move to new efficiencies, the more likely they are to jeopardize their own jobs or their friend's jobs. As United Auto Workers' Local president Peter Kelly said: "It's like being on the *Titanic*. You climb to one upper deck after another, but eventually you know you're going under." Though some technologists will survive, it appears that the vast majority of workers are being asked to do more for fewer rewards in order to help themselves out of a job. Though this doomsday scenario may be more perceptual than actual, it is the perception of reality that Roger is asking his people to redefine in his terms. Each GM person must buy into Roger's perception, to make it his or her own, if it is to stand any chance of genuine success. So far, that hasn't happened.

Seven years into his quest, the vision has become a sight. Instead of the 70 percent market share Roger predicted his revitalized company would achieve, GM has all but given up on maintaining 40 percent and fell to just 35 percent of the domestic car and truck market in the first half of 1987—only slightly more than half of Roger's espoused goal and the lowest level of GM market penetration in half a century. A single point of lost market share means about $1 billion in lost revenues and about six thousand lost jobs in GM and its supplier community. The 13 percent drop in market share experienced under Roger is the equivalent of losing six assembly plants, four stamping plants, and an engine plant and the end of seventy-eight thousand American jobs.

Despite massive technology investments, or perhaps because of them, GM has plummeted under Roger's leadership from the lowest-cost domestic producer to the highest, without gaining any competitive advantage in quality. The company's breakeven point has risen more than 30 percent, which means certain disaster unless it can be corrected before the next cyclical downturn in car sales. That's not likely, partly because of the products themselves. Plagued by look-alike cars since Roger took office, the company is in a panic to make quick fixes to new models by tacking on fender extensions and reshaping a little sheet metal.

Profits in 1986 were virtually nonexistent and would have been worse but for Roger's genius for juggling numbers and squeezing through tax loopholes. That's especially damning since 1986 was the year General Motors finally achieved its long sought goal of breaking the $100 billion revenue mark. Yet even Ford Motor Company, with only two-thirds of GM's revenues, made more money than the giant for the year. It was about that time that institutional investors began speaking of GM in terms of its "breakup value" and referring to the giant as the "sick old man of the auto industry."

Roger began a massive corporate cost-cutting effort in 1986, announcing 13 plants to be permanently closed, 25,000 salaried workers to be permanently furloughed, and critical future product programs to be curtailed or dropped entirely. Yet in the midst of all of this, Roger spent three-quarters of a billion dollars to buy out Ross Perot and three other EDSers, an action that buried GM's legal department in shareholder "greenmail" lawsuits.

Roger, surprised by the depth of public sentiment, made a concerted effort to appease the major portfolio and pension fund managers, the only people with the potential combined voting power to depose him. He took refuge behind the walls of a Manhattan public relations agency that specializes in repelling takeovers, even though the odds of any group actually amassing enough to challenge General Motors' sovereignty were a million to one. Still, the threat was enough. Roger dropped everything and concentrated on pleasing the investors. When they said his cost-cutting plans didn't go deep enough, Roger announced a $10 billion reduction drive, eliminating 15,000 more jobs than he had previously announced. "Fifteen thousand jobs to keep one chairman in office," one personnel manager said. "Boy. That makes him one damned expensive employee."

Roger promised the investors he would not buy any more market share with incentive programs that, in effect, meant publicly giving up on retaining GM's industry dominance. The capitulation came at a time when the dollar devaluation in relationship to the yen was forcing the Japanese to raise their prices by as much as 30 to 50 percent. To finally beat the Japanese back would have taken nothing more than a reduction in GM prices, yet GM raised prices by 7 percent instead. The high-tech quest had placed GM in a position where it could not take advantage of a major opportunity to regain lost market share. Public response to all of this has been dramatic, and the vote has gone overwhelmingly against Roger. As author-editor Brock Yates said in a *Washington Post* analysis: "If he [Roger] were the prime minister of a parliamentarian nation, he would have long since been deposed. . . . Had he been the captain of a Navy ship, he might have been court-martialed."

Is Roger deterred by these setbacks? Hardly. As he told me recently, "If I owned 100 percent of this company, I would have gone further and faster." In one breath he defines the massive investments in high technology as "one-time expenses that are largely behind us now," then with the next breath he talks about the wondrous technology GM is developing in Saginaw and how even GM's newest plants will have to be redone soon to accommodate these breakthroughs: "When you look at the advantages, we have no choice but to bring this technology in right away." Above all else, Roger is determined to hold to the course he set in 1981 and to create an entirely new corporation in the process.

To media and investor criticism Roger has become philosophical. He is taking a broader view, and he concludes that the very nature of the American culture is at fault. (Previously he blamed labor, then his senior executives, then "the frozen middle" managers, for GM's problems.) In one of his major speeches, which he frequently quotes from now, Roger puts his long-term perspective into focus:

> Truth is that much of America is like the college student who wrote his father complaining: "The food at the school cafeteria is terrible. I wouldn't feed it to pigs for fear they would turn blue and die. And not only that, they serve such small portions!" Too many of us want it both ways—we want the improved standard of living that is the eventual result of reinvestment and industrial modernization. But we don't want to reduce our current consumption.
>
> In virtually every aspect of society—from three-minute fast-food restaurants, to empty savings accounts, to slipknot marriages—it is clear that we have become a society of short-term pleasure seekers with a very low tolerance for delayed gratification of any kind. The clearest example of our live-for-today culture can be seen in our unparalleled lack of personal savings . . . this country's savings rate ranks well below that of most other developed countries. . . . Now, you need to save more to invest more. It's simply not possible to save more and consume more at the same time. In fact, the only way to increase both the level of savings and the level of consumption is to get your economy to grow faster. . . . That requires investment.
>
> We haven't accepted these simple mathematical realities. In fact, from 1983 onward, America has spent more than it produced . . . by borrowing from abroad. That's the other side of our trade deficit. We got the goods from abroad and

borrowed the money from abroad to pay for them. So by 1986, we went from being the world's largest creditor to becoming the world's largest debtor. Worse, we [America] didn't utilize this excess spending to retool to make us more productive. . . .

Many capital investments—especially ones with significant productivity improvements attached—take as long as 5 to 10 years to reach fruition. Yet, under the pressure of quarterly earnings statements, many managers feel that they cannot risk making such long-term commitments. . . . Contrast our situation with that in Japan or Germany where business has access to lower-cost capital and doesn't have stringent demands on quarterly returns. The disincentives to long-term investments in America are obvious. . . . [Someone must] tell the American public the truth, that you can only reap what you sow.

Roger goes on to argue that "long-term strategic planning in a nearsighted society" is the challenge to business leadership today and that, because we are an immediate-gratification culture, any attempts to take the longer view will inevitably bring criticism. "Ask any American coach who commits his team to a season of team rebuilding. You are bound to get a lot of criticism from the sidelines."

And on the morale problems from within, he says, "When you start changing things, people get shook up. How do you tell a guy at Norwood [a plant Roger is closing] that he's in trouble? You know what he's going to say? He's going to say, 'No one told me we were in trouble.' That's not true. We went down time and time again trying our best to communicate that his job was threatened [by world competition]. Or how do you tell a timekeeper at Hamtramck [another plant] who is making $60,000 a year that the same job at the local bank is paying $30,000? How do you tell them if they don't wake up and get competitive, the forces of change are going to sweep them away? Not even Clint Eastwood or Elizabeth Taylor could communicate that kind of thing and make them like it."

Roger may be right. He may be the industrial leader with the longest, most perceptive vision in America today. His factory of the future may be the only American factory that can eventually function in a world market in which some undeveloped nation is always willing to do it cheaper—Japan at $18 an hour today, Korea at $1.72 an hour tomorrow, China at $.10 an hour the day after tomorrow. Or he may be a generation ahead of his time. Roger's 21st-century corporation may be like the ill-fated Chrysler Airflow introduced in 1937—about 20 years too early. The majority may follow a leader who is marching a few feet ahead of them, but if he is marching a mile ahead, they cannot see him or his vision and will not follow.

Roger may be right, but he may never have the chance to prove his hypothesis. For to get from where General Motors is today to where he envisions it being tomorrow will take the total dedication of his massive world organization—people who are on his payroll but are not now on his team. As we shall see throughout this book, people are Roger's problem. Far from motivating and inspiring, Roger's chairmanship has been marred by an endless array of insensitive acts and public utterances that have devastated morale and turned cooperation into confrontation. And Roger has lost sight of GM's most important constituency—the customers. By downplaying the psychological side of America's love affair with cars, he has placed GM years behind on styling, which sells, yet years ahead on unseen manufacturing sophistication, which doesn't sell.

Perhaps the greatest roadblock to his vision is the man himself. He is the product of an elite corporate culture that, by design, has denigrated the concept of highly visible motivational leadership. And he has had the misfortune to be juxtaposed against two of the best examples of symbolic leadership in America today: Lee Iacocca, the man who saved Chrysler Corporation from bankruptcy, and billionaire Ross Perot.

In 1980, when Roger was planning his technological renaissance, Iacocca was enlisting the support of his people. Iacocca rejected his Chrysler salary and publicly announced he would accept "a dollar a year" in salary until he turned his troubled company around. "I wanted our employees and our suppliers to be thinking: 'I can follow a guy who sets that kind of example,' " Iacocca explained in his book. Iacocca called it "equality of sacrifice," noting that the human spirit is such that an individual will endure almost anything if everyone is suffering together. "When you find yourself in a position of leadership," he says, "people follow your every move."

Perot, the super salesman who invested $1,000 to start a company that within 10 years was the leader in its industry, set up his salary initially at $68,000 a year. "I have never accepted any raises or bonuses or special privileges," Ross says. "Instead, I've let the growth of the company itself [his share of the stock] make the difference. Let the market determine your success or failure." It worked for Perot, who is now one of the wealthiest men on earth with a net worth of more than $3 billion (most of it from selling his company, and later his stock, to GM). More important, his philosophy worked to maintain a symbolic commonality with his subordinates.

In an interview with Roger and his PR vice president Jack McNulty, Roger became visibly annoyed when I brought up these examples of symbolic leadership. Of Iacocca's dollar-a-year, he said: "Would I tell people I'm going to work for a dollar a year when I know I've got $20 million coming over here on the side that I know I'm going to get? You'd better find someone else for that one." He was referring to Iacocca's guaranteed stock options, which Iacocca would receive based on the company's eventual profitability. In 1986, those options amounted to $20 million Iacocca received in net income. And on Perot's $68,000-a-year gesture, Roger said, "Anybody who's got $3 billion, and you know that 10 percent of that gets you $300 million a year at the bank, and he says he's only going to take out $68,000?" McNulty injected: "It's almost dishonest. It's pandering to people's ignorance." And Roger added: "General Motors is the most ethical corporation in the world. GM can be everything it wants to be without breaking the first law or being deceptive. And that's the way it's going to be as long as I'm here."

The point, of course, is not whether Iacocca's taking a dollar a year in a failing company with the outside chance for a killing is deceptive or whether a $68,000-a-year salary when Perot was just starting out was gimmicky. The point is that these men were able to garner respect and commitment to the level of absolute devotion in their organizations through the use of such masterful symbolic gestures and leadership by example. And if some leadership acts might be viewed as showy, or even somewhat manipulative, well, as Eric Hoffer said, "Charlatanism to some degree is indispensable to effective leadership."

Within General Motors today much is happening to build the kind of team approach that the Japanese have used so successfully against American industry. Under Roger's chairmanship the Saturn contract was developed, an ultimately flexible working agreement that may become the standard for union-management cooperation in the future. Under Roger, there is a new GM-UAW program called JOBS (Job Opportunity Bank Security) that provides retraining for people who have been displaced through automation. Under Roger, participatory management techniques are being attempted in many plants and offices. Under Roger, union leaders have more direct access to management than ever before. Yet morale is languishing, and many plants that have tried team approaches are beginning to back away from the effort. The rank and file, now thoroughly convinced of the severity of world-competitive challenges, genuinely want to help, yet they express frustration that Roger's administration will not let them have a full voice. As Peter Kelly, Tech Center UAW president, says, "It's difficult to help row when they won't let you in the boat."

Not that it is essential to be a charismatic leader like Ross Perot or Lee Iacocca. There are many styles that can motivate people to achieve. At Ford Motor Company, Chairman Donald Petersen is a Mensa intellectual whose laid-back style would appear to be more at home behind the rostrum in a Harvard lecture hall. The essence of Petersen's style is participatory. His primary goal is "to remove the artificial barriers that are built into the classic corporate structure" to create "a spirit of teamwork throughout the organization." As the story goes, when Petersen first became president he asked the Ford designers if they liked the cars they were planning. They said "no," so Petersen asked them to come up with their own designs, and the rounded look of the late 1980s was born. While his approach is radically different from that of the hard-charging Perot or Iacocca, the results are equally impressive. Ford has gone from the deepest well of losses in its history to gaining a greater share of the U.S. market than anyone else in the decade.

What is lacking under Chairman Roger Smith is not so much leadership as the perception of leadership—the symbolic leadership that is the precursor to great deeds. "The appearance of leadership is extremely important," says David Cole, director of the Transportation Research Institute and the son of a former GM president. Cole gives an example of what he means by referring to a visit to an engineer friend at Chrysler. There is a picture of Chrysler chairman Lee Iacocca on every office wall. "You know," the engineer said, "when I even think of goofing off for an instant, I get the feeling that Lee's eyes are watching me from the picture." That, Cole says, is an example of the symbolic influence that a leader like Iacocca can achieve. "Roger doesn't understand *how* important that is," Cole says. "The leadership issue has to be resolved. He should find someone else to be GM's spokesperson and show leadership qualities." The chances of Roger's placing someone else in the charismatic leadership role are slim.

F. James McDonald was originally picked to be GM's president and Roger's management mate partly to install an articulate and likable spokesperson. Jim McDonald was an excellent speaker, who came across as he was, a straightforward and morally absolute man who worked his way up from the iron foundry floor. Jim's favorite quote, and the one he lived by, came from Emerson: "Nothing astonishes men so much as common sense and plain dealing." Yet Roger did not put Jim out front. Roger consistently placed himself in the spokesman's role, giving nearly three times as many speeches and rarely handing over significant announcements to anyone else. And Roger had an even more charismatic leader in Ross Perot, yet never considered enlisting Ross's public relations magic for GM's cause.

The tragedy of Roger's story is that he possesses the sensitivities, the warmth of character and ability to inspire, that are more than amply manifested in his personal and social life. Yet Roger seems unable to bridge the gap between the sensitive private man and the corporate personage. We are, after all, products of our experiences. And while Roger has the intellect to see much that is wrong with the largest corporation in the world, and has the courage to attempt unprecedented change, he has not shown the ability to overcome his own rigorous upbringing in the callous financial culture that spawned him.

To create an entirely new corporation out of the remnants of a decaying smokestack industry may require a charismatic leader, a person who can inspire intense loyalties and courageous actions. "Society is founded on hero-worship," Carlyle said, and that's equally true for great corporate societies. Terrence Deal and Allen Kennedy, in their book *Corporate Cultures*, studied numerous American corporations and concluded that the most successful ones develop cultures in which great individuals provide the role models. As Deal and Kennedy put it:

"Managers run institutions, heroes create them."

2
Sloan's Pallbearer

"Everybody says, 'Boy, if Mr. Sloan could see what you're doing now, he'd turn over in his grave.' Well, I say, 'Heck, if he was here, he'd be doing exactly the same things.'"

Roger Smith

Roger was methodically groomed for 31 years to be the philosopher king of a culture that no longer existed by the time of his coronation. About the only uncompromised aspect of the GM culture by 1981 was the rigorous process of methodically nurturing leaders like Roger . . . and Roger himself eliminated this last link with the past shortly after his ascension.

Peter Drucker, in *The Concept of a Corporation*, had analyzed General Motors during World War II and revisited the company in 1959. He concluded that the corporation's success principles had become "fuzzy beyond recognition." That's significant, because the old culture was immensely successful for General Motors—propelling the corporation to the top of American industry and keeping it there for more than half a century. In fact, many within General Motors still quote chapter and verse from the old text, chiefly because Roger has not been able to communicate a new text. Roger himself has added to the confusion, saying, "We're getting back to Mr. Sloan's principles" at times and "Sloan is no longer applicable" at other times. The result is a cultural confusion and mass

41

identity crisis of epic proportions—a company that, in the words of Matthew Arnold, is "wandering between two worlds, one dead, the other powerless to be born."

Corporate culture, along with *synergies* and *participatory management*, is a buzzword of the 1980s, yet the culture of a corporation is of critical importance to the well-being and productivity of its participants. Companies have always had cultures, of course, but they are more aware of them today because their cultures are in a state of flux. Harvard anthropologist Michael Maccoby says, "People become aware that they have a culture when they have to change."

The culture—essentially the net value of company goals, traditions, loyalties, and assumptions—has a profound impact on the quality and productivity of one's work. In *Corporate Cultures*, authors Deal and Kennedy made an in-depth study of the cultures of more than three dozen major U.S. corporations. They concluded that consistently high-performing companies have strong cultures, while weak or confused cultures "waste a good deal of time just trying to figure out what they should do and how they should do it." Deal and Kennedy estimated that having a strong culture can make as much difference as two hours a day of production time per employee. Former Harvard Business School professor Michael McCaskey concludes that the corporate culture provides the "conceptual maps." The defined culture is the "employee's guide to reality within the corporation—the dos and don'ts, the code of behavior . . . the road to success." While there may be a few who can live with uncertainty and, in fact, prefer the excitement of it, the vast majority of people need "well-defined maps to orient themselves." The culture provides the traditions that, in the words of Tevye from *Fiddler on the Roof*, tell us "who we are and what God expects us to do."

GM's traditional culture, the one that gave the corporation such fundamental stability that it could weather the Great Depression and numerous recessions without red ink, was the brainchild of a single man's life's work. The man was Alfred P. Sloan, Jr.

Sloan is the George Washington of the General Motors culture. In Deal's and Kennedy's cultural parlance, he was, and to many remains, the culture's philosophical hero, the founding father. Sloan didn't create General Motors. A man named William "Billy" Crapo Durant did that. Durant went around buying car and component companies like a man trying to see how many slot machines he could have spinning at one time. They didn't pay off for Durant, who, after being forced out by the New York bankers twice, ended up his career running a bowling alley. Durant's buying sprees brought together 30 or so companies, but he was unable to order the pieces in anything that looked like a cohesive whole. Sloan, who ran one of the pieces Durant bought, quietly came to the forefront with Durant's final departure in 1921. Sloan was GM president (when that title meant chief executive officer) from 1923 through 1949, GM chairman from 1937 through 1956, and he continued on the board and was leader emeritus until his death in 1966 at age 91. Sloan went on influencing GM from the grave, thanks to his autobiography, *My Years at General Motors*, a bone-dry yet solid definition of his management concepts.

Sloan was a slight, somber man with a pronounced Brooklyn accent. He was a graduate electrical engineer but had such a decided genius for detail and dollars that many historians mistakenly refer to him as a financial man. "Silent Sloan," as many called him, was largely without redeeming vice. He didn't smoke, drink, or gallivant and thought recreation and sports a waste of usable time. His only memorable human quality was tremendous personal philanthropy. He was once the largest shareholder in General Motors, yet he gave virtually everything he earned and most of his stock to cancer research and to endowments for Massachusetts Institute of Technology, his alma mater. Sloan's genius was not in inspirational leadership, but in organizational structures. He established the GM management system that has been taught in every major university and emulated by corporations around the globe.

Sloan is credited with bringing the American industry such innovations as installment sales (a dollar down and a dollar a week), annual model changeovers (planned obsolescence), and fattened sales by loading the buyers with options (more car per car). He is also typically given credit for the GM strategy of providing a full range of cars of every size and luxury level (a car for every purse and purpose), though this was actually Billy Durant's contribution.

By far, Sloan's greatest contribution to GM's culture was his concept of organization. Sloan did not pattern his structural design on any other model, but Drucker notes in *Concepts of a Corporation* that it bore close parallels to "two institutions most renowned for administrative efficiency . . . the Catholic Church and that of the modern army as first developed by the Prussian General Staff between 1800 and 1870." There are essentially only four tenets to Sloan's structure:

- policy by committee
- balance between financial oversight and operational autonomy
- centralized policy and decentralized administration
- guided progression and succession to develop leaders

Sloan's first concept of management by committee had devolved over the years from rational to unreasonable to ineffectual. Originally, Sloan's committee system was restricted to setting broad policies. As he saw it: "Policy may originate anywhere, but it must be appraised and approved by committee before being administered by individuals." The concept was not unlike participatory management approaches today, except that, like every aspect of Sloan's system, it dealt only with the executive cadre. (Sloan never addressed the company's relationship to the workers except in terms of labor costs or problems therewith.)

Under Sloan's organization there were two main committees in General Motors, one on policy and one on administration. Drucker called the committees "the government of General Motors . . . the court of last appeal should there be serious disagreements on policy within the organization." The two major committees were supported by a number of subcommittees, comprised of both staff and field experts. Total openness was encouraged in the committee process, and one definition of a GM executive Drucker found was "a man who would be expected to protest officially against a policy decision to which he objected." The committees under Sloan were fundamental in what was essentially a federalist system of management.

The committee system got out of hand in the 1960s and '70s, when every request for appropriations or approval on product developments or purely administrative personnel matters ended up going before a committee. This was a distortion of Sloan's concept. "I have never believed that a group as such could manage anything," Sloan said. "A group can make policy, but only individuals can administer policy." As discussed in the last chapter, the senior committees under Roger Smith's chairmanship are largely fact-gathering, not policy-making, exercises. There is still a plethora of committees meeting throughout General Motors, or committees by newer names such as *task forces* or *teams*. But for good or ill, the Sloan committee concept no longer exists.

Sloan's second management concept was to maintain a balance between financial oversight and operational autonomy, much like the checks and balances in a loose federation. Financial control was centered in the board of directors and personified in the chairman of the board in New York City. The chief executive officer ran the operating side from GM headquarters in Detroit, at the epicenter of actual manufacturing production. The concept was simplicity itself—an engineer or a product man would oversee the manufacturing company, and a financial guy would watch the money to make sure the engineer didn't give away the store. In his autobiography Sloan said: "Whoever is in charge of operations should be delegated with real authority. . . . It will probably be best if the president of the corporation could absolutely have charge of operations."

Slowly, at times imperceptibly, the financial side, more commonly called "bean counters" in GM, took charge. The first, and most decisive, step in that direction came in 1958 when Frederic G. Donner, a finance man who many said perfected the art of winning by intimidation, became *both* chairman and chief executive officer. In effect, the presidency received a major demotion. Old-timers tell me the shift in power came about because of Harlow Curtice, the dynamic and universally popular leader who was the last chief-executive president. As the story goes, Curtice visited GM's European operations and approved several product and capital expenditures without checking back with the bean counters in New York. The financial people decided that the only way to prevent that from happening again was to assume the reins.

Yet another explanation given for finance's taking full control was the times themselves. General Motors in the 1950s was so large and prosperous—with more than half of the domestic market and a third of the world market—that the company began to be perceived as a possible monopoly and a threat to competitive trade. Indeed, in 1949, when Roger Smith joined the company finance staff, General Motors and DuPont were defending their 30-year relationship in federal courts. (DuPont owned 25 percent of General Motors until 1956.) The quest to break up the giant corporation was fanned by such outspoken advocates as George Romney, head of American Motors and one-time U.S. presidential hopeful. The effort intensified until, in 1971, there were 18 different antitrust actions going at once against General Motors. Eight were criminal indictments, 10 civil complaints. So as early as the mid-1950s it was clear that for GM to aggressively pursue an even greater share of the market would invite extinction. The emphasis logically shifted from making more and better cars to making more and more money from a relatively stable number of sales. That put the ball more squarely in the financial side's court.

John Z. DeLorean, former GM group executive vice president, in his book (as told to J. Patrick Wright) *On a Clear Day You Can See General Motors*, blames the Corvair disaster on financial dominance. The 1959 Corvair, a revolutionary rear-powered small car with an aluminum-block engine, was introduced to compete with the ubiquitous Volkswagen Beetle. Soon after introduction it was clear that the car had major stability problems in power turns. It was so unstable, in fact, that it tended to flip over and crush its occupants. Ralph Nader, the then little-known consumer advocate, attacked the Corvair's problems in a best-selling book, *Unsafe at Any Speed*, that set off a congressional investigation, an attempt by

GM to discredit Nader, and a successful lawsuit against GM by Nader. GM had hired detectives to investigate Nader, and the investigators had gone a bit too far in harassing the young consumer crusader. GM chairman James Roche publicly apologized, but the incident went a long way toward undercutting auto industry credibility and invited regulation.

DeLorean says that Chevrolet's engineers knew that the Corvair had problems and suggested a number of fixes, all rejected by the financial staff as too expensive. Finally, when Bunkie Knudsen became general manager of Chevrolet, he insisted that Corvairs be equipped with a $15-a-car stabilizer bar. DeLorean says, "Bunkie threatened to quit if he didn't get that stabilizer bar." In 1964, the financial staff relented, but it was too late to save the car's image or the lives that had been lost to save a few dollars.

"What was happening," DeLorean said, "was a predictable result when the control of a consumer goods company moves into the hands of purely financial managers." The emphasis naturally shifted from people and products to short-term profits.

During the 1970s, other subtle changes in reporting and authorizations appeared that continued to solidify the financial side's control (and undercut the participatory committee system as well). One small, yet significant, change took place around 1977, when it was decided that the executive assistants to operating executives had to be financial men, who were to report not to the executives they served but to the treasurer's office. Executive assistants have been known by any number of demeaning nicknames over the years, including "spear carriers" and "dog robbers," after the servant who scoops up droppings from the family pet. Currently, the nickname is "bag men" because they carry the boss's bags and open his doors. Yet executive assistant is actually an extremely important position. Traditionally, the sharpest young men, with the greatest potential for eventual leadership positions, were given the spear carrier tasks. Roger Smith and his predecessor, Tom Murphy, both served in this function. The essential nature of the role is to be the executive's primary assistant, to do the investigating and be the executive's eyes and ears in the company. The change in reporting meant that the ears would now be listening and the mouth reporting to the finance staff. One GM manager who was an executive assistant at the time was taken off the assignment because he was not a finance man. "There's no question that the treasurer's office wanted control of the function," he said. The rationale for their being financial men was that they could make up for the limitations of a president and other executives with engineering backgrounds who simply weren't up on the numbers. The reality, however, was that finance found a way to keep tabs on what the operational executives were doing and saying.

One former financial staff bag man crystallized the situation for me. "The operating exec I was assigned to had a pet project in his skunk works [an unofficial project] that he didn't want finance to know about until it was ready," he said. "My boss [in the treasurer's office] found out I was holding back, and next thing I knew I was in farm country as comptroller for a jerkwater widget plant. The executive was one of the top five executive committee guys, but he didn't have the clout to bail me out. That taught me whom I *really* worked for."

In writing speeches for senior operating executives, I worked with the bag men. I learned that to give any one of them a copy of a private document was to assume it would be duplicated and circulated throughout the treasurer's operation within the hour. And when my executive wanted to make a point that didn't sit well with them, the bag man would politely guide me to his actual boss, assistant comptroller John Mischi. Mischi was what I assumed Sister Woman's no-neck kids had turned out to be—broad-bodied and abrasive. Even when he was attempting civility, Mischi would call in a finance guy or two and chew them out in front of me, just to stay in practice. It always amazed me that Mischi seemed to know more about every operating executive's job than the executive did. Mischi, under treasurer's staff directions, attempted to bully finance's perspective into everything. I found the only way to avoid these browbeating sessions was to tell him to take up any problem he had with the executive who would be giving the speech. That always stopped him cold. The treasurer's office style was to influence inconspicuously, to use fine enough puppet strings so that they never showed on camera.

When Roger, a financial man, became chairman in 1981, the first thing he did was to sell the General Motors Building in New York and move much of the financial operations to Detroit. Under Roger's leadership a significant number of financial men have been appointed to very unlikely positions as the heads of operating divisions. One was named public relations manager of a group; another, vice president over marketing. When I asked Roger about the financial dominance, he said: "Times have changed. There is no longer any way to efficiently run the company with the financial staff separate from Detroit. . . . There's a lot of talent in the finance staff, and you've got to consider each man by what he can do. . . . Sloan would have understood and approved my action. He understood the need for change." Later Roger said of his job: "It doesn't take a finance man to sit in this office, but it doesn't hurt, either."

One interesting side point gives an indication of the financial staff's position within General Motors today. The treasurer's staff is positioned on the 13th floor, in the wing directly under the chairman's office. The financial people have the only way of getting up to the 14th floor without going through the elaborate double-door security system—a back stairway that comes out on the 14th floor across from Roger's office. Since this stairway was quicker than the conventional route, I got into the habit of going that way until a senior treasurer's office executive made it clear that the private stairway was strictly for finance. No one else was allowed direct access to the stairway to corporate power.

It's interesting to note here that a similar transition to financial dominance was happening down the road at Chrysler Corporation in the 1960s and '70s. Lynn Townsend, a man with financial staff experience only, became the darling of Chrysler when he started turning a large profit by drastically cutting into the product development and operating side of the business. Because of his efforts, Townsend was named president in 1961, then both chairman and chief executive officer of Chrysler in 1967. He loaded top Chrysler management with financial men without giving them any meaningful management experience on the operational level. For 20 years Chrysler had been known for excellence in engineering and innovation. Townsend abandoned this and instead emphasized outside acquisitions as a faster track to profits. The result was that Chrysler lost contact with the marketplace and was at bankruptcy's door before a marketing and product man was brought in to save the corporation.

Sloan's third corner of his management structure, and by his own analysis the most important for success, was "centralized policy and decentralized administration." Sloan considered decentralization the only realistic way of coping with the enormous management nightmare of a corporation the size of General Motors. As Sloan put it:

"General Motors' long-term survival depends upon its being operated in both the spirit and the substance of decentralization."

Under Sloan's decentralization each division was a separate moderate-sized company. The division was self-contained, with its own manager, engineers, designers, suppliers, sales staff, and research activity. Each division—or company within the company—was responsible for its own return on investment. With only one exception, Fisher Body, which built the skins for all of the autonomous divisions on order, decentralization was complete. Decentralization fit beautifully with his predecessor's, Billy Durant's, desire for diversification to cover many possible engineering and design futures and to avoid the all-or-nothing approach that would result from one centralized company.

Divisions were gradually stripped of their autonomy during the 1960s. By 1971 a new General Motors Assembly Division had complete control of all car making, Fisher Body controlled design, and the various engine, transmission, and components divisions pieced out their segments of control. The divisions became little more than marketing and public relations operations.

A new concept called "badge engineering" emerged. With it, a single car was designed, then each division was allowed to ginger up its version slightly with trim modifications to make it into a Chevrolet or Pontiac or Buick or Oldsmobile or Cadillac—but customers were not fooled into thinking that the same car by a different name was anything but a clone. The original concept of the divisions was that each one represented a step up in quality and price. Over a lifetime, a family could start out with a little Chevrolet, then move up to Pontiac, then Buick, then Oldsmobile, and ultimately, if things went well, to Cadillac luxury. And there were many who developed lifelong loyalty to a single division—"Dad's always driven a Buick." Sloan emphasized how extremely important it was to GM's success to have each division "so distinctive that you can tell one division's cars from another at a glance." It was a brilliant marketing approach that kept buyers inside of the GM community for generations. Badge engineering ended all of that, and it speeded up the trend toward multiple-company dealerships. Traditionally, a GM dealer could combine the products of two divisions for a wide showroom range. But it didn't look nearly as good to put look-alike cars side by side and attempt to sell them as distinctive. So dealers moved to contracting with a second company, often a foreign car company, for variety. Badge engineering has done more to devastate GM's successful marketing strategy than any other single factor.

Badge engineering was unquestionably the invention of finance staff as a way of vastly increasing profits through uniformity. Some also say that the move to corporate-wide manufacturing divisions and look-alike cars was a way of discouraging the federal antitrust gang. It's harder to break up a single corporate whole than to break off autonomous car divisions.

The Arab oil embargo in 1973 also did its part to push General Motors into ever-increasing centralization. Long lines at gas stations, rationing, and skyrocketing prices sent the market looking for economy cars. The only place they could be found in GM was at Chevrolet. So GM quickly gave Pontiac, Buick, Oldsmobile, and, later, Cadillac versions of the Chevrolet economy cars. This was done both to assure sales for devastated big-car divisions and to increase the proportion of small to large cars sold overall in order to meet stringent federal fleetwide fuel economy goals.

Roger has yet another explanation for the demise of decentralization. He says it was the victim of "increased product complexity and excessive government regulation." In other words, it was too costly to do everything that needed to be done in the 1970s in a decentralized manner. The decade of the 1970s certainly can be considered the era of regulation and reaction. By 1979 GM complained, more than 24,000 employees were doing nothing but filling out triplicate forms to respond to federal bureaucrats. Independent sources estimated that regulation cost the auto industry about $10 billion a year from 1974 through 1981.

The two toughest regulations were the federal emissions standards, which sought to eliminate smog by mandating reductions of tailpipe hydrocarbons, and CAFE (corporate average fuel economy) standards that required automakers to produce fuel-efficient cars. The problem was that with conventional technology whatever improved fuel economy also increased emissions, and vice versa. Catalytic converters could solve the problem, but these depended on the use of rare noble metals found primarily in unfriendly or unstable countries. To produce 15 million cars a year with uncertain sourcing was a major gamble. GM chairman Richard Gerstenberg decided to take the chance with noble metal catalysts across GM's entire production, and at the same time downsize its full size cars in 1977. Simultaneously, the corporation was doing extensive research on alternate fuels, on electric, turbine, diesel, and Wankel (rotary) engine concepts—all just in case gasoline tanks dried up or emissions regulations tightened further.

The demands of the 1970s spurred General Motors in the direction of computer-based technology. "There simply were not enough engineers in the world to do everything we needed done," former GM president Jim McDonald says. GM became the world leader in computer-aided design and computer-aided manufacturing. And, in 1980, GM took the greatest leap of all in deciding to install in-vehicle engine control computers across its entire 1981 car line. "That was a technological miracle," Roger says. "To put computers on a few thousand cars and test them out for a couple of years would be one thing. They [government] didn't give us the time. So we put computers in six million cars at once without any chance for trial and error. That put us a couple of years ahead of anything the Japanese had, and our engineers did a miraculous job bringing that together."

The emphasis on technological solutions and on rapidly downsizing all car lines, according to Roger, forced the company to become more centralized. It simply was not the kind of challenge that smaller, autonomous divisions could have met. Nor was there time for a great deal of individuality. Yet, whether it was regulated expediency, financial staff greed, or antitrust paranoia, the fact remains that decentralization ceased to be even a remote operating principle of General Motors by the time Roger became chairman.

"Progression and succession" was the final aspect of Sloan's management system. This was the methodical process of nurturing GM's top leadership through a series of carefully defined steps of ever increasing difficulty. Sloan considered succession of utmost importance, and while he would sometimes skip executive board meetings, he was always present and involved in the rigorous process of selecting managers. Every quarter he was said to have spent a full three days doing nothing but reviewing staff appointments. "The perpetuation of leadership," Sloan said, "is sometimes more difficult than the attainment of that leadership in the first place. This is the greatest challenge to be met by the leader of an industry. It is a challenge to be met by the General Motors of the future."

Performance reviews were regular, eventually settling on six-month intervals, so that progress of the high-potential employees could be carefully watched and guided. The several hundred high-potential people on the fast track learned loyalty and team play, and, above all, they learned to accept the paternal nature of the system that was guiding them upward. Jim McDonald, for example, was general manager of the Hydra-matic (transmission) Division in 1964 when the selection committee decided he should take a step down to become works manager at Pontiac. It was clearly a demotion, yet he was told the step was needed to round out his experience. Jim swallowed hard and accepted the demotion and eventually rose to the GM presidency. The lesson was as much one of accepting authority as of broadening his potential for leadership.

As Sloan envisioned it, the slow and methodical process through a dozen jobs over 35 to 40 years would prepare the best man for the chairmanship or presidency for a three- or four-year term. The fact that the individual who rose tended to be uniformly without charisma, or even discernible personality, was intentional. The ideal GM leader would place the image and goals of the group before his own. Through committees he would be able to speak as "we" instead of "I." He would be objective rather than self-styled and subjective. It was as elaborate a leadership scheme as Plato's rigorous preparation of the philosopher king, only the GM philosopher king would preside over an empire that spanned 39 countries, far larger than any city-state.

In essence, two lines of succession developed under Sloan's balanced leadership concept. The succession up through engineering, manufacturing, or marketing would lead to the presidency. The individual on this track would typically have been born within a couple of hundred miles of Detroit in a small, but industrial, community. He would graduate from General Motors Institute (GMI). The West Point of General Motors, this fully accredited engineering college in Flint, Michigan, sent more than 95 percent of its graduates directly to work for the corporation. He would start in a plant, as all GMI co-op students must, then work his way up through staff engineer, chief engineer, then a succession of ever larger division managerships before finally moving on to "The Building."

The chairman's succession was somewhat different. He could be either an easterner and come up through the New York hierarchy or a midwesterner and come up through the New York hierarchy. Typically, he should have graduated from a Big-Ten school, University of Michigan preferred, and have a master's degree in business administration. Somewhere during the dozen or so financial jobs in the progression was an obligatory stint of 18 months to two years as an actual manufacturing division general manager for the hands-on experience. ("That's like teaching someone to play football by making him coach," DeLorean protested.) Only one man in the past 30 years did not follow this pattern to the chairmanship. He was James Roche (1967-71), who was neither a financial man nor an engineer. Roche was a poor farm boy without benefit of a college degree, who came up through the Cadillac Motor Car Division organization. Roche was such an outstanding leader that the exception had to be made for him (but a vice chairman was named from the financial staff to keep the proper focus at the top).

Much has been written about the closed community of GM's philosopher-kings-in-training. They were all tall, Caucasian, and conservative in dress and religion. No dark little Mediterraneans, and certainly no Jews, had a chance. They married attractive cheerleader types, who would be enthusiastically supportive during their husbands' long climb. And as they neared the upper echelons, they were expected to take up residence amid the posh rolling hills and private lakes of Bloomfield Hills, Michigan—a community of 40,000 with one of the highest average per-capita incomes in America. All were expected to join the Bloomfield Hills Country Club (though few played golf). They were generally jocks and good ol' boys and not the type to read a book unless it was assigned to them. (Roger's two favorite books, for the record, probably suggested by a speech writer, are Adam Smith's *An Inquiry into the Nature and Causes of the Wealth of Nations* and Richard Bach's *Jonathan Livingston Seagull*.) And they were thoroughly GM. Less than 1 percent of those who rose to the 14th floor had ever worked anywhere else. As Brock Yates said in *The Decline and Fall of the American Automobile Industry*, "They live together, they work together, they drink together, they play golf together, they think together."

It is interesting to note here that the stereotypical image of GM's management did not exist in the clearly decentralized culture under Sloan. In evaluating GM in the 1940s, Peter Drucker said: "There is no 'General Motors type' . . . in fact, I am greatly struck by the difference of atmosphere between divisions, and by the variety of personality and background between individual divisional managers." Drucker believed that this was fundamental to Sloan's decentralization in the assumption that "every man will do his best job when he does it his own way. . . ." Decentralization meant diversity. The centralized GM of the 1960s and '70s meant uniformity.

Yet, in fairness, the stereotypes of GM's inbred culture were only partially accurate, at best. The norms themselves were never as hard and fast as outsiders have suggested. Conformity certainly was there, a natural by-product of any large institution, and the stereotypes provided the conceptual maps for the upper 5 percent of the GM culture. Yet there were always a handful of exceptional leaders on the track who tended to run in their own style. Men like Jim Roche were talented enough to demand a great deal of latitude. Roger Smith is hardly a tall Nordic type, is not married to a cheerleader, and doesn't know zip about the NFL and NBA.

John Z. DeLorean was perhaps the greatest critic of the regimented GM culture. In his book DeLorean said that he was considered a rebel with his Italian-cut suits, long hair, fast cars, and the flashy young models he dated. Yet the fact that DeLorean rose from entry-level engineer to group executive vice president in just 17 years belies the force of discrimination and conformity he experienced. Yes, the GM system tended to weed out the radicals and nonconformists—the non-team players—long before they might reach the pinnacles of power, yet great latitude was allowed to men of exceptional talent.

The aspect of the GM culture that has fascinated me, and has never been explored adequately, is the sexual puritanism of those who reached the top. The greatest taboo of all is sexual expression, or even innuendo. In the mid-1970s I was the start-up editor for a new magazine circulated to a million high school seniors. The magazine, called *American Youth*, was sponsored by General Motors exclusively and had the express purpose of communicating the wonders of American life, in particular private enterprise, to emerging adults. One of the articles I put together was an interview with "Wonder Woman" Lynda Carter. I planned the cover with a full-length shot of Lynda in her Wonder Woman costume. PR vice president Jack McNulty circulated the galley around the 14th floor. They had a collective coronary over Lynda's cleavage.

"We can't show breasts," Jack said. "It's just not something

GM execs can deal with." I explained that millions of school-children watched Lynda daily on television and none seemed shocked that she, indeed, had breasts. That didn't sell on the 14th floor. Lynda ended up with a photo of her shoulders, neck, and head—no bosom.

Another time I had an article by a bright writer named Kate Phifer. To deal with growth hormones, Kate had to mention the impact of the menstrual cycle in the text. "Can't you use some other term?" Jack asked. "They'll never buy that up-stairs." How about "the monthly curse," I suggested, but they didn't see the humor in that, either. After a protracted battle over whether we should tell 18-year-olds that women had menstrual cycles, I won. It was a major victory for science.

Yet another experience was related to me by a fellow speech writer about one of the top four GM executives (not Roger). He was to make a keynote speech at the world design conference, but hadn't realized that in addition to auto de-signers there would be clothing designers, interior decora-tors, etc. Some were decidedly gay. This shook up the 60-year-old executive so badly that he bungled his speech, spent an hour sliding his back against walls, and excused himself as early as possible.

Human sexuality was not something the GM executive could, or yet can, deal with. Roger has removed from his speeches jokes containing even the slightest sexual inference, and it didn't help to explain that they were jokes that former U.S. presidents had used before Congress. Aside from drawing the obvious conclusions about sublimation and displacement aggression into business and sports (GM primarily sponsors team sports advertising), the conclusion that you could draw is that this was—and is—a fraternity of remarkably unsophisti-cated men. You automatically get that idea when you hear the chairman of the board say "gosh, gee, and holy Toledo" when his enthusiasm gets the better of him.

The culture itself was archaic. The fast track presented no major problem in an era when operations changed little, if at all. But as the need for change increased, the system's funda-mental shortcomings became painfully obvious. Moving exec-utives around at dizzying speeds disrupted ongoing operations. "When you move the stars around constantly, it's hard for those below to get their bearings," a Pontiac plant superintendent said.

The original concept of evaluating leadership performance was lost in the rapidly rotating whirligig. Fast-track runners didn't stick around long enough to reveal their ability to effect permanent change. In a plant setting, for example, you could churn out junk to increase production and profitability, knowing full well that you'd be promoted and gone long before the warranty claims returned a year or so later to haunt you.

Sloan's succession process did foster a great deal of think-alike management. Roger recognized the error of inbreeding and set out to change it. As finance vice president in the late 1970s, Roger began hiring outsiders into significantly high positions—unheard of in a system in which virtually all promotions had been from within. In 1979, for example, he hired Dr. Marina v. N. Whitman as vice president and chief economist. Dr. Whitman had previously been Distinguished Public Service Professor at the University of Pittsburgh and served on the President's Council of Economic Advisors. She had no industry experience.

After his election to the chair, Roger stepped up his fresh-blood hiring of outsiders. In 1982 he approved the appointment of Dr. Robert Frosch, former head of NASA, as vice president over GM's prestigious research laboratories. Frosch is a Jew, the first Jewish GM vice president in the corporation's modern history. But the most startling appointment was when Roger hired Elmer Johnson in 1983 to be vice president and general counsel. Johnson was a Chicago lawyer and had participated as a consultant in the reorganization of International Harvester and the breakup of AT&T. In 1987, with just four years inside General Motors, he was promoted to executive vice president and member of the GM Board of Directors—a position that places him one step away from the GM chairmanship.

Another shock to the succession process came in 1987, when Roger promoted a brilliant black plant manager to vice president of personnel, jumping him a half dozen succession steps at once and passing over a dozen designated fast-trackers. That set executives mumbling about "reverse discrimination" and made it clear that promotion from within GM could no longer be assumed.

A more direct statement of Roger's intention to break up the club came only a matter of weeks after his ascension. He withdrew GM's financial support from GMI, the company-owned college. GMI had been the source of operational talent for 60 years. A long string of GM presidents, including Jim McDonald and his predecessor, Elliot "Pete" Estes, were GMI graduates. Roger saved $16 million a year by withdrawing support, not a great deal of money by General Motors standards; but, more important, it was a message that the traditional progression and succession no longer applied.

Sloan's four-legged system was ideally suited to support a stable industrial platform in which everything, and everyone, was interchangeable. It was a purely elitist concept, as witnessed by the fact that it never addressed the functionings of anything other than the top 5 to 8 percent of the total General Motors culture. The vast majority of the General Motors organization had quite a different culture.

For the rank-and-file salaried employees, the vast majority of the foremen, engineers, and clerks with no entreé to the fast track, what went on at The Building had little to do with their ongoing existence. They were Chevrolet people, or Buick people, or, the mark of excellence, Cadillac people, with no identification with the GM parent except to assume that the corporation, "Generous Motors," as many called it, would give them a bit more than the hourly wage people received with every new union contract. So they identified far more with the hourly workers than with the distant stars in the corporate galaxy.

Moving the fast-trackers frequently in and out of positions of authority had the curious effect of negating their leadership. Plant and staff people understood the drill. The stable salaried people knew that the fast-track manager would be in and out of their area in a couple of years. They also knew the fast-tracker would make dramatic changes in order to impress the powers that be; thus, they fully expected to be inundated with new programs with each newcomer and to quietly drop those programs the moment he moved on. "I've seen it all before" was a realistic survival attitude. The idea was to placate the fast-trackers but not to change anything so much that you could not change it back the day after tomorrow. To operate successfully this way, the rank-and-file salaried people depended on a network of informal communications—the "good ol' boy" network. Networking is present in every organization, of course, but in GM it became fundamental to survival.

As for union-represented workers, they were blue-collar migrants without the benefit of the travelogue. Labor was hired or dismissed in direct proportion to the harvest of new car and truck orders. And in an industry where big-ticket items meant extreme sales cycles, life for the auto worker was one of uncertainty. There are few auto workers, even today, who have not had several extended layoffs in their first 20 years of employment. Nor did it matter a great deal to the company if it got back the same people it laid off, since virtually any man or woman could be trained in the assembly task in a matter of minutes. A counter girl at McDonald's needed to know more than the assembler at Pontiac. Sloan could summarize all one needed to know to manage the hourly worker in one brief sentence: "Give a man a clearly defined task and let him do it."

Labor was a commodity. For the vast majority of Detroit's people, that fostered an uncertain, and largely demeaning, existence. Sociologists have pointed out the downside of isolation and ignorance, of frustration that has kept Detroit the murder capital of America in most years. Yet there was also an upside of a people who, having lived with uncertainty, reached out to help one another along the way. Detroit was the birthplace of the United Foundation, known in most communities throughout America as the United Way or the Torch Drive. Major philanthropic organizations, including the Kiwanis Club and Exchange Club, were founded in Detroit. And there have been many less-publicized humanitarian efforts emanating from the Motor City, such as the Care-Givers, a national organization to help shut-ins, and a relatively new national effort called Homes for Black Children. While life for the masses in Detroit was demeaning, it was not without dignity and charity.

Detroit, of course, was only the hub of the auto empire. Its plants spread out like the spokes of a giant wheel that stretched from Saginaw, Michigan, to Dayton, Ohio, and from Buffalo, New York, to Chicago, Illinois. Most of the auto towns, places where the manufacture of cars or parts thereof determined the community's overall economy, had much the same unsettled situation of uncertain employment and more certain downgrading of individual relevance. Satellite plants from California to New Jersey and from Montreal, Quebec, to Shreveport, Louisiana, also were affected by Detroit's culture, in diminished proportion to the distance from the hub and in direct proportion to the number of auto workers in the larger community.

The most successful auto companies, with GM at the top, were those that could keep the best ongoing adjustment of the human commodity in relation to production schedules. Management wanted no part of the worker's participation. In 1970, UAW leader Irving Bluestone suggested greater worker involvement and participation and was politely told by General Motors to "go to hell." Sloan himself objected to the rise of labor's demands on increasing profits, saying: "In the end, increased efficiency flows not so much from the increased effectiveness of the workers, but primarily from more efficient management and from the investment in capital and labor-saving devices."

No industry was more ripe for unionism than the auto industry. Yet when unionism came, nothing seemed to change. Labor remained a commodity. Peter Drucker said General Motors "was dead from the neck up in public relations since 1937," the year, of course, that the United Auto Workers expressed their will in a sit-down strike against GM in Flint.

The gap between the top management and the blue-collar workers has historically been greater at General Motors than at either Ford or Chrysler, largely because of the distances imposed by Sloan's system. Owen Bieber, UAW president, has said: "Historically, workers have always distrusted GM because the company looks out for its executives, not its workers."

The only significant change that occurred between 1937

and 1977 was that labor became an *expensive* commodity. The only time General Motors fully resisted union demands was in 1970, and that resulted in a 77-day strike which emptied the UAW's bank accounts and cost GM in the neighborhood of $5 billion in lost sales. Doug Fraser, former UAW president, remembers the strike well. "A strike against anything the size of General Motors isn't a strike," he says. "It's a crusade." That strike was primarily over whether GM would take the cap off the cost of living allowance (COLA). COLA yoked compensation to increases in the overall cost of living as measured by the consumer price index. It was protection, within limits, against inflation. The strike removed the limits. It took the cap off the COLA, and cost competitiveness has fizzled since. With COLA *and* obligatory pay hikes attached to every new contract, there was no keeping the balance between costs and productivity improvements.

In 1979, when Roger, then vice president of finance, was asked about the negotiated contract that year, which was clearly inflationary, he simply shrugged and said, "There are some things you just can't control." Roger and most other auto executives blame a gluttonous union for their industry's competitiveness problems. Lee Iacocca, however, sees management as the culprit. As he says in *Iacocca*, to fight meant risking downtime, lost revenues, and a loss of individual executive bonuses. "Our motive was greed," Iacocca says. "The instinct was always to settle quickly, to go for the bottom line."

Sloan's clearly elitist concept worked well enough in a stable market in which maintaining order and modest profitability in a far-flung empire was the goal. The centralized elite could progress through their stages of development without having their inexperience and enthusiasm do too much damage, as long as there was the committee system to keep them in bounds and a justifiably cynical decentralized white-collar cadre was in place to resist dramatic departures from the proven norms of production. It worked as long as the demands placed on the blue-collar workers were as minimal as the rewards and they could be kept as unskilled and interchangeable as the 15,000 parts they hung together to build a car.

Sloan's system had a number of advantages. Operating decisions were made quickly in the autonomous divisions. There was a tremendous sense of personal security in a system in which everyone knew the limits of each person's authority and factionalism was kept at a minimum. And perhaps most important was the absence of management by corporate edict. Frequent "Sloan meetings," as they were called, were used to explain overall policy decisions, and the most junior of managers was encouraged to participate.

While Sloan's system was already becoming fuzzy in the late 1950s, two major events were developing—one highly publicized and the other largely overlooked—that made Sloan's elitist system as obsolete as tire tubes and running boards.

The first, of course, was high-tech. The microprocessor removed the physical limits of engineering and made it possible to actually extend the human mind into the machinery around us. Data could be processed, transmitted, and sorted in infinite variations. Alvin Toffler called this the beginning of the Third Wave, the information age. Yet it was not information that held out the potential, but communication. Information meant simply that more facts could be accumulated, more reams of paper in what was to be the paperless society. Communication implies the human ends of the information connection, the sharing of human-refined data and ideas. Traditionally, information was hoarded as a source of personal and professional power in our institutions. Guarded knowledge kept the elite executive (who had to prepare for a third of a century to gain access) above the white-collar cadre and eons above the factory-floor laborer. With high technology, communication knowledge was still power, but now it flowed to nearly anyone who could garner access to a terminal and a telephone. Knowledge, which, in an elitist culture meant power, was now available via computer links to virtually anyone. The communications revolution did what the Gutenberg Bible had done to religion: it made the source of knowledge available and removed the mysticism that was the priest's lock on his elite knowledge. Communications brought egalitarianism to the workplace. Decentralized decisions could be made on the job site with computer-supplied knowledge, thus eliminating the need for a centralized elite.

The same high technology fostered smart machines. These machines, if not quite as clever as *Star Wars*' R2D2 and C3P0, could at least ape human motor tasks and, for the first time, unchain the man from the machine. There were two ways to look at this event, of course. One could view it in the context of upgrading the required skills of people who would supervise, maintain, and orchestrate a number of smart machines at once. Skill levels once reserved for the elite (or at least for the skilled tradespeople who were the elite among the working ranks) now had to be mastered by the line machine operator. In this scenario the blue-collar worker could no longer be a commodity. He or she could no longer be trained in five minutes and be expected to function in this sophisticated environment. The worker, thus, had to be viewed as more of a fixed asset, someone to invest in and utilize more fully.

As Alvin Toffler said in a 1981 visit to the auto capital: "If Detroit is going to continue to be a lunch-bucket, mass-production town, I'm sure there's a niche for that, but it isn't going to be a very important place. . . ." Detroit must learn "that the essential resource is not coal or steel but what is in people's heads."

Sloan's steadfast belief that productivity gains came from investing in capital (technology) that traded off labor was no longer a viable concept. In fact, Peter Drucker in *Managing in Turbulent Times* says, "There is little evidence that this 'trade off' ever really worked as a way to increase overall productivity." What happened was that each time capital equipment was purchased to trade off against a reduction in labor rates, the skill levels required, and therefore the cost of labor, actually rose. And as the electronic revolution vastly increased the need for knowledge workers instead of muscle laborers, the cost of labor—and its value as a fixed asset—logically should have increased.

Yet another way of viewing the smart machines was to take a leap of imagination into what Toffler calls the Fourth Wave, the era of artificial intelligence and the insertion of humanlike thought into the clockworks. (The First Wave was the invention of agriculture, the Second Wave was the Industrial Revolution, and the Third Wave was technology yoked to electron-

ics, the "technetronic age.") The Fourth Wave, according to
Toffler, would result from incorporating human thought into
the machines, eventually bringing about the total automation
of the factories. The Fourth Wave could be viewed, as Roger
seems to have, as a way of removing much of the unpredict-
able human element from the equation in the 21st-century
corporation. The Fourth Wave, however, is still a great distance from a solid shore. The technology simply isn't ready.

The American Production and Inventory Control Society
recently concluded that even state-of-the-art computer implementation fails to meet expectations from 30 percent to 75
percent of the time, largely because of failures to meet the
.Third Wave requirement of improved human communications. Manual systems, in fact, are proving to have far higher
uptime because there is simply less that can go wrong with the
biological operator. And the machine vision so essential for
the robots in the factory of the future has proven far too complicated to be practicable. As Robert Shillman, president of
Cognex Corporation, a maker of vision machines, said in a
recent *Electronic Business* magazine article, "There is no generic solution to machine vision problems . . . each task requires its own solution, and eventually people will figure out
that the market payback is not large enough to invest in the
solution." In Roger's new General Motors the thrust to advanced technology has simply created an incredible array of
new toys for the engineers and has succeeded in creating
Rube Goldberg devices that, as Goldberg said, are "symbols of
man's capacity for exerting maximum effort to accomplish
minimal results."

The second evolution, taking place far more unobtrusively
than high technology, is in management techniques. In *Innovation and Entrepreneurship*, Peter Drucker captures the essence of this movement when he says that the most important
technology of our age, at least the one that has created the
greatest increase in American jobs and prosperity, is "not electronics or genetics or new materials. The 'new technology' is
entrepreneurial management." He is referring to new and innovative ways to more fully develop and utilize human resources, which, of course, should be the essence of any pro-

ductivity-oriented institution. There are numerous new approaches such as statistical process control, team action, quality circles, just-in-time flow-through systems, participatory management, parallel or synchronous engineering, ad infinitum. They have a common characteristic in that the focus is placed on helping the individual make improvements to his own job. It is micro, rather than macro, orientation. All of this centers on respect for the individual and a belief that he or she wants to do excellent work, to share in the rewards of that effort, and to increase personal dignity in the process.

Most of these innovative management techniques were, as were the vast majority of inventions in this century, American creations. They have been tried, and discarded, at one time or another by one company or another. Statistical process control, for example, is a way of continuously measuring the variations from the norm of a machine's output to systematically narrow the range of nonconformance and thus improve the product. Fast-track GM executives introduced the method in a number of plants during the 1950s, but, as with most innovations, the idea was quietly dropped when the executives moved on. Failing in the U.S., men like Dr. W. Edwards Deming and Dr. J. M. Juran took their concepts to Japan, where a culture without adversarial divisions found them most amenable. As Ross Perot says: "I can remember when if your parents gave you an apple for Christmas, you understood. But if they gave you a Japanese toy, you wondered if they still loved you." Japan was producing junk in the 1950s, yet through the new people-oriented management techniques the Japanese became the world's leading quality and low-cost manufacturers.

"It's the difference in national culture," the American manufacturers maintained and went on with business as usual. But in the 1970s Japan opened its first plants on American soil, and for the first time we could see what they could do using American workers and materials. The first plants produced color television sets. That was a shock. For the U.S. television manufacturers had already given up on trying to compete with Japanese imports and had moved their operations offshore. The Japanese produced the same sets with high-cost American workers—and with low technology—and were cost- and quality-competitive.

Honda and Nissan followed in establishing U.S. plants, again with relatively low technology and outstanding results. GM's own quality audit showed that these transplants in the American South had less than a fifth as many defects as the average GM plant. In fact, the Honda cars and Nissan trucks built in the U.S. achieved even higher quality evaluations than the same vehicles built in Japan. *The difference was management alone.* I had the opportunity to hear Shoichiro Irimajiri, president of Honda of America in Marysville, Ohio, talk about the operation. He became immensely enthusiastic about how an associate (Honda's name for workers) had realized he was walking 70 feet to pick up each part, when, if the machine was moved, he could reduce the effort to 55 feet. For this the associate received a small award and much recognition. I remember thinking at the time that such a small accomplishment would have been considered far too trivial for a GM executive even to mention, let alone rave about.

The ultimate lesson should have come for General Motors with Roger's own experimental joint venture in California with Toyota. The 50-50 joint venture created a company called New United Motor Manufacturing, Inc. (NUMMI). They would produce the Chevrolet Nova using GM's defunct Fremont plant and former GM workers, yet with a Japanese vehicle design, a Toyota Corolla, and Japanese management. When Roger had signed the order to close the Fremont plant, he was eliminating a management nightmare. The labor force was considered "uncooperative"; some called them "hellions."

Work stoppages, absenteeism, grievances against the company, and outright acts of sabotage were commonplace. As one reporter said, "When GM locked the plant [in 1982], the greatest surprise was that they bothered to save the keys."

Bringing back some of the most belligerent of these workers, the new Japanese managers were able to produce a car with higher quality levels than any other plant in General Motors and with higher production and lower costs than even Roger's most high-tech plants. We'll look at the lessons of NUMMI more closely in a later chapter, but for now NUMMI serves to make the point that there have been plenty of examples, even within General Motors, that the problem is not so much the

lack of high technology as it is ineffectual management techniques. Yet even seven years into his administration, Roger
continues to place his bets on the dramatic high-tech solutions to fundamentally simple human performance problems.

The best expression of how this relates to the Sloan elitist
structure came with the 1986 GM Executive Management
Conference. I worked with Howard Kehrl, then vice chairman,
to capture the essence of the problem in his presentation to
the top 600 manufacturing managers in the corporation. Howard was one of the most intelligent and reflective executives I
had the opportunity to write for. He had started his GM career
as a researcher at GM Research Labs, had several patents to his
credit and two master's degrees, one in engineering and
another under a Sloan Fellowship in management at MIT. As
vice chairman, Howard was Roger's chief of high technology.
Roger used Howard's engineering depth largely to set up new
ventures like Saturn Corporation, Saginaw's factory of the future, the Hughes acquisition, and the Lotus deal. Howard reminded me more of an absent-minded professor than of a corporate power broker. He would become so engrossed in
thought at times that if you spoke to him, he would nearly
jump out of his chair and snap your head off for the interrup-
tion. Howard built his career on asking questions. Sometimes
he asked thoughtless questions, like the time he inspected
GM's latest locomotive, climbed into the cab, and asked,
"Where's the steering wheel?" Yet more often his questions
cut to the heart of the issue and devastated elaborate presentations. Once I accompanied Howard to GM Research's Competitive Assessment Center, where the research operation had
compared its own expertise in each area such as polymers,
fluid dynamics, and acoustics to the best research in the field.
Howard took one quick look at the room full of charts and
asked: "Who did the comparisons?"

"Why, we had our own experts evaluate them," the scientist
said.

"Ridiculous. No one can grade his own report card," Howard snapped and walked out.

Though Howard was the corporation's chief technologist,
he found himself focusing more and more on management as

the one area where General Motors, and he felt all of American industry, was in deepest trouble. Formerly, as head of GM's Overseas Operations, he had reestablished recognition programs to encourage innovation and more recently had set up the Kettering Awards to honor and encourage outstanding inventions and innovations. However, he felt much more was needed. He formulated the fundamental premise of his Executive Management Conference speech from his evaluations, then, in traditional GM fashion, had me solicit insights on his perspective from all of the top scientists and engineers in the corporation. To my surprise, they were unanimous in their agreement with Howard's thesis. The problem was, they agreed, inherent in the corporate culture. Howard used a baseball analogy to make his point:

> All of you are home-run hitters, or you wouldn't be here. Many of you may be frustrated because something's gone wrong with the game—the fence has been moved way back, and a strong wind is blowing from the outfield. What was home-run performance a few years ago doesn't even get you on base today . . . you're frustrated. And I don't blame you. . . . Today, I'd like to tell you about the new reality that's causing your frustration. . . . It goes by many different names—continuous improvement, incremental innovation, gradualism, and *Kaizen*. . . .
> Continuous improvement comes only when individuals are motivated to achieve regular improvements in all areas of their work. It is acceptance of the reality that people and their brainchildren—like their own children—require years of patient nurturing before they reach the potential that was there at birth. Technology is important . . . but even more important is what we do in the years after we get the new machine or process in place. . . . With continuous improvement, the benefit of the major step in technology is multiplied by many small steps. And that holds true whether you are dealing with improvements in quality, or marketing, or design, or productivity, or human development. . . .
> Why? Because in a continuous improvement approach the emphasis is on the total team effort. The steady accumulation of small hits, walks, bunts, base hits, little sacrifices—all add to the total score. In the traditional

American way, we place most of the emphasis on the home
runs—on the heroes of the game. And if you follow baseball,
you know that the home-run hitters vary all over the lot in
overall performance.

Howard went on to give numerous examples of how GM's
home-run culture stood in the way of establishing a culture in
which incremental improvements were the norm. The GM
Suggestion Program, for example, pays off in big rewards such
as several thousand dollars or a free car and takes six months
to a year to process a suggestion. Toyota gives very small
awards frequently. The Toyota suggestions are evaluated by a
worker's peers and implemented by the individual or team
that made the suggestions. The result is that the Toyota employee makes 38 suggestions each year—more than one every
two weeks—and has better than a 95 percent acceptance and
implementation. The typical GM employee averages less than
one suggestion a year, and actual implementation compared to
suggestions is at 5 percent or less.

Sloan's management system, of course, places all of the emphasis on developing superheroes (the home-run hitters)
who make all of the significant decisions. The result is block-
buster change without operational follow-through. The continuous improvement approach is change from the bottom—
the workers—up, not from an elite down. Masaaki Imai, a management consultant, says in his book *Kaizen* that this approach is "the single most important concept in Japanese
management—the key to Japanese competitive success." The
typical Japanese manager, according to Imai, spends 50 percent of his time working to support his people in implementing typically small improvements.

One example that we didn't use in Howard's presentation
because of the anxiety level associated with it is the group
within General Motors that has long been committed to a
continuous improvement approach. They are called *industrial
engineers*, and their job is to work with small groups in the
plants to find improvements in the processes. "When I was
told they were assigning me industrial engineering, I asked
what I had done wrong," one young engineer said. Industrial

engineering is second-class citizenship in General Motors because its participants do not come up with the gee-whiz changes that capture senior management's attention. No industrial engineer in General Motors has ever reached the vice presidential ranks, though their entire existence is committed to improving quality and reducing costs.

As a postscript, Roger's response to Howard Kehrl's presentation was to praise him "as a brilliant *engineer*" and to say, "I can always depend on Howard to have a different way of looking at things." Far from an endorsement, Roger's reaction amounted to an "Isn't that cute?" pat on the head in front of the entire manufacturing team. Nearly two years after the presentation, none of the examples of GM cultural roadblocks that Howard pointed out in his presentation have been changed. On the 14th floor the general feeling was that Roger didn't see the argument as significant. And as Howard spent more time discussing improvements in management, Roger began to favor Vice President Donald Atwood for high-tech projects. Atwood was far more of a pure believer in technological, not motivational, solutions. Howard retired a year ahead of schedule and was replaced in the vice chairmanship by Atwood.

A new GM production system incorporating many of these new management techniques is in the works. *Production system* is probably the wrong term, for it is fundamentally a comprehensive management approach that can be used in virtually any interpersonal situation. It incorporates most of the lessons learned from Japan and GM's own NUMMI experience. Yet development of the production system has been allowed to languish. "Don't expect too much from this," a vice president told me. "Hell, they were allowed to take nearly a year just to pick the committee members. That doesn't sound like a priority project to me."

The new management technology amounts to a complete negation of Sloan's concept. It means trusting in people whom you recently perceived as a commodity to make most of the decisions that were the exclusive domain of the elite. That can happen only with management leadership that supports the enlightened approach and builds a level of trust so that the rank-and-file employees will be convinced that this is not just another example of what Don Ephlin, the UAW's GM Department vice president, calls "GM's tradition of management by fad."

Yet giving up the old system, even though the legs that supported it have been weakened, is going to be a major challenge. Three Harvard business professors—Mal Salter, Dave Dyer, and Alan Webber—have recently published a major evaluation of the U.S. auto industry in a book, *Changing Alliances*. They concluded that a major problem is going to be convincing managers to give up what they believe are their rights to manage. "Many managers today are staunchly defending a fallen citadel," they say. The experience in new management technology clearly shows that the advantage is to the companies that make allies out of their employees. Salter, Dyer, and Webber believe that, in the auto industry, defending management's rights will incur "the costs of trying to make an old myth perform in the context of a new reality."

Yet within GM today none of this is clearly articulated. The future culture of the corporation is nebulous at best. The old culture is dead, yet most GM managers do not even know that it was ill. They continue to praise Sloan in current, not historical, terms. Roger has added to this confusion, saying at times that "decentralization is what our new GM is all about" and "Alfred P. Sloan, Jr.'s, contributions are very much with us," and at other times that "Yes, we've gone a long way away from Sloan. His methods just wouldn't work in the new competitive world."

Ross Perot heard Sloan quoted chapter and verse when he explored General Motors. He realized that the new approaches were a great distance from the founder's vision, and Ross felt GM had to change if it was to become world competitive. As Ross Perot says:

"Too many people in GM are still reading Sloan's book."

3
Ledger-Ink Blue

"I think somehow we learn who we really are,
then we live by that decision."

Eleanor Roosevelt

W hen he parked his brand-new 1949 Ford at a 30-
minute meter and walked into the palatial vaulted
entryway of Detroit's General Motors Building,
bells should have tolled and trumpets sounded. For if ever
there was a man born and reared to succeed in the elite GM
corporate culture, it was Roger Bonham Smith.

Roger's father, Emmett Quimby Smith, had taken as much
care in establishing the path behind Roger as Alfred P. Sloan,
Jr., had in preparing the way ahead. No passage from family to
corporate culture could have been more natural or preordained.

The Smith family home was one of privilege and discipline,
and it emitted an inner sense of propriety that came of distinguished and exceedingly deep roots. On his father's side, Roger's genealogy is traceable to William de Huntingfield, a signer
of the Magna Carta in 1215. Roger is the namesake of William's
son, Roger de Huntingfield of Frampton. Roger's mother was a
Daughter of the American Revolution, and traced her ancestry
back to Samuel Fuller, who came over on the *Mayflower* and
married a Bonham (Roger's middle name) in a ceremony con-

ducted by Myles Standish. Wherever this side of the family settled, it seemed a town or boulevard was named after one of them. There is a city of Bonham in New Jersey named after his maternal great-grandfather and an Obetz, Ohio, from his mother's surname. In a town like Detroit, where most inhabitants can trace their lineage back one generation to either "somewhere in the Appalachians" or "the old country," the Smiths were an anomaly. "We were always aware of our ancestry," says Marilyn Engstrom, Roger's older sister. "We were taught to carry ourselves well and not to do anything to disgrace the family names."

If their blood was blue, it was the blue tint of ledger ink. Capitalism and the entrepreneurial spirit were bred into the lineage. Emmett Quimby Smith, son of a Chicago doctor, came to Columbus, Ohio, after World War I. He came back from the war with a pocketful of French francs and trudged from bank to bank trying to exchange the money. No bank in Columbus could do it, so Quimby (as he was called) talked one of the banks into letting him set up a foreign-exchange window. In 1921, the young businessman married Bess Bell Obetz, a teacher who became assistant superintendent of the Columbus schools, and soon they established both a family of four children and a bank of their own. Roger was born on July 12, 1925, a middle child tucked between an older brother, Quimby, Jr., and a little brother, J. Walter. The children all looked like Rockwell characters, with red or blond-red hair and round cherubic faces.

Roger was five years old when the Great Depression closed the family bank. They moved to Michigan. Quimby got a job as comptroller for Bundy Tubing Company, an auto industry supplier. Soon Quimby worked his way up to vice president and part owner of the company. He also established his own company on the side, Agalloy Metal Tubing, which made parts for the atomic bomb and parachute hand rings during World War II. Even well into retirement Quimby bought up small businesses, improved them, then resold them at a profit.

"We weren't wealthy by any means," Roger says of his youth, which comes as something of a surprise to those who knew his family when he was a boy. The family bought the stately home of former Michigan governor Wilbur Brucker, in the prestigious Indian Village community of Detroit. They maintained a second family home in northern Michigan and memberships in the better clubs, including the Detroit Boat Club. And all of this occurred during the deepest years of the Great Depression.

Quimby possessed the two qualities most essential for success in industrial Detroit, a strong business sense and a knack for invention. "Dad invented systems and methods and even invented some parts on machines," Roger says with obvious pride in his father, who established several patents in the tubing business. "He didn't believe you couldn't do things better." Sister Marilyn said, "Dad used to teach us kids how to be creative. He'd bring home some item and put it in the middle of the kitchen table and give us a problem. It might be a handful of spinach leaves and the problem was how to package it so that the leaves would not be ruined. Each of us had to think through the problem and come up with a creative solution."

Quimby's inventive mind also added a sense of adventure to family life. He would blow a bugle on a Saturday morning, and, when everyone was assembled, he'd tell them to get packed for a trip. "Where are we going?" they'd ask. "Follow your nose," he'd answer, and they were off on a new and, typically, educational adventure. The Smith children revered their father, a rare man who committed as much time and thought to developing his children as he put into nurturing his businesses.

Both parents were like gurus, who turned every activity into a lesson of one kind or another. Each child was required to learn an instrument (Roger, the least musical, played the drums), and they had regular band sessions on Sunday afternoons. Even religion was an educational experience, as the children were taken to many different churches to learn the broader implications of faith. Quimby's religious philosophy was decidedly Calvinistic—"Fear God and take your own part."

The Smiths would take winter breaks to Florida and spend entire summers in northern Michigan, away from the city's hay fever and the threat of polio. When they traveled, which was often, the children were required to take their schoolbooks and read in the car. The children were frail, and not always healthy, yet even in sickbeds their mother would have the others gather around and take turns reading youthful adventures such as *The Hardy Boys*. There was a blackboard in the bathroom, and each week five new words were posted (spelled phonetically for ease of retention), and before the week was out the children were expected to make the words their own. They were even financially motivated to achieve good grades—a dime for an A, a nickel for a B, and below a B you got trouble. All of the Smith children were outstanding students and typically skipped a grade somewhere in their elementary school years.

Firm discipline was as much a part of the scenario as educational fun. While they were wealthy by any measure in Depression-torn Detroit, the work ethic was sacred. Each child had chores and was expected to earn his extra money (Roger had a Sunday newspaper route). Though they had a black nanny to care for them, they had to wash dishes, make their own beds, and mind the nanny's instructions as carefully as if the orders were coming from a parent.

One of their father's lessons that Roger and his siblings would carry through life was the importance of disciplining their time. "No wasted motion" was a family mandate. "Dad was always conscious of how he used every minute," Marilyn says. "Time was used wisely, even when he was relaxing. That's how I learned to play golf. He'd say, 'We have 10 minutes to play this hole.' You had to hit the ball straight down the fairway to get it done in the allotted time."

As you'd expect in an almost storybook family, the children were close to one another. Although Quimby encouraged competitiveness in everything they did, there was also a strong sense of unity. Roger fit comfortably into the structure. He was never the rebel, and in his middle position was generally the appeaser, smoothing out disputes among the others. Left-handed and clearly not a gifted athlete, he always avoided team sports. He preferred to compete with himself in singular activities—horseback riding, hunting, fishing, and, most of all, sailing.

Roger was brought up in exclusive circles. He attended University School, now University Liggett, a small prep school in Detroit's wealthy Grosse Pointe crescent. At the Detroit Boat Club Roger and his brother competed in sailing races. Yet in true Smith family fashion, the children had their sleeves rolled up. Roger frequently worked with his older brother, Quimby, Jr., who had three paper routes—*Detroit News*, *Detroit Times*, and *Detroit Free Press*. One summer Roger worked in a Chrysler assembly plant installing roof insulation, and he worked at other times in his father's tubing plant until he was fired by his father for "having too good a time," Roger says. "He sent me back to the books."

Like his father, Roger had a natural interest in mechanical things. He dismantled his first car and put it back together at age 16 "with not too many parts left over," Roger says. His favorite subject in college, he said, was auto mechanics. Yet Roger showed his greatest abilities in business. "He was always the businessman," Marilyn says. "He'd charge you interest if he lent you a penny." Roger had a natural mind for numbers, and when he attended University of Michigan, he took differential calculus "to improve my grade-point average." He reviewed each professor's credentials and teaching reputation before taking a class so as not to waste valuable time.

In going to University of Michigan and majoring in business, Roger didn't know that he was following the traditional route to the chairmanship of General Motors. He, in fact, had the same teachers as GM chairmen Albert Bradley, Fred Donner, and Richard Gerstenberg and vice chairman Oscar Lundin. Roger graduated near the top of his class, with a bachelor's degree in accounting and a master's in business administration.

And he took a couple of years out from school to serve as an enlisted man in the navy. It was the first time he showed his career-long ability to get close to the top people wherever he went. Roger ended up as a radioman on the USS *Montpelier*, serving Admiral Arleigh Burke directly. Burke was called "the sailor's admiral" because he was protective of his enlisted men. Roger became close enough to the admiral to talk him into granting leaves for himself and Quimby, Jr., so they could go home for a holiday together.

Throughout his early adulthood he was thought of simply as a solid but overall typical student. He was a Phi Delta Theta fraternity brother who drank beer and sang songs with the bunch. His classmates, those who remembered the slight young man with the colorless hair, said he was "just a regular good Joe." His accounting professor, Dr. William Paton, said Roger had "an amazing amount of grit."

Grit and determination are fundamentals of each of the four Smith siblings. They have all gone on widely diverse career paths, yet each has been successful. Quimby, Jr., became a scientist in the aerospace field, J. Walter was successful in the rubber business, and Marilyn, after raising three girls and "being a room mother 13 times," has recently received her investment broker license and, in her early 60s, is launching a brand-new career.

Perhaps the greatest indication of Roger's reverence for his father was how he would relate to his own family. Roger married Barbara Ann Rasch, an attractive clerk in the GM Public Relations Department. They met at a Grosse Pointe Hunt Club party where Barbara knew no one. "He just took over," she recalls. Barbara had none of Roger's blue blood lineages (though she is a "very distant cousin" of the popular American poet Edgar Guest). Barbara was simply a working girl who had had more than her share of misfortune in her youth. Her father had diabetes, which, back then, was not controllable. He was unable to work, so, when she was 12, the family moved in with a grandmother. Barbara's mother supported the family by working as a clerk in traffic court. Barbara went to Detroit Commercial College—a secretarial school that no longer exists—and, after a few short-lived jobs, ended up at General Motors.

Roger and Barbara married in 1954, the same year they met, and settled in to create a family. They would have four children like his own father—Roger, Jr., Jennifer, Victoria, and, eight years after the others, Drew. "The children are Roger's closest friends," Barbara says. "There is nothing more important to him."

Like his father, Roger always made time for the children. They frequently traveled together, summers in northern Michigan and Christmases in the Caribbean, and were exposed to the adult community at every opportunity. Roger taught them all to sail, hunt, and fish (his own pastimes) and how to cook (wild game and French cooking were two of his passions). And he gave them the same firm, but affectionate, lessons in self-discipline and commitment he had received. He spent far more time with his children than any other fast-track GM executive, though his great anxiety has always been "I never get as much time with the kids as I'd like."

There was never any question that Barbara would be a full-time homemaker to "be there when the kids got home every day." Barbara, now matronly, and gentle in manner, talks of the children the way any mother would. "I practiced on my oldest one [Roger, Jr.]," she says. "I didn't know anything about raising kids. Mother worked, and Dr. Spock was new and untried then. And there was no second car in those days. It wasn't easy."

All four children are remarkably well adjusted for having been raised in a home with abundant money and social standing. Roger, Jr., graduated from Albion College, a private and highly academic Michigan school, then insisted on paying much of his own way through University of Michigan graduate school. He has the same degree, accounting and business, as his father, yet refused to work for General Motors, joining a small supplier company downriver. "Roger is most like his father," Barbara says. "He's more internal . . . I guess more introverted than the others."

Jennifer, the elder daughter, went to Kingswood, a prep school, then graduated from Albion also. She married and now pursues a career as the chief financial officer of a small company.

Victoria, "Tori," was the rebellious one. She went through a series of short-lived college experiences at DePauw, then Oakland University, and finally graduated from Northwood Institute. "When she came home after dropping out," Barbara said, "she thought she was just going to hang around for a while, but her father immediately enrolled her in a business school."

Tori found her niche as the "salesperson of the family," is now married, and works as a salesperson at a local clothing store.

The last child, Drew, came along much later than the others and got more of his father's individual attention than the first three. Roger and Drew are constant companions. They fish and hunt together regularly and play gin rummy nearly every night. Says Jack McNulty, GM public relations vice president, "I've been on trips with Roger when he insisted that we fly back at night, getting in at 2:00 or 3:00 A.M., just so he can be home in the morning to go to McDonald's for breakfast with Drew before his paper route."

Arriving late in Roger's career, Drew, now 18 years old, bore the brunt of being the son of the chairman of the largest corporation in the world in a town where about half of the people one meets work for General Motors or its suppliers. Yet Drew is a surprisingly normal young man who does his chores, asks for permission to go out, and is at ease, yet respectful, with adults. "Drew thinks the guy next door is rich, not us" Roger says. Last year, at about the same age Roger had been when he'd had too much fun in his father's factory, Drew was beginning to wander from his high school studies. "Roger put him back on track studying," Barbara says. "Drew even had to carry his books on their hunting trips and do his schoolwork before they'd go out in the woods." Drew entered Princeton last fall as a freshman.

Al Parrish is a friend of the family, close enough that the Smith children call him "Uncle Al." He says, "Roger works hard at being a father. He feels he has a commitment to do for his children what his father did for him."

Here, then, was the Roger Smith who parked at a 30-minute meter and confidently ran in to apply for an accounting job at General Motors in 1949. At 24 years old he already had a sense of propriety and purpose and a role model with well-defined edges. Later, when people asked him who influenced his career most, the politically astute answer would have been to name some GM luminary (and Roger was political), yet he would always answer "my father." His father would guide his thinking for most of his life and even directed him on this first step into General Motors. Roger was planning on leaving soon to take up a career in California's aviation industry and had stopped at General Motors only because his father had told him it was a "well-managed company" and that Roger should look into it.

During that employment interview, Roger's self-assurance impressed Arthur Sarason, the GM assistant comptroller who interviewed him. There was only one job open at the time, and Sarason told Roger it was a tough one and he doubted if the fresh graduate could handle it. "I was going to go in and show them I felt pretty sure I could do it," Roger recalls. After he was hired, Sarason later recalled telling his secretary: "I just hired a guy who *thinks* he's going to be chairman of General Motors."

Art Wisely, who recently retired from General Motors as an executive director of administration, became Roger's first friend in the corporation. They met on Roger's first day on the job and worked at desks facing one another for four years. "Within a month of joining," Wisely says, "Roger told me straight-faced, 'I'm going to be CEO of General Motors.' I laughed and said, 'In that case, I'll bet I become president.'" The difference, Wisely says, is that Roger wasn't kidding.

In those early years, Wisely was overwhelmed by Roger's seriousness about the job. "He had an uncanny ability to know what was important to the bosses and what wasn't. For example, we had these record cards that we were supposed to alphabetize before we turned them in. Roger refused to do that. Too menial. He said his time was too valuable to waste on clerical work. So I ended up doing it for him. The same with his subledgers.

"But Roger realized that the 10-K Report [a federally required report filed with the Securities and Exchange Commission] was important. So he took the massive 10-K documents home and became our staff expert on it."

Roger always outworked everyone on the staff. One of his earliest assignments was to evaluate foreign subsidiaries. He overwhelmed his boss by turning in a hundred-page report on Opel. "I used to work on anything I could get into, and it didn't matter whose department it was. That's the way you learn." It was also the way to make points with higher-ups, which some who knew him in his early career felt was his only objective. University of Michigan professor David Lewis, who worked at GM then, said of Roger, "All that mattered in the world to him was that briefcase he had in his hand. He was a cold S.O.B." A still-employed GM secretary remembers Roger back then as "someone who wouldn't say 'good morning' and would never have said a word to a cleaning lady because there was nothing in it for him."

Thomas Aquinas Murphy, called "Murph" by his friends, got to know Roger in 1950. Murphy was ten years Roger's senior and would lead the way to the chairmanship, occupying it and eventually naming Roger in his place. Back then, Murphy was in the New York treasurer's office and Roger was in accounting in Detroit. They spent endless hours on the phone working on facts for congressional testimony. Murphy flew to Detroit frequently to work on details on one project or another.

"When I'd come to Detroit, I found that if I needed anything in a hurry, Roger was the one to go to. He knew just where to go to find the right facts, no matter whose department it might be in."

Murphy and Roger worked most closely on GM president Harlow Curtice's antitrust testimony for the sensationalistic Kefauver hearings. Roger didn't just come up with the facts for Curtice; he developed a brilliant rationale justifying GM's existence in terms of jobs and economic stability for the entire nation. That one event was enough to gain attention from top management for the young accountant. He jumped on the fast track.

Contrary to popular opinion, to get on and stay on the fast track in General Motors requires some show of imagination. Roger showed off his creative side frequently. "He had more good ideas in the space of a day than most have in a lifetime," Murphy says of him.

At several stops on the way up, that imagination served him well. The first time Roger addressed the Greenbrier Management Conference in 1972 was just such an occasion. Greenbrier was a top-level conference held every three years in a posh convention facility in West Virginia. While it was a business conference, the real essence of it for most was that it represented the ultimate time for middle-level, fast-track executives to impress those who mattered. Executives would work for months on a single presentation. The presentations, however, were generally straightforward and predictably dull. Roger's was different. He worked with photographers to develop an opening visual effect of stars rushing at the audience as if coming off the screen. By *Star Wars'* standards it was commonplace, but in 1972 it was well ahead of its time. Then he had a woman on film opening a refrigerator and talking—directly off the screen to Roger. The film lady would ask questions, and Roger would answer them. "I think that one event convinced everyone that he was going to the top," says Hugh Welles, now corporate advertising manager who at the time of the conference was an executive speech writer. "I'd say it was a real turning point."

One of Roger's greatest innovations was bringing strategic planning to General Motors. The obsession was with 60- and 90-day reporting, and Roger felt intuitively that long-term planning was essential to run a business. "Those who do not plan end up working for those who do," he says. Roger tried three different times to get it going and finally succeeded through a circumvention revealing that Roger understood how to beat the bureaucracy when it was to his advantage. "Management was so against the concept," Roger says, "that I had to call it by a different name to get it going. I called it the 'Corporate Directions Group' . . . whatever that means."

Roger found a brilliant young man to head up the effort, an Englishman named Mike Naylor. Naylor was an engineer who had apprenticed at Rolls-Royce and worked for several years in the California aerospace industry before joining GM. Naylor wrote a futuristic study about transportation systems, "Scenario 2000," which caught Roger's attention. The initial study dealt with applications of turbine engines in the future. Roger saw the potential for a far broader concept—a strategic plan for all of General Motors through the end of the century. It could be the basis of his 21st-century corporation. Naylor agreed to "have a go at it."

Hiding Naylor away in a data processing area, Roger gave him an innocuous title that meant nothing at all. Naylor developed a very special relationship with Roger. They met regularly for breakfast, and Naylor talked in far-out, futuristic terms. Roger delighted in each new turn of thought and encouraged Naylor to keep working. Even after Roger became chairman, Naylor continues to work under an innocuous title, but carries a letter from the chairman giving the free-thinking Englishman access to any division's most guarded records. His special status in the corporation, naturally enough, has fostered a great deal of jealousy, and some call him "Roger's Rasputin." In reality, Naylor is Roger's futurist, the man he talks to when he wants to wander along distant horizons.

"Roger is visionary," Naylor says. "He has the unique ability to see the big picture, yet the details as well. He doesn't paint in broad brush strokes or with a roller, but constructs his picture with detail upon detail."

Imagination certainly is one of Roger's great strengths. "He gets absolutely giddy over new ideas," one research scientist told me. He becomes ecstatic should the idea include technology. When Roger was working in the New York treasurer's office, he and a younger associate, Jack Smith (no relation), worked a deal with the head of GM Research Laboratories to patch in and use a portion of their mainframe computer. They set up a terminal in a coat closet and proceeded to learn programming on their own.

"We were working on government securities portfolios," Roger recalls. "There were thousands of them, and they changed almost daily. So if we wanted to know which government bond had a yield of 2.4 percent, or which of our holdings were nearing maturity, we could punch it up in a minute."

Much of Roger's creativity had to remain, like his computer and his futurist, in a closet. General Motors was, and largely still is, a semimilitary organization. Creativity is encouraged only to a point. That point is when you present your idea once. If it doesn't find favor with the boss, you drop it immediately. Being a good soldier, doing your boss's bidding, is of utmost importance. Roger knew when not to be too imaginative or idealistic.

A typical example of Roger as the hard-line soldier came with the *Jesus of Nazareth* movie. Chairman Jim Roche had

approved $3.5 million to develop a full-length movie depicting
the life of Jesus. Developing one's own movie for a TV mini-
series was, and is, a sound marketing technique. The company
that does this has an advertising exclusive for a prime-time
special. Sponsorship also assures the company that there is
nothing in the film that could be embarrassing to the corporation. Recently, GM has developed two mini-series on the life of
George Washington that have been highly successful advertising vehicles. Roche's *Jesus of Nazareth* promised to be a
classic.

"Every executive who saw the film while it was being shot
was in awe," says Tom Adams of Campbell Ewald Advertising
Agency. "It was going to be brilliant." But the project wore on
for three years, long enough for Murphy to become chairman.
Murphy is a devout Catholic, stopping every morning at the
parish chapel before coming to work. Without seeing the
movie, Murphy decided it was a mistake because it might appear as if General Motors were commercializing Jesus. Murphy
told Roger to get rid of it.

"Roger wouldn't even consider going back to Murphy and
telling him the film was good," Adams says. "He had his
orders, and that was that. Roger sold the movie to Procter and
Gamble at a loss of a couple of million dollars. Procter and
Gamble has aired *The Story of Jesus of Nazareth* every Easter
on national television since then. It's been both profitable and
good for their image." Adams recalls many similar instances,
when Roger carried out orders rather than worry about the
good of the corporation.

Roger did what he was told, no matter what his personal
feelings or thought might be. Richard Gerstenberg, former
GM chairman, once said, "If you asked Roger to move the
General Motors Building across the street, he would say,
'Which way would you like it to face?', then do it." According
to Murphy, what counts most in General Motors is consistency
of performance and "making your boss look good." Those
were Roger's strong points.

Roger had a knack for knowing not only *what* was important, but *who* was. His way to the top was assured by attaching
himself to those who counted, as he had done with Admiral

Burke in the navy; only these admirals were every CEO in succession from the time he joined GM: Curtice, Donner, Roche, Gerstenberg, and Murphy. And when he saw anyone on the way up, he would make friends. For example, Jack McNulty was brought in as Roche's speech writer through the financial side to shield McNulty from public relations influence. Jack had been John D. Rockefeller III's speech writer, then had served President Lyndon Johnson as speech writer during his term. Jack is in every conceivable way Roger's opposite—a hard-playing, fun-loving Irishman, who was as at home with a deck of cards, horse-racing forms, and good bourbon as Roger was with actuarial tables and accounting ledgers. Yet Roger befriended Jack, anticipating he would quickly rise to the top of GM public relations.

Despite all the right moves, it took Roger nine years to get his first big promotion and break away from the competitive pack. There was another lull during the mid-1960s when he sat as director of financial accounting in New York for seven years. Other than those two flat spots, his upward thrust was meteoric, marked by a major promotion every two years until he reached executive vice president of finance, in 1974, one step from the top.

One characteristic of the fast track was that you had to do something dramatic along the way to assure the final lunge to the top. That something came when Roger paused for two years as the group executive for Nonautomotive and Defense Operations, his only real contact with a manufacturing job. There he realized that the Frigidaire Division, which made household appliances, and the Terex Division, which produced giant earth-moving equipment, were not competitive. He decided to sell them. The Terex sale, as it turned out, came back to haunt him, for he sold it to IBH Holding Company of Germany, a shaky enterprise that eventually went bankrupt; and a disclosure in 1987 that GM had been slipping the company money to make it look better resulted in a criminal suit filed against Roger Smith.

Selling off divisions wasn't the kind of move a finance fast-tracker would normally come up with. It meant admitting defeat. "I told Eddie Cole [then GM president] that those two divisions were not worth saving," Roger says. "Eddie said, 'Come on, Roger, we can make them work.' I think it was the first time anyone in GM had admitted there were some things we just couldn't do." The timing of the sales, as it turned out, was perfect, as they were finalized during the sudden drop in fortunes brought on by the 1979 oil embargo. It was suddenly a time of contraction, and Roger was there with two demonstrations of his ability to make Draconian decisions. It clinched Roger's nomination as chairman—ironically, for the wrong reason. "The recession was obviously going to deepen," says a GM director who took part in the nomination process. "Smith looked like a traditional finance guy, a conservative who could hold the line on costs and raise capital should we need it."

Roger was anything but conservative. He was a visionary and dreamer with both the energy and imagination to work his way around obstacles in a bureaucratic system to achieve personal goals. Roger was, in essence, an entrepreneur like his father. An executive committee member described Roger before his election to the chair as "a closet iconoclast."

That he could climb the conservative ladder, with 10 major promotions to the top, and at 55 years old look forward to a full decade as CEO of General Motors, was, in itself, a rebuttal to those who conclude that entrepreneurship and large enterprises are as incompatible as fire and ice. Peter Drucker, in *Innovation and Entrepreneurship*, explores this misconception. He points out that the small corporations, once they get established, spend most of their time dealing with the day-to-day operations. They do not have the resources in time or money to be entrepreneurial. Large companies like General Electric, 3M, Johnson and Johnson, and Westinghouse have shown that size is not an automatic barrier to innovation.

Risk taking was not uncommon for General Motors during Roger's career. It was a risk to enter the Space Age, with GM's Delco Division developing guidance systems for commercial aircraft, cruise missiles, the Apollo flights, and the space shuttle *Columbia*. It was a risk to put the first car on the moon—Delco's rover, which made tracks on the lunar surface on July 31, 1971. It was a monumental risk to bring computer graph-ics into the engineering design shop at a time when downsizing was placing untold demands on the corporation. And installing an engine computer two years ahead of the world industry posed a significant risk of recalls and warranty overload. (Worth noting here is that most of the successful risk taking for GM in the 1970s involved high technology, a fact not wasted on Roger.)

And there was risk taking that failed, like the multimillion-dollar investment in the rotary engine designed for the Chevrolet Vega even though it was not out of the laboratory yet (this risk also hurt American Motors Corporation, which planned its Pacer around the rotary's small engine characteristics). Far from risk aversion, General Motors has shown entrepreneurship even in an era of overregulation and extreme market turbulence.

And at least one side of Roger, perhaps more than any other chief executive in the past half century of his giant corporation, reveals every characteristic of an entrepreneur. An entrepreneur tends to be aggressive, imaginative, disdainful of red tape and rigmarole and thoroughly impatient with keepers of the status quo. The entrepreneur does not look for security within the institution, but is ready to take large risks to achieve his ends. Roger Smith has every one of these characteristics in superabundance. "He thrives on challenges," Jack McNulty says. "I remember once when someone told Roger his idea would meet a lot of resistance, Roger told the guy, 'When the *Nina*, *Pinta*, and *Santa Maria* sailed from Spain, nobody was on the dock waving good-bye.'"

Yet in all this, there is also a classic flaw. For Roger's family training and Sloan's ladder were both based on individualistic entrepreneurial qualities, not leadership qualities. Those who shared his youth and fast-track career were highly self-motivated men and women. Roger never appeared to strive for the two great corporate motivators—money and power—yet he achieved both because of a built-in homing device that pointed him always toward achievement. To Roger, the intensity is built in. "I don't know of anyone who lives up to my standards," he says, "least of all me." As his close friend, and one of the few who know him both as private and professional, says of Roger's intensity, "He is simply the guy who always had to get the *A*s in school. He's always working for those *A*s in achievement."

Self-motivation is Roger's family inheritance. Like his father, he controls every minute even in recreation. Ben Thompson tells of the time when at an Executive Conference at Greenbrier, he used the only hour of free time he had allowed himself to find and fish the local streams. The story is that he stunned everyone there by making 10 casts with his fancy lures and reeling in 8 trout.

Self-motivation is typical of anyone climbing the financial staff ladder to the chairmanship. A problem is that these supercharged young executives are especially isolated from the requirements of motivational leadership. In my own experience working with both financial and manufacturing sides of the corporation, I was struck by how the financial staffers seemed to be intense, harried, and totally callous toward those who worked for them. A senior executive who shared my observation explained the reason, based on his 30-plus years in General Motors, finance staff were the company storm troopers:

"On the operating side you deal with things and people. It's damned obvious if you're good or not by looking at how well you motivate your plant and division people and relate to your product and consumers. You work with loyalties, team spirit, and tough interpersonal challenges. Financial just doesn't have a well-defined yardstick. I mean, you can't distinguish one man from another based on whether he can add or subtract, right? So you have a bunch of brilliant, driven men clawing for the top, and the only standards you can measure them by are arbitrary."

The competitive environment can be brutal, the infighting bitter. Evaluations become ends in themselves. Achievements tend to be individual, not group, accomplishments, like Roger's independent end run to establish strategic planning. Or individuals are measured by how well they can follow orders, not achieve goals. And all this has little to do with the corporation's primary goal of making world-competitive cars and trucks. But, then, Sloan's model never intended the financial progression and succession to end up as chief executive officer. The chairman, in Sloan's concept, was to control the purse strings, not guide the hands of the artisans. GM's financial culture dealt with the vast majority of workers only in terms of numbers that would sit still on a ledger page. Labor was more often an abstract concept under "variable costs," an annoying category that conjured up anxieties, unending benefits, and exorbitant wages. The common man tends to become, like Plato's "oxen of the world" or Edmund Burke's "swinish multitude," something quite distant and alien.

Strategic planning, Roger's largest contribution before becoming chairman, has been almost universally criticized because it underscores an elite, top-center organization. Only a few people at the pinnacle of the organization have the knowledge and power to initiate strategic plans. It stresses centralization, where major decisions can be made, and reduces the importance of field and factory activities, where achievements are measured with micrometers, not with yardsticks. Talent and rewards tend to gravitate to the central office, where the important decisions are made. As Harvard management professor Robert Hayes wrote in *The New York Times*: "Planning's top-down orientation has emphasized the development of grandiose strategic leaps, rather than the patient step-by-step improvements that are difficult for competitors to copy."

For operating executives used to sudden shifts in markets and economic cycles, strategic planning is the antithesis of flexible management. "A road map is useful if one is lost in a highway system," Hayes says, "but not in a swamp whose topography is constantly changing." Strategic planning restricts the individual's ability to use his ingenuity to deal with the challenges as they arise. Roger's strategic planning does require that plants and smaller staff units create their own five-year plans, but since only the major steps are visible from such a time perspective, the end result is to elevate and perpetuate the elite.

Roger, then, is in many respects an anomaly. On the one hand he is a man who was born to the entrepreneurial spirit of risk taking, a man who thrives on fast action. "Somewhere in the background of every successful businessman," Roger says, "you'll find some big risk taking." Yet he is also the personification of the corporate man—an ultraconservative who wears a seat belt while riding in his chauffeur-driven limousine and feels it is necessary to have every aspect of life planned for the next 5 to 10 years.

Elitist or not, by any standard the young man who parked his Ford in front of the GM building in 1949 was a prize for any employer—well-born, energetic, and innovative. There is little question that, had he gotten into that car and headed for California or for the financial gold coast of Manhattan, Roger would have been successful. "Yes," Roger agrees, "had I gone into entrepreneurial things like my father, I probably would have done better financially." That may sound strange coming from a man earning $2 million a year, but considering his energy and upbringing, it is probably true. "But I think the challenges of a big corporation have been worth a lot," he adds. The cost of those challenges began for Roger on the day he was hired in 1949, when he went out to his car and found an expired meter and a $2 parking ticket under the windshield wiper.

4
Cookie Cutter Cars

"You can often fool the people above you, and you can sometimes fool the people at the same level as you, but you sure as hell can't fool the people below you—they can read you like a book."

F. James McDonald
GM President, retired

Christmas music played over the car radio as Mary Louise Poshek left the Flint Engine Plant parking lot and drove toward home. It was the last day of work before Christmas, and Mary was tired from eight hours of tightening manifold bolts on the moving engine line, but it was a good kind of tired, for she had the money now to buy presents for her four boys. Nineteen eighty had not been a good year for Mary. Her husband had been laid off from Chrysler in February and, after several family fights that rose out of restless anger, had left to look for work in Texas. Mary got lucky three months ago when she found the job at the GM plant. Things were going to work out now. As she turned onto her own street, the news came on the radio. Fourteen of GM's plants would be closed as of today, the announcer said, and the workers would be notified about the layoff by mail. It was certain to be a prolonged layoff, the announcer added, with the recession deepening daily. No one had said anything to her at the plant about a layoff, so the report didn't upset her. Then the announcer read off the list of plant closings. Flint Engine was one of them. Mary pulled her car to the curb and wept.

Mary and some nine thousand other GM employees heard they were out of jobs over car radios and the nightly TV news on their first evening of Christmas vacation in 1980. Christmas parties throughout the GM headquarters had slowed down the announcement's travel through the elaborate clearance process, yet the public relations staff was able to get out its closings news release without checking with personnel, which had not yet sent notification to the affected plants. The Detroit-area media made little of the insensitive act; that was simply the way GM operated. Instead, the papers were trying to make a story out of the GM chairman-elect who would take office on New Year's Day. In the meantime, the Smiths were taking the Christmas holiday with family in the Caribbean. Wasn't it fascinating how Barbara Smith packed the family turkey and a small Christmas tree to take along! Wasn't she resourceful?

Roger's appointment had been a foregone conclusion for two years. It had been announced three months early to ease the transition of power. The progression and succession to the throne was utterly predictable. *Automotive News* started its first article on Roger's ascension by saying "Alfred Sloan would have loved it." And while editors felt the election of the most powerful CEO in the world was worth a series of pieces, so little was known about Roger's visionary plans that the stories appeared to arouse little interest.

If a poll were taken about Roger's appointment—which the press, in fact, informally did take—Roger would have won hands down as the chief executive least likely to change anything or impress anyone. Roger had done such a superb job of staying out of the limelight throughout his career that the press didn't have much to go on. He had made a few minor speeches during the 1970s, mostly condemning the high cost of the industry's overprivileged labor force, but other than this standard rhetoric, not much was known about him. No one expected the squeaky-voiced little accountant with the permanent case of hives to do anything out of the ordinary. Oh, there was a recession going on, but recessions were another fact of life in Detroit. It would simply entail some layoffs and perhaps selling off some ineffectual operations. Nothing serious. (Some even suggested that GM could easily have avoided losses in 1980 but decided to take them in order to pressure the unions into taking GM's pleas of poverty seriously.) After all, for the past two years GM had experienced record profits. The corporation awarded its six thousand bonus-eligible executives more than half a billion dollars in bonuses from 1976 through 1979. And despite the 1980 downturn, GM actually gained market share, achieving 49 percent of the U.S. market. All this hardly seemed like the profile of a troubled company.

So, while Chrysler and Ford seemed to be in serious trouble—in fact, some said they had fallen off the typical cycle and were lying in the ditch—the small loss at GM looked like nothing to fret about. Indeed, the American Big Three automakers, as they were traditionally called, were becoming a thing of the past. It was the big one and the Japanese. As Lee Iacocca said in 1979, ". . . the imports and GM cracked 70 percent of the market. You wonder who the Big Two and the Little Two were."

That 12 of the top 15 executives in the company were being changed with Roger didn't raise many eyebrows except among a few astute industry insiders. It was business as usual with a soporific transition of power at Mother Motors. The fact that Roger was only 55 years old, and would therefore be at the helm of General Motors for a full 10 years, and on the board of directors for 15 years, was recorded as being a bit out of the ordinary for the giant. Roger's term would be exceeded in duration only by Alfred P. Sloan, Jr.'s 20 years and Pierre S. duPont's 13 years (though duPont's role was less direct). "Well, the thing about that," Roger said, laughing, "is that at the end I won't be able to look around and see anyone else's work. It will be pretty much mine." Yet even a long tenure didn't convince anyone that Roger would make an impression. And Roger himself reinforced the uneventfulness of the occasion by telling the press not to expect any sweeping changes from the previous GM administration. "I'm not looking with any great desire to make a mark or anything," Roger said. "I've been part of the management team for six years, and I've contributed to the decisions. . . . Don't expect me to do anything differently."

Within days, however, Roger was shaking up the corporation as never before. He held an executive meeting and said, "We are behind our foreign competition right now . . . in quality . . . in technological design . . . in plants and facilities . . . and, yes, even in our management." Roger made it abundantly clear that things were going to change quickly. He held meeting after meeting appointing task forces to look into changing nearly every aspect of the company and approved the use of outside consulting firms in virtually every case.

Roger was determined to streamline the organization. "It takes five years for GM to bring out a new product," he said. "That's longer than it took us to fight and win World War II." His first step in what would be massive reorganization was to combine product engineering, manufacturing engineering, advanced engineering, and advanced manufacturing into a single advanced engineering activity. Then he approved a worldwide reorganization of the truck, bus, and van activities into a single group. And he consolidated major divisions, combining Rochester Products and Diesel Equipment into a new division and Harrison Radiator and Delco Air Conditioning into another new division. And all activities were put under the microscope for additional restructuring.

In the meantime, Roger would make child's play out of turning the corporation's 1980 $750 million losses into a $333.4 million profit—a $1 billion turnaround in one year. He did this in the conventional Detroit manner of distributing the burden among the employees. Roger laid off union people by the tens of thousands. He would add more than 90,000 layoffs to the 108,000 already laid off in 1980. The lower-level salaried work force also made its sacrifices. In addition to layoffs, they lost 10 vacation days, merit pay was suspended, COLA allowances were set aside (COLA was worth 9 percent of income at the time), and medical coverage and the stock-benefit program were reduced for another 5 percent pay cut. Add the value of all losses, and they amounted to a stiff 18 to 20 percent pay cut (roughly equivalent to Roger's pay raise for the same year). There was a public outcry from the salaried workers, not so much because they had to make sacrifices as because the decisions were made without telling them. Many read it from a posted memo or heard about the reductions in the newspapers. "It was especially galling to read in the papers that Roger said, 'The salaried employees are cooperating in this,' " one secretary said. "I distinctly remember no one asking me. They didn't even tell me. They just sent around a bulletin telling me my paycheck would be cut. That had us all upset for weeks." Some grumbled about starting a salaried union, as they always did at such times, but nothing became of it.

Roger also increased company income by selling off some unneeded real estate and canceling a new-car program. He sold the New York GM Building for $333.4 million, closed down several plants permanently, and sold a Hyatt Roller Bearing plant to its workers. Then he backed out of support for GM Institute, the corporate college, saving another $16 million a year. He canceled the much-publicized S car project, the development of a U.S. minicar that would transport four people 50 miles on a gallon of gasoline. The S car would have cost GM about $2,000 more per car to make than its Japanese-made competitor. Roger knew that GM was not cost- or quality-competitive, so he set out on a strategy to get there.

One of his strategic approaches was what I like to call the LUV strategy. In the 1970s, GM had bought a small Japanese Isuzu pickup truck to sell under the Chevrolet nameplate LUV because GM didn't have anything comparable. So it used the Japanese truck to fill its market gap and in the meantime developed its own small pickup to replace it. This was the extremely successful S truck series introduced in 1981. The same strategy could work across the board. So even while the company was down, Roger borrowed money to make a 5 percent investment in Suzuki to develop a minicar for export to GM (the Sprint introduced in '84) and invested another $200 million to develop a second Japanese import, the Spectrum from Isuzu, also introduced in 1984. GM also expanded its dealings with its South Korean 50 percent subsidiary, Daewoo Motor Co. The LUV strategy could buy the company time to work on a small car of its own. Roger authorized the reorganization of advanced engineering, which picked up the pieces from the S car program he canceled. It was the start of a new small car project, tentatively dubbed Saturn.

With the total company involved in the transition to front-wheel drive, Roger saw the opportunity not just to bring the new plants that had to be built up to state of the art but to risk a technological lead to gain cost competitiveness through extensive automation. He upped the authorizations for plant modernization teams and encouraged them to be entrepreneurial in looking well ahead in buying technology. "I don't just want to buy technology," he said. "I want to find areas where we can make a genuine contribution to advancing technologies."

Much of the technology Roger approved in these early days was, if not still experimental, certainly on the leading edge. Instead of just buying new stamping presses, for example, GM opted for trans-axle transfer presses. The 5,000-ton monsters, each as large as a house and a city block long, cost $450 million a copy. They are incredible devices. Replacing six or seven conventional presses, they have the capacity to be changed over from one automotive part to another in 10 minutes instead of the traditional six to eight hours. This was well beyond anything the Japanese had, or were likely to get, since General Motors in 1981 had placed orders for 95 percent of the world's total capacity for building them. Several Japanese companies had considered transfer presses non-cost-effective. "Right now, they're not," a GM engineer says, "but we're not concerned with that now. We're concerned with still being modern at the turn of the century."

GM became the first U.S. car maker to use automated guided vehicles (AGVs), computer-operated vehicles without a human driver. Used initially in body shops, the AGV operates via wires buried in the floor and can deliver parts, engines, or entire bodies to work stations when needed. Since these 10,000-pound robot trucks are not connected in a continuous train, nor do they have to follow each other in sequence, they had the potential to eliminate the traditional assembly line, bringing the right parts to the right station when needed.

And Roger approved a daring move to an entirely new paint booth concept. The modular painting system had bodies stopping in computer-controlled booths (traditionally they continue to move) for better control over the process. Tom Meschievitz, a paint systems engineer, said: "We're taking a risk in going to modular paint . . . the Japanese still use individuals with spray guns so they can control quality. We feel GM can get even better quality with this more sophisticated system."

When Roger took charge, GM had 300 robots in operation. He committed to having 14,000 robots by 1990. And they wouldn't be just conventional hydraulic robots, but seventh- and eighth-generation electronic androids, many with touch sensors, vision, and machine intelligence. To achieve this, in 1981 Roger worked out a deal with Fujitsu-Fanuc, the leading Japanese robot manufacturer, to enter into a 50-50 joint venture. They created GMF Robotics, which would build robots for the American market (about 70 percent to go to GM). Overnight, GMF Robotics became the number-one robot maker in the world.

Much of what Roger was backing advanced the state of the art. GM would have some forty thousand computer-based manufacturing machines, but, when he took office, each machine maker was using its own computer languages and program codes. The result was what Roger called "the tower of Babel that exists among robots and other computer-aided programmable devices." GM set out to develop a set of universal communications standards, called *manufacturing automation protocol* (MAP). GM not only used its buying muscle to encourage its suppliers to use MAP, but it encouraged others—duPont, Eastman Kodak, McDonnell Douglas, and four hundred more—to join in the endorsement.

With MAP, Roger was erroneously confident that the ultimate factory of the future would be ready. In 1982, while negotiating with the United Auto Workers on a new three-year contract, he took time out to hear a group of GM engineers outline the potential for a fully automated plant utilizing all of the advanced robotics, MAP interfaces, and assembly line machine vision. He approved a $52 million budget for a pilot plant in Saginaw, then returned to the union to ask for more wage concessions. With hundreds of thousands laid off at the time, the Detroit newspapers were saying, "Will the last person to leave Detroit please turn off the lights?" Roger saw the way to turn out the lights in the factories without leaving town.

Another aspect of Roger's corporate strategy was to acquire new businesses that would offset the cyclical nature of GM's auto business. "I'm not looking to spend another $40 billion on equipment, but I wouldn't mind spending $40 billion on electronics or electric cars or some of the other things I see coming down the road." The target was to diversify into high technology. He believed that "the electronics industry is on the verge of making the Industrial Revolution back in the 1800s look like peanuts." "Electronics," Roger said, "is our future." The plan was to be about 10 percent nonautomotive by 1990. That may not sound like much, but in a $100-billion-sales company that's $10 billion a year in electronics, putting GM among the top three electronics companies in the world. Roger sent his senior executives out on a scavenger hunt for high-tech investment opportunities. His plan was to use high-tech acquisitions both for diversification and to bring more electronic talent into GM's manufacturing and product developments.

Ford and Chrysler had traditionally followed whatever direction GM set. This time they simply did not have the financial resources to do so. Instead, Ford and Chrysler would both look to their people to improve productivity, using as much new, yet far from advanced, equipment as they could afford and enlightened management techniques that did not cost anything to implement. Ford and Chrysler would commit what little income they had, plus whatever they could borrow with reduced credit ratings, for future product programs. Chrysler, for example, committed $6.5 billion over the next five years to come out with a new car each year (all based on a single structural platform and power train), even while they were losing vast sums during 1981. Ford's product programs were also growing, with a dozen new vehicles planned for the next five years while their fortunes languished. New products and people had to be the strategy, because they could not afford to do more than cover the basics. High technology was the in thing in American industry at the time, the golden child of the venture market, and with the GM giant leading the way, it is more than likely that Ford and Chrysler would have pursued a similar strategy had they had the wherewithal.

Roger, too, was planning for future car programs, but his plans were a bit more elaborate. While Iacocca planned to put out a whole new string of cars and a minivan for Chrysler's $6.5 billion, five-year effort, Roger authorized $7 billion for a single car project—the GM 10, the replacement for GM's mid-size cars. It was by far the most extensive new-product program in auto history. He also approved development of a new plastic-bodied sports car and a plastic-bodied van, but all of these projects would not materialize for several years (and some never), so in the meantime the goal was to sell the products designed under his predecessors.

Almost from the day Roger started putting his strategy into action, there were problem rumblings from GM's product side. Already the press was criticizing GM for making cars that were so much alike in styling and size from one division to the next that the consumers couldn't tell the difference. This was confirmed in 1982 when a study by J. D. Power and Associates, a California research firm, found that the public could no longer link the GM models with their divisional nameplates. Predictions inside of GM were that this would hurt luxury-car sales—GM's major source of profit—more than the sales of base cars, simply because with the look-alikes you could gain the status of driving a Chevrolet that looked like a Cadillac, but it made no sense to spend money on a Cadillac that looked like a Chevrolet.

While the logic would throw the advantage to Chevrolet, Roger's predecessors found a way to shoot themselves in the foot even with their most successful car line. At one time, Chevrolet represented more than half of GM's total car sales. In advertising, they'd say, "One out of every four cars on the road is a Chevrolet." By 1981 that was down to one in five. To save Oldsmobile, Buick, and Cadillac during the late 1970s and early 1980s, Chevrolet was not only forced to share all of its small cars with other divisions, but the 14th floor also took away Chevy's traditional price advantage. That meant the consumer could buy a higher-status Oldsmobile or Buick for virtually the same price. The Chevrolet X car in 1981, for example, was priced only $100 below the Olds-Buick-Pontiac versions of the same car and just $97 less than the larger intermediates.

The confusion of models and prices had all but destroyed Sloan's concept that each division should be a step up in luxury, size, and price from the division below.

A few years later Roger would receive a barrage of criticism for not dealing immediately and decisively with the product-line confusion, particularly the emergence of look-alike cars. Yet few realized how complex the problem actually was. With some 35 to 40 manufacturers producing more than 600 different models for the U.S. market, the future clearly lay in finding smaller niches for each model. Chrysler, in fact, would make its dramatic comeback by using the same vehicle platform, the K car, to build an array of limited-niche vehicles, from convertibles to minivans. Roger's long-term strategy was to compete successfully in the niches by moving to flexible automation, in which the assembly or stamping line could build a number of widely different models through the same process (using computers to identify each model and modify each process along the way). The problem was that the computer-based manufacturing technology—even the leading-edge technologies Roger was rushing into his plants—was not equal to the on-line differentiation task. Also, the new unitized body designs made it far more difficult to design in differences. When cars had frames, the skins could be changed easily to create new and different appearances. Thus it was possible in the 1950s to achieve annual model changes that made every model distinct. But the unitized body *is* the frame, so making variations in an overall design that all divisions would share was far more difficult. In essence, the look-alike problem was thought to be a temporary side effect of the eventual high-tech cure for all of GM's cost-competitive ills.

The J car, introduced in May 1981, was Roger's first experience with marketing look-alikes. All divisions got nearly identical versions, appearing as the Chevy Cavalier, Pontiac 1200, Oldsmobile Firenza, Buick Skyhawk, and even a Cadillac version, the Cimarron. Besides being variations of a single design, the new cars had an unfortunate choice of a standard engine, a 1.6-liter four-cylinder model, which was said to run like a sewing machine and propel the car from zero to 60 miles per hour in a day or two.

What really hurt the J car was a bizarre marketing strategy, which Roger approved. The J experience reveals the shallowness of GM's market understanding. Japanese cars came with dozens of standard items, which were extra-cost add-ons in American cars. The idea was to incorporate all of the extras into the J cars and up the standard price. The flaw in this logic was that the U.S. market was already suffering from sticker price shock after a prolonged period of double-digit inflation that forced price increases. To add all the extras into the base price not only shocked the consumer; it sent him into a coma.

Initially the J car was a major sales flop, even though it was a solid design. The extras were placed back on the option list. It took two years of incentives and the addition of a more powerful engine to bring the car's sales up to original expectations.

The Js were followed by the A-cars months later (Chevy Celebrity, Pontiac 6000, Oldsmobile Cutlass Ciera, and Buick Century). These new front-wheel-drive cars were very close in size and appearance, to two other major lines of GM cars (Gs and Xs). A return of low-cost gasoline soon added a demand for traditionally large cars, so GM decided to keep the older lines going alongside of the new ones. The result was a profusion of GM models, many nearly identical in size and cost, which confused the buying public.

Instead of turning to product developers to straighten out the look-alike mess, Roger's finance-dominated team came up with low-interest loans to sell the unpopular models. That seemed logical, since Roger had concluded that what kept buyers out of the market in 1980 and early 1981 was not lack of product appeal, but high interest rates on consumer loans. Roger's first cut-rate offer was a 13.8 percent rate (low at the time) in August 1981. It would be followed by low-finance offers that defined the market over the next five years. Low interest rates, however, did not make up for designs that were simply uninteresting, and so GM began its long slide in market share.

If the product offering was beginning to show insensitivity to public tastes, some of the company's sales activities were even more callous. GM offered to underwrite new-car loans at 12.8 percent in the spring selling season. The day after the two-month sale, people who had placed orders but had not yet received their cars were told that the company wouldn't honor the lower interest rates. That made sense to Roger, since the offer was defined as being for two months only. It made no sense to buyers, who threatened lawsuits and saw their complaints get into the newspapers. Roger backed off and made good on the 12.8 percent, but by that time the damage to the corporation's image had been done.

The greatest of all strategies of the new chairman, the one he had become obsessed with, was to reduce labor costs. American labor must shoulder much of the blame for the fierce beating the auto industry was taking, Roger told the press. He pointed out at every opportunity that Japanese auto workers made $8 less per hour than American workers. He neglected to consider, however, that Japanese auto workers also received subsidized housing, subsidized food, subsidized recreation, and lifetime employment guarantees. Nor did he calculate the cost of a ratio of one-to-10 supervision in the United States compared to one-to-30 in Japan. And he didn't mention that U.S. management systems were such that it took twice as many American workers to build a car. Apart from these oversights, his labor comparison was correct. Noncompetitive hourly wages, he insisted, were the major reason for GM's sale of Frigidaire and Terex. And the 1981 sale of the roller bearing plant was used repeatedly as the ultimate example of what was wrong. He told an audience in Detroit in October:

> Noncompetitive costs were the prime factor in our recent sale of the New Departure-Hyatt plant at Clark, New Jersey, to the plant employees. And there may be other sales and closings of facilities in GM if that is the only way to get our costs under control.
>
> The Clark experience demonstrates the potential for improved efficiency in our operations with the proper employee and union cooperation. The employees who now own that plant expect to make a profit—and they plan to do this by taking an average cut of 30 percent in salary and benefits and by reducing their work force by about a third— while still producing the same number of bearings.

When asked how the average employee at that plant could
expect to be 50 percent more productive than he had been
working for GM, the chairman of the Clark union local told
Forbes that the "employees would do a day's work for a day's
pay. . . . It's no secret that the union helped create an
atmosphere where people who were in the plant eight hours
did four hours of work. . . . That's appropriate when GM is
making billions in profits—you make more jobs, and you
make work easier for your men. But it's no longer
appropriate."

Roger's strategy was to force the United Auto Workers into
reopening contract negotiations early because of the recession, and much of his aggressive criticism of labor was posturing to that end. Doug Fraser, UAW president, said: "The guys in
the plants knew the companies were having trouble and were
willing to help. I, personally, was in favor of reopening the
contract because I was worried about Ford, not GM." (The
Ford and GM contracts were, and still are, yoked to cover the
same contract periods.) "But Roger's talk was getting people
angry. He was doing his cause more harm than good."

The UAW did open the contract more than a year early, but
Roger personally took charge of the negotiations. He offended
everyone with his tough talk, and the union canceled the negotiations after just 17 days. "Someone ought to put a zipper
on Roger's mouth," Fraser said in exasperation. Bill Hoglund,
the charismatic GM vice president who would later head up
Saturn Corporation, said of Roger, "Within six months, he
[Roger] had offended just about everybody he came in contact
with."

After a cooling-off period, the UAW again agreed to reopen
the contract talks early. This time Roger was conspicuously
absent from the bargaining team. But that didn't stop Roger
from talking, and this time his rhetoric cost the company sales.
Roger, thinking he was helping the union sell its members on
concessions, made a joint announcement with UAW vice president Owen Bieber that any concessions would be reflected in
lower prices on GM cars and trucks. As any marketing man
could have predicted, the effect of the announcement was that

people postponed purchasing new GM cars until the contract was sealed and the price cuts announced. It virtually destroyed the fall selling season. And the wait was a long one, for the contract wasn't completed until the following spring.

The early contract was all to the benefit of the company. The union agreed to freeze COLA and numerous other benefits and accepted a profit-sharing concept instead so that they might benefit when the company's profits rebounded. In all, there were more than $2.5 billion in concessions over the three-year period of the new contract. On the very day that the UAW was to announce the unprecedented concessions, another Roger Smith public relations disaster was in the making. The GM Board of Directors had approved a plan two years before to dramatically fatten the executive bonus program. The new plan offered far more lucrative cash payments plus an extra 5 million shares of stock for the top 600 executives. The plan was to be voted on at the 1982 stockholders' meeting and, therefore, had to be included in the proxy statement sent to all shareholders in advance of the meeting. The proxy notice announcing the fattened bonus plan was to be mailed on the same day the union would announce its people's concessions. "I told my bosses that the problem was coming," a stockholder relations manager told me, "but no one seemed terribly concerned."

"When we got the word of what was happening," Fraser says, "our people were distraught. Owen Bieber even threatened to resign out of embarrassment. We looked around for a way out and finally went to the GM bylaws. They said that just because a proxy was passed, the CEO doesn't have to put the thing into effect. So I sat down with Roger and told him we were mad. He was apologetic and said that he hadn't planned for this to happen. There was no malice aforethought to it, he said, and I believed him. I told Roger that he'd have to make a statement promising not to give the increased bonuses during the new contract. He said he'd go back and work it out, then issue a statement. I said, 'No way. You sign a letter right now to that effect, and we'll meet the press in five minutes to make a statement.'

"What gets me most was not that the mistake was made, but

that Roger was so insensitive to what the consequences would be. Roger kept his word, and the bonuses were not given during the contract, but they might as well have been for the damage they did. Six years later I still get plant people telling me about the bonuses Roger gave out in '82. The way they remember, it happened and Roger did it."

As if that were not enough bungling for one contract session, Roger made one more colossal public relations blunder to top it off. He had docked the six thousand GM bonus executives (including himself) by $135 a month—equaling the COLA allowance that the average factory worker was losing. Roger bragged about the gesture and had the public relations department issue a national release. It doesn't take a degree in accounting to realize that $135 a month out of the paycheck of an executive who earns upwards of $100,000 a year is not the same thing as $135 out of a $14,000-a-year laborer's check. The outcry was loud and sustained. The absurdity of Roger, who was then making $56,250 *a month*, giving up $135 of it as a sacrificial gesture was pointed out by virtually every newspaper columnist in every town where GM had a plant. Lee Iacocca, who at the same time was drawing only $1 a year in salary, said, "Now there's a company that doesn't understand equality of sacrifice."

To make matters worse, shortly thereafter the word got out that Roger and his senior executives would receive significant base pay increases for 1981. The chairman got an 18.8 percent raise during a time when hourly and salaried nonexecutives were making major sacrifices to support the corporate recovery. Gary Edwards summed up the reaction in a Letter to the Editor in the *Detroit News*, saying, "Imagine the sacrifices, suffering, and cutbacks that were made in the Smith household when they found out there would only be a $200,000 raise for 1981."

If Roger wasn't making any points with the workers, he was making even fewer with the small stockholders. The GM Annual Stockholders' Meeting held in the spring was the one opportunity that small investors traditionally had to express concern to the stewards of their life savings. The former chairman, Tom Murphy, understood this and was tolerant even of

the annual outcropping of a few kooks who regularly showed
up. But, in general, the meeting was a cordial occasion in
which top management got a chance to hear, and joke a little
with, some of the people who actually owned the corporation.
Roger wanted none of this democracy in action.

At his first annual meeting in 1981 Roger demonstrated
how tough he could be. A massive clock was set up, and each
speaker was allowed no more than two minutes. If he or she
ran a second over, Roger had the attendants shut off the microphone. He was abrupt with individual stockholders: "Your
facts are totally incorrect," he told a man, without answering
his questions. He said he'd forcefully eject others if they didn't
behave themselves. And he told another man: "If you want
cooperation with GM, the way not to get it is to disrupt our
annual meeting." All the man had done was ask to be heard.

As the 1982 meeting drew near, Roger decided he wasn't
going to put up with rabble-rousing again. "It's a circus," he
said. So Roger devised a plan to avoid facing the multitude,
announcing that the 1982 annual meeting would be conducted in a new way. There would be two meetings. A first
meeting, which Roger would oversee, would be a bare-bones
gathering in which the agenda, including election of board
members, would be run through with minimal discussion
from the floor. The first meeting would start at 9:30 A.M. and
be over in plenty of time for Roger to hold a press conference
before lunch. Then there would be a second annual meeting
held 15 miles away from the GM building. GM President Jim
McDonald would officiate over the second meeting, in which
shareholders could have their two minutes each to speak. But
Roger wouldn't be there to hear them. Instead, he'd be at a
board of directors meeting at the GM building. And at the
afternoon meeting, only written questions would be considered.

Again, the shareholders objected, and Roger seemed surprised that they would have such strong feelings about the
event. The *Wall Street Journal* ran a cutting editorial about
the effort to avoid shareholder governance. And Tim Smith
(no relation), head of the Interfaith Center on Corporate Responsibility, called Roger's restructuring "a very arrogant act

of corporate irresponsibility." In the end, Roger backed off and held the meeting in the traditional way, but he kept the cutoff switch to the microphone poised at all times.

The cumulative impact of Roger's utterances dropped his overall acceptance rating into the basement. So, in the winter of 1982, with the company in the midst of drastic change, the general feeling toward Roger in and outside General Motors was one of disdain. "He's a disaster," a Flint union man said. "I don't know anyone who likes him," a salaried clerk said. At a mid-level management meeting at the GM Technical Center, one participant started off the meeting with a round of applause by asking, "Is there any way we can trade Smith for Lee Iacocca?" David Smith (no relation), one of the most astute auto editors on the Detroit scene, said, "It looks like one of Roger's robots could do as well on the 14th floor."

Roger's initial reaction was pure GM—to blame the media. GM had traditionally looked at the media in Nixonian terms, and Roger was following the tradition of paranoia. "The media have given us a black eye, particularly in Detroit," he told a group of GM managers in Pittsburgh in May 1982. "As a result, many people inside and outside of our corporation perceive General Motors as lacking integrity, as being guilty of double-dealing with its employees." Yet by and large, the negative image was not directed so much at the corporation as it was at the new chairman himself.

"I don't like the phrase 'cold and calculated'," Roger told a *Nation's Business* reporter in reaction to his overall image. But he equated it with being realistic. "Being part of the finance staff," Roger had said, "you're a little bit back from all the gung-ho spirit you normally get in the other divisions, and you develop a more pragmatic attitude."

The image of callousness and uncaring leadership, however, doesn't do the complex Mr. Smith justice. In 1978 Roger established GM's Cancer Research Awards, which would prove to be an important motivational tool for the fight against that disease. For Christmas in 1981 Roger had the board issue a $300 special payment to all laid-off workers to lessen the holiday burden. And for Christmas in 1982 he came up with the "Care and Share" program. Joining with the UAW and International Union of Electrical Workers (IUE), GM's two major unions, the corporation sponsored a program whereby every can of food that the union people donated for laid-off workers would be matched by a 50¢ donation by GM, and money contributions would be matched dollar for dollar. More than $1.3 million in food and cash was distributed in this way.

Uncaring might be the wrong word; *arrogant* would be more appropriate. Roger was in charge and saw no reason for patience with anyone who was not getting in step with his drummer. *Arrogant* had always been the word that best described General Motors. I remember when I was an automotive editor for *Better Homes and Gardens* magazine in the early 1970s, GM scheduled each of its one-day divisional press conferences during separate weeks, so magazine journalists had to make several trips to Detroit to get the story piecemeal from five car divisions. The California car buff magazines, never long on money, complained about this. I was present when the public relations manager told them, "GM is half the industry. If you want to cover our new products, we figure you'll find a way to get here." The regulated 1970s and the rise of superior foreign products had taken some of the arrogance out of the giant, but not much.

To the criticism, Roger was impervious. "I look at the bottom line," he said. "It tells me what to do." As Roger saw it, the bottom line was moving up during his first two years in office, and that is what mattered most. In 1982 GM would make almost $1 billion profit, not impressive considering earnings of only 1.6 percent of sales. But this was after deducting $9 billion in capital investments, so things were looking better. GM would recall some 214,000 employees, and once they returned to work, much of the anxiety over Roger's arrogant management would subside, as it typically had under past GM elitists. Roger could continue to ignore the critics and say:

"What the board tells me is what counts, and they tell me I'm doing a good job. I don't worry about the other stuff."

5

A Billion Here,
a Billion There

*"Whenever you see a successful business, you can
bet someone once made some courageous
decisions."*
Roger Smith, paraphrasing Peter Drucker

As the economy bounced back from 1983 through 1985, Roger sprang into action. He announced radical changes with such rapid-fire regularity that he became the darling of the news-famished press corps. He built an uneasy rapport with the journalists, teasing them with each new announcement that there was an even bigger news break ahead, that *"the* lulu was yet to come." Roger earned a new image as "the innovator," the "visionary," and "21st-century futurist." And since 85 percent of his efforts and acquisitions were in the U.S., and GM was the most vertically integrated of the auto companies, making about 75 percent of its own parts, Roger could claim the title of champion of employment— "We're saving jobs for Americans." For a brief period, he caught the public's imagination and became an unlikely media hero.

Roger was showered with praise and awards in 1984 and 1985. He was named *Automotive Industries* magazine's Man of the Year. *Financial World* honored him with its Gold Medal as the best chief executive in America, he was named Ad Man of the Year by *Advertising Age* in 1985, and was designated as one of the 10 best executives in America by the *Gallagher Report*. Responding to the recognition, Roger said, "Where were they when I needed them a couple of years ago?"

But Roger was moving too fast to pay much attention to his newfound public status. He was moving so fast, in fact, that he was continuously frustrated, and often enraged, at the soporific pace of the corporation. "I always feel like I'm running around pounding the fingers of the people who are clinging to the rock, to get them to let go and swim across the damn stream. 'You'll make it; don't worry how fast the current is.' "

His theme was to bring entrepreneurship into General Motors. "We, in the past, just haven't done the right job in getting all the innovation out of the people," he said. "That's the job of the future." He called the approach his three Rs—risk, responsibility, and reward.

Risk taking took center stage as Roger went on the greatest short-term spending spree of any CEO in industrial history. As he saw it, General Motors was running out of time to become competitive. One study, for example, said U.S. industry would have to achieve a 5 percent improvement in productivity per year for the next five years just to catch up and get even with the Japanese on costs. A 25 percent productivity improvement in five years was not likely in a company that averaged less than 2 percent productivity improvements in 1983. To go so far so fast, Roger felt, was impossible without drastic, high-risk measures.

The economy was recovering from the deepest recession since the Great Depression, and Roger was predicting (correctly) that there would be at least four years of solid growth. Interest rates were falling, and consumer confidence was rising. Moreover, Reagan's deregulation of key industries, and the administration's slackening of ongoing regulatory controls, meant resources would be freed. "We've got some wonderful expertise in technology that's been all tied up in safety, emissions, and fuel economy [regulation]," Roger said. And, perhaps most important, the administration intimidated Japan into easing up on its U.S. invasion. Japan announced it would voluntarily limit vehicle exports to the U.S. for three years. The limit would amount to 1,680,000 per year, effectively halting penetration at 1980 levels. Since there were some 120 protectionist bills in Congress at the time, the Japanese considered self-limitation preferable to more stringent U.S. trade restrictions. With the Japanese in abeyance, and Reagan in Washington, the stage was set for Roger's frontal thrust.

Roger was ready to step up his strategic plan. "We're not just wandering around in the dark," he said. "We've got the most complete plan for the future of any company that I know of." His two-pronged plan was on one hand "to achieve exponential growth in the technological areas—to leapfrog ahead either by our own research and development or by buying into leading-edge technology wherever we can find it," and on the other hand to diversify into new businesses. "I don't know where the new businesses are going to come from," he said, but he was certain they would be in areas where GM could "achieve natural synergies" with businesses that complemented and contributed to the transportation business.

The list of newsworthy GM program and acquisition announcements grew so rapidly that by the fall of '85 it was no longer possible to include them all in a 30-minute speech and still have time to say anything else. The sequence goes something like this:

1983

- NUMMI announced. A 50-50 joint venture with Toyota to build cars in California. Roger calls it a "learning lab" to find out more about Japanese management. (Privately he considers it a test of whether the methods will work with fiercely independent American workers.)
- Six billion dollars in new technologies for the year. Lake Orion, Michigan, and Wentzville, Missouri, assembly plants open. Both are high-tech plants with more robots and automation than any other plant in the auto industry.
- Saturn project announced. A new small-car project aimed squarely at beating the Japanese at the cost and quality game. Set new precedent also by bringing the union into the product-planning stage.
- Ground breaking for GMF Robotics Headquarters in Troy, Michigan. The robot company announces plans to build a major development facility in the state.

- Buick City bows in the press. The idea is to make all suppliers gather within 30 miles of a core manufacturing cluster so that plants can operate without inventories, depending on suppliers to deliver parts when needed.
- Factory of the future in Saginaw is officially revealed to the press. Called "the ultimate in automation" and "the model for all industry."
- Quality Institute is established in Detroit. Week-long school for GM managers and union leaders to teach quality decision making. A major investment in Philip Crosby Associates, Inc., is the basis for the effort.
- Project Trilby is leaked to the press. A secret project to go as far ahead in electronic vehicle concepts as possible. Nothing-sacred project, including whether the future car should have four wheels.

1984

- Nine billion dollars spent on new technologies. Hamtramck plant (in Detroit) begins slow (and troubled) start-up. This plant is the next generation in high technology for the industry.
- Reorganization of car divisions announced. This massive effort is intended to bring all small-car development into one group and all large-car development into another. It is the equivalent of creating two Ford Motor Companies.
- Electronic Data Systems purchased. A special class of common stock is created to "keep EDS independent." The Texas-based company will take over GM's $2 billion-a-year data processing activities.
- Saturn Project becomes Saturn Corporation. Commitment of $5 billion to create the first new vehicle nameplate for General Motors since the creation of Pontiac in 1927.
- Daewoo Motor Company Ltd., GM's 50 percent partner in Korea, receives $427 million to build a version of GM's German Adam Opel car in Korea and ship to the United States as the Pontiac LeMans.
- New innovative contract with the UAW provides job protection and retraining for those displaced by technology.
- Equity investments announced in applied intelligence systems, Automatix, Inc., Diffracto Ltd., Robotic Vision Systems, View Engineering—all either machine-intelligence or machine-vision companies.

1985

- Ten billion dollars earmarked for the year in capital expenditures for new technologies and plant modernization.
- Hughes Aircraft Corporation accepts GM's high bid of more than $5 billion to purchase the major military electronics and satellite company based in California.
- GM Hughes Electronics Corporation is formed, a new company that combines GM's Delco Electronics Division and Power Products & Defense Operations with Hughes in a new advanced electronics subsidiary.
- Project Trilby, a major multiyear research project, is broken out of the GM Research Laboratories and given top priority.
- Two mortgage companies are purchased. GM enters this totally new business to take advantage of GMAC's data processing capabilities.
- Magnequench—a GM Research invention—is approved for development into a new subsidiary. The super-strength material can make magnets smaller and lighter. It will be manufactured for commercial sales.
- GM/Volvo joint venture formed. GM will combine with Volvo to build and market medium and heavy trucks in the U.S. and Canada.

In 1985, after two years of whirlwind spending, Roger sent executives to Europe to see what he still might buy. He made inquiries as to whether Fiat, Alfa Romeo, and BMW might be for sale. And he eventually bought Britain's Group Lotus. When a reporter asked if he was finished spending, Roger responded, "The last time I looked, the little green box [cash box] wasn't empty." Indeed, with record car sales in 1984 and 1985, Roger was sitting on a pile of money—$7 billion in cash reserves in '84 and $9 billion in '85. Talking about technology investments, he said, "It's frustrating that we just can't spend the money sometimes as fast as we'd like."

Logically, every one of the actions fit neatly into Roger's overall strategic plan. He was moving to high technology, diversifying into electronics industries, and covering his bet by expanding relationships with Japanese, Korean, and Mexican allies. Some of these acts were truly innovative, such as NUMMI and Saturn (discussed in later chapters). And all appeared to relate in some way to GM strengths or needs. GM's entry into the mortgage services business was a good example. GM Acceptance Corporation, Roger's financial wing, purchased Norwest Mortgage, a Minneapolis-based company, for $11 million and then paid $190 million for the seven companies of Corestate's financial corporation group on the East Coast. The mortgage servicing business is one of paper-thin profit margins that can be achieved only by companies that can push huge volumes of paper through a computerized system. Since the data process for mortgages and automobile receivables was essentially the same, there was money to be made by taking advantage of GMAC's massive data processing network. It was an excellent example of finding natural synergies.

The scope of GM's spending appeared to be a source of fun for Roger. He delighted in comparing GM's massive spending with the conservative capital outlays at Ford and Chrysler:

"Listen," Roger said in a press conference when told that the other companies were rebuilding plants, too. "You could paint the doorknobs on some of those facilities [other companies' new plants], but that doesn't compare with the $450 million we spent on each of our new plants. We will soon have the first lights-out factory of the future, flexible automation beyond anything in this country. The computer software alone costs tens of millions of dollars. I'm talking about *real* investment.

"There's a story told—I didn't hear it directly—about Iacocca announcing his Liberty Car project [a Saturn imitation] after we announced our $5 billion project. Some newspaper guy asked him how much he was going to spend. Iacocca said, '$150 million.' From the back of the room came a voice that said, 'Give him one white chip.' "

Such genial hostility only partly masked Roger's dislike for Lee Iacocca. They had been on opposite sides of numerous issues because what was good for number one wasn't necessarily good for the small and struggling Chrysler Corporation. Iacocca, for example, went to Washington to file protests and testimonies against Roger's joint venture with Toyota. When that didn't work, he filed a private lawsuit. Lee was opposed to the largest domestic car maker joining forces with the largest Japanese automaker. The potential for price fixing seemed too great.

Roger's animosity toward Lee seemed to run much deeper than business issues. He resented the fact that the head of a company a fraction the size of General Motors should receive so much more public attention. Iacocca's personal support of the project to rebuild the Statue of Liberty garnered him more press coverage than all of the Saturns and NUMMIs and reorganizations had gained for Roger. An executive committee member told me Roger almost snapped his head off at lunch one day when he said something positive about Iacocca's television ads (Iacocca was his own company's on-camera spokesman). The popular Iacocca for President movement that developed in 1986 set Roger's teeth on edge. The last time I saw Roger, he went on at some length about an Iacocca ad that left out some figures to prove a point. Roger said it was dishonest.

Finally, Roger blew up in a press conference and attacked Iacocca personally. Because Chrysler had stuck primarily to compact cars since its recovery, the company was able to meet the strict federal corporate average fuel economy (CAFE) standards, while GM and Ford faced fines for selling too many large cars. Roger appealed to the government to repeal the CAFE standards, but Iacocca testified that the standards should be kept in place and his rival companies should pay the price for their indifference to the law.

"He [Iacocca] is responsible for a lot of the trade problem," Roger told reporters. "He has gone overseas to buy parts and cars. He's exported American jobs. . . ." Roger went on to say that "he [Iacocca] has given up on half the families of America." He was referring, of course, to Chrysler's decision not to reenter the large-car market even though the price of fuel was declining and pent-up demand for large cars was growing. Underneath it all one got the feeling that what irked Roger most was really Iacocca's flamboyant style, his methods were too blatant and blunt for the understated Mr. Smith.

Bragging about massive spending, even to undercut an old rival, probably was not good public relations, since a great number of people, inside and outside of GM, felt that Roger's spending spree did not bring home equal value. There was a great deal of grumbling, even on the executive committee, that Roger was spending far too much for everything he was buying. The Saturn Corporation announcement was a case in point. Roger announced that he had earmarked $5 billion to build an all-new line of economy cars. Estimating a sale of 500,000 cars per year over a six-year period (ambitious, at that, in a crowded market), and deducting the cost of permanent plant equipment, that still would have worked out to $1,000 in development overhead per car. That was far too large a burden for an entry-level vehicle. A competitor said: "It's like spending $50,000 on a kitchen that will turn out only hamburgers. Expensive hamburgers."

And the same thing occurred in Europe, where Roger spent $2 billion to bring out a new small car, the Corsica, for a crowded market in which the projected production of 270,000 cars a year could not possibly offset the initial investment. "We're not just coming out with new cars," Roger explained. "We're buying a piece of the future."

The Hughes Aircraft acquisition was another example of exorbitant spending. Hughes Aircraft was the leader in the defense electronics industry, the company that invented the laser, put more commercial satellites in space than anyone else, and was recognized master of large systems integration, having set up the entire air defense networks for both the U.S. and NATO. Someone had said that Hughes was a larger brain trust than MIT and Cal Tech combined. Hughes had operated for most of its existence under a tax-exempt status under its parent company, Howard Hughes Medical Institute. The institute relationship, however, was more like a tail wagging a dog, for Hughes Aircraft decided on its own how much it would hand over to the medical institute each year. In fact, most of the resources were pumped back into advanced research so that the company functioned as a nonbusiness brain trust. When the government put an end to the tax shelter, Hughes went on the auction block. It was a genuine plum for anyone who wanted high technology.

Roger was salivating over the opportunity and went after Hughes as early as 1983. Ford Motor Company and Boeing

Aircraft were also bidding on Hughes at the time. On the morning that the Hughes board was to meet to decide whose bid it would accept, Roger sent it a final offer that was so far beyond that of any other bidder that there simply was no contest. Irving Shapiro, former chairman of DuPont, expressed his admiration for Roger's action in a *Fortune* interview, saying: "GM had the resources and the guts to play table-stake poker and make its bet at the last minute." The $5 billion-plus bet, however, was at least fives times Hughes's assets, and insiders said it was at least $1 billion above the most exaggerated estimates of Hughes's value (and that came directly from a Hughes vice president). Hughes had been having major quality problems, particularly with its Tucson, Arizona, missile plant, and the Air Force had halted $37.9 million in contract payments, placing the future of the entire corporation in doubt. And Hughes had never actually operated in a profit-oriented mode before, so there was no definable track record to indicate whether the brain trust could be trusted to become an income source.

Roger justified the acquisition by saying, "Almost everything I've seen at Hughes you can find an application for in the future of the automobile business." Yet others pointed out that Ford Motor Company had been in the aerospace business for many years, and that affiliation had not shown up in its products or plants. "In all, Hughes is a solid company," a board member told me. "But there wasn't any reasonable justification for paying so much for it."

Whatever the cost, the deluge of changes in such a brief time span carried with it the price tag of internal chaos. *Confusion* is the word most used to describe GM from 1983 through 1985. There wasn't a nerve anywhere in the entire corporate body that wasn't severed, pinched, or frayed. Tens of thousands of employees were being moved around so rapidly that a personnel director, in all seriousness, suggested printing a weekly telephone directory to keep track of them. In the midst of the movement there were all-new projects, new equipment, new processes, and long-term quality and warranty problems still unresolved.

More disruptive even than his rapid acquisitions, Roger's

reorganization of the car divisions created utter havoc. "Decentralization is what reorganization is all about," Roger said. "We've got to move faster in designing new products and bringing them to market. . . . We have to uncork individual talent by giving our people the opportunity to take risks, assume responsibilities. . . . We're pushing responsibility down in the organization to the people who are directly involved and therefore most able to make the right decisions on the spot."

There were many outstanding reasons to do something about GM's organizational structure. Centralization had robbed the divisions of any clear-cut authority. The platform group, bringing engineers together from each division to design a car, was developed as one way to resolve the weak product image, but it hadn't worked out. The lead division concept, in which each division is given responsibility for a single aspect of a car design (Delco Electronics the lead division on instruments, Hydra-matic on transmissions, Oldsmobile on front-wheel drive, etc.) hadn't worked either. The continuous clearances and running changes in new product development were not only time-consuming; they resulted in actual loss of control over the process.

"You approve a two-door convertible, and four years later it comes off the line as a four-door sedan," an engineer said. "The entire system is a mess." Alex Mair, the vocal vice president of advanced engineering, pointed out just how much of a bottleneck it had actually become. "In 1962 it took less than a year to get the Chevy II from clay models to production. There were five body styles, and everything on those cars was new, except the transmission. . . . Now with CAD/CAM it should be better, but we are running up to five years to move from drawing board to production."

Besides product development, the two massive manufacturing divisions—GM Assembly Division and Fisher Body—had gained so much power and independence that they ended up calling the shots on far too many product decisions. "Fisher was so independent and powerful that it would think nothing of countermanding any division's request for a design feature. They'd just say flat out we couldn't do what we wanted," a former Buick general manager said. The need was certainly present to return some control for products to the individual division managers.

Yet looking at GM's reorganization plan, it is difficult to see how decentralization could ever have come out of it. Essentially, the plan involved creating a new level of management in the form of group vice presidents, tightening the span of control at the time from five operations to two. Buick, Oldsmobile, and Cadillac were lumped together as the large-car group. Chevrolet and Pontiac were assigned to the small-car group, with GM of Canada added to fill it out. (Adding Canada was illogical, since it made no cars, only parts; and, by Canadian law, GM of Canada must remain a separate corporation, with only dotted-line connections to the states.)

The powerful Fisher Body and GM Assembly divisions were eliminated entirely. Their plants were divvied up between the two car groups, B-O-C and C-P-C, or handed over to component divisions, removing them entirely from direct car group control.

Engineering functions would be centralized for all car divisions in each group, leaving the divisions with only a marketing operation and a chief engineer without significant staff. Consolidating, not decentralizing, engineering was part of the plan from the start. "We didn't have enough engineers," Roger said, "and we weren't using them effectively." Further, the B-O-C division would make standard and large-sized cars for all five car divisions, and the C-P-C would do the same for compact and small cars. In other words, one source would still produce all of a certain model, thus perpetuating the fundamental problem of product sameness resulting from centralization.

As for driving decision making downward, that simply has not happened. Initially, Roger did stick to a hands-off policy, letting the groups make decisions for a few months. But when costs continued to climb and cost cutting was not immediate, Roger took back the authority and centralized it again in the executive committee. Two-and-a-half years after the beginning of reorganization, a conference of the top 600 manufacturing executives was held. The number-one question on everyone's lips was "When are we getting the authority to do the job?" Roger answered by scolding the executives: "The executive committee is ready to push down more responsibility—just as soon as you show you can handle it. Frankly, the results we've seen so far don't warrant additional responsibility. In fact, just the opposite, they show this management group hasn't properly discharged the considerable responsibility it already has."

Reorganization was a disaster in human understanding. Instead of streamlining decision making, it had the effect of scattering it like bits and pieces of shrapnel. People were moved from one job and location to another at breakneck speeds. In the confusion, buildings were leased that were never occupied. "Our staff rented a large house in Detroit as temporary quarters for a move that was threatened four times in six months," an Advanced Engineering manager told me. Existing buildings were overcrowded to the point of absurdity. C-P-C headquarters, formerly Fisher Body headquarters, became such a snarl of humanity that visitors had to park a half mile away to make an appointment with someone who was probably at a desk in a hallway or vestibule. Suppliers were totally confused as to whom to contact, who had any actual authority. By the time they had pinned down the right person, there was another wave of movement, and he or she was gone. Even GM of Canada, which had operated more efficiently than its U.S. counterpart while independent, was complaining about the 14th floor taking over its functions and screwing things up royally. Dealers were complaining that the car divisions had lost so much control that it was pointless even to work with them. The UAW GM Dept. leader Don Ephlin, two years into the reorganization, told me: "The union wants to help in any way we can, but it's impossible when we can't find out who's in charge on any given day." The confusion went on—not for a few months, but for years. "I still haven't unpacked the boxes," a B-O-C manager said, "and I don't see that the dust has settled enough to consider doing so."

"Things went screwy in '83," Joe, a data processing specialist, said. "I'd just been transferred from Harrison Radiator to Fisher Body and hadn't yet learned where everything was when they wiped out Fisher and transferred me to C-P-C. The place was utter confusion, but it didn't matter 'cause they transferred me a few months later to EDS. That's when I quit. How do you figure it? I mean, I'd been a GM guy for 19 years and had all superior performance ratings, yet they jacked me around for 3 years. . . . I can tell you, not a hell of a lot of work got done anywhere with all the goddamned confusion.

"Painful, short-term local disruptions of people's lives and careers," Roger said, "are the unfortunate price for long-term competitiveness for the entire organization."

"The companies that seem best able to change with the times are those with the most internal stability," Thomas J. Peters, of the McKinsey and Company management consulting group, has said. "Management that is already chaotic and unstable is apt to be only further confused and discomfited by such activities." An ironic statement, since it was McKinsey and Co. that was the primary outside consultant on GM's reorganization. Most insiders blame the group for confusing reorganization with a matrix system no one understood.

One psychological aspect of reorganization that Roger misread was nameplate loyalty among workers in the separate car divisions. Since he had always been on the corporate track, he had never experienced the pride people had in being part of a definable entity. I remember one assembler telling me he planned to quit rather than be transferred to a corporate operation. "I've always been a Chevrolet man. I know the products, and I believe in Chevrolet. But it's all gone now." When I brought up divisional loyalty to Roger, he said: "Yes, that's what's been killing us. There was a hole in the wall, and Fisher Body was on one side and Assembly Division on the other. Each had their own way of doing things, and it was screwing up the works. It was making it hard to pass anything through the wall. It was killing us." Interdivisional rivalry is a fact of life in a large organization, but there are ways of dealing with it short of major surgery. Reorganization appears to be a quick fix for a management unequipped to deal with the subtleties of human interaction. Granted, the downside of divisional loyalty is divisiveness, but the upside is pride of workmanship and identification with end products so essential to maintaining quality in a manufacturing setting. Very few people away from The Building could identify with anything as large and impersonal as the General Motors symbol.

By centralizing engineering functions under reorganization, individual innovation under the old system was lost. In the traditional car division, senior engineers always kept their own "skunk works"—unauthorized projects in which the engineer tinkered with a new idea, which could be anything from a new widget to a complete car concept. The system was loose enough to allow this divisional experimentation. And it paid off in numerous ideas that suddenly appeared out of nowhere. The space-frame Pontiac Fiero was, in a very real sense, a single engineer's skunk works project that caught everyone's imagination.

Perhaps the worst aspect of reorganization in the midst of major modernization efforts and offshoot projects was that it required significant staff increases with no basis for continued employment. Instead of streamlining, C-P-C alone added 8,000 additional people. This added more overhead, making the group's products even less cost-competitive. By 1985, for example, C-P-C Group produced 3.5 million vehicles a year—roughly the same number as Toyota. But C-P-C had 160,000 people, while Toyota had only 60,000, and that's not counting the fact that Toyota builds more of its own components and includes its worldwide sales group in its numbers.

What was devastating GM competitively was not hourly rates, as Roger contended, but the number of workers GM employed to build a car. That number grew like Topsy throughout Roger's series of lulus. Worldwide GM employment went from 691,000 in 1983 to 748,000 in 1984 to 811,000 in 1985—an increase of 17.4 percent in just three years. In sharp contrast, Ford and Chrysler had reduced their employment levels in 1980, '81, '82 and, despite dramatic production increases, had kept their work force lean. "Cost reduction and lean staffing have become a way of life now at Ford," Don Petersen said in 1985.

"We knew that reorganization was going to take extra expense and extra time going in," Roger says. "We could have shut down GM for a year and opened up on the new system, but I don't think that's the right way to do it." If that is what the game plan was, then it was a gross act of deception to thousands of new employees who were never told that they would be needed for only a year or two at best. But the facts indicate that Roger had no idea that employment numbers had gotten so far out of hand. A full two years into the plan, executive speeches, all of which Roger reviewed, continued to talk about reorganization as streamlining, trimming staffs. I recall hearing the reverberations in the PR staff on the day Roger reviewed C-P-C's and B-O-C's numbers in the summer of 1985. And I personally choose to believe employment got out of hand rather than accept the premise that Roger could be capable of so fundamentally dishonest an act as hiring tens of thousands of people under false pretenses.

Reorganization was not the only wholesale restructuring of thousands of jobs during this period. When Roger purchased Hughes, for example, he created a new wholly owned subsidiary called Hughes Delco Electronics. He transferred 18,000 people from the stable, and highly profitable Delco Electronics Division into the outside company, without clear explanation of what their benefits or status would be. At the same time, 10,000 data processing employees were transferred out of GM and into the newly acquired Electronic Data Systems. The disruption of careers and lives was immense, and talented young employees began deserting the corporation at an alarming rate. To this, Roger said: "We won't lose a single good man."

Roger's new theme of "bringing the entrepreneurial spirit into GM" was capturing headlines. Yet few journalists stopped to appraise exactly what Roger meant by entrepreneurship— which he called "interpreneurship," to emphasize the improvement from within. Management experts were teaching companies that the way to encourage risk taking was to reduce the consequences of failure, create a no-fault environment in which people would dare to be different. Roger's definition was somewhat different. "I want to give the guy out there an opportunity to build his own car, and if he fails, he loses his job."

In Roger's mind and rhetoric, the entrepreneurial drive was

needed in every office and plant. That, however, shows a genuine lack of understanding of the disruptive nature of entrepreneurs. Peter Drucker calls the entrepreneurial personality *rerum novarum cupidus*, greedy for new things. This drive for innovation in all things is the antithesis of stable, high-volume production. Drucker, in *Entrepreneur*, gives companies that would attempt to bring entrepreneurial attitudes into their operations three primary warnings:

1. "Do not ever put the entrepreneurial into the existing managerial component.
2. "Innovation should not be diversification—out of your own field.
3. "Don't buy into other businesses . . . unless executives are prepared to put in their own management quickly."

Roger violated all three guidelines in his quest for entrepreneurship within General Motors. He made risk taking a virtue on every staff and plant, bought up companies such as Hughes in aviation electronics and space technologies, and assumed that he was buying the management talent along with the stock certificates. "One of the reasons we bought Hughes and EDS," Roger said, "was that we wanted their management teams."

Had Roger actually had plant management experience, he would have understood that entrepreneurship doesn't lend itself to quality production. Manufacturing, by its production-oriented nature, strives for consistency, not innovation. The function is not to come up with one idea that might work, but to produce tens of thousands of complex vehicles that won't fail. Roger's primary competitors, the Japanese automakers, understand this well. They were able to copy U.S. inventions and bring them to market first, and at higher quality levels, by keeping entrepreneurship out of the clockworks. Research and development efforts were kept away from manufacturing until the machine or process was thoroughly proven technology. Honda even went so far as to create a separate R & D company within its company to assure independence. Once it has been decided to make a product, the Japanese blueprint is set in stone. Manufacturing people are encouraged only to find ways to follow the blueprint more precisely and save money in refinement, not redirection.

But these matters were never discussed. Roger's quest captured the headlines and diverted attention from the chinks in his armor. The media generally did not report the downside of Roger's rapid-fire spending and project spree. For years the media had sniped at GM for being an immense bureaucracy impervious to change. Thus, any man with the courage to challenge entrenched thinking deserved recognition. Few seemed to notice that the problems Roger was challenging were not endemic to the old system, but problems created by the new one.

A few questioned throwing money as a way to fight. As the old joke goes, "You spend a few billion dollars here, a few billion dollars there, a few billion over there, and first thing you know you're talking about real money." Roger's spending was adding up. In three years of record incomes, with sales climbing 22 percent, GM's earnings fell 35 percent. Gross margins on annual revenues were falling steadily—from 18.5 percent in 1983 to 16.3 percent in '84 to 15.3 percent in 1985. Roger's little green box was emptying rapidly.

The major investments were not yielding proportionate increases in productivity. The new technology was proving far more costly and cantankerous than union labor had been for Roger. GM's ultramodern Orion plant had 157 advanced robots, a full complement of AGVs, and bar-coded stock controls as in a supermarket checkout. It was supposed to produce 270,000 cars a year with 1,500 workers on two shifts. That was 3,000 fewer people than a conventional plant would have required. The technology, however, was balky. Robots painted walls instead of cars, and welding robots welded doors shut. The high-tech machines were down far more than they were up and working, and the plant's quality on the high-priced Cadillac DeVilles and Oldsmobile 98s was near the very bottom of all GM plants.

Buick City was another example of unfulfilled dreams. This 1.8-million-square-foot facility in Flint, Michigan, combined a Buick and a Fisher Body (eliminated in reorganization) plant to come up with a new kind of facility. There was less management supervision, and workers were given buttons to stop the line if they spotted quality problems. It was a borrowed technique from the Japanese that was working well with Toyota management in GM's Fremont, California, plant. In Flint, however, there was still the old pressure to pump the metal through the system and out the door. "I saw the same door hinge problem on several cars and pushed the button," an assembler said. "The line stopped, and the supervisor looked at the problem and said it was a design flaw. We couldn't do anything about it. Then I pushed the button to stop the line on a lousy paint job, and that's when they put me on a different job where I couldn't be so concerned about quality. It's the same old story—they talk quality, but it's all yak and no shack." Buick City went to a modified system whereby the button lit a yellow light to signal a problem, so the assembly line could keep moving along.

If technologies and techniques were balking, so was the attempt to speed up the process of bringing on new products. Every new product or component development from 1981 onward was plagued by delays, patchwork fixes, and customer complaints. The new C-cars—Cadillac DeVilles, Buick Electras, and Oldsmobile 98s—were scheduled to appear in the fall of '84. They actually began deliveries in December of '85. The innovative Pontiac Fiero project, a two-seat plastic-bodied sports car, ran a full year late. New engines were from six months to a year behind projected schedules, and new transmissions were even later (some finally were shelved, never to appear). Roger inherited many of these problems with the programs approved under previous CEOs, such as the diesel engines and transmissions offered in 1980 models that "self-destructed after three thousand miles," as one owner said of her 1980 Cadillac Seville. The problems included fuel-injector and head-gasket failures, early camshaft wear, radiator and heater core leaks, and cracks in the engine blocks. GM was spending more and more time in courts and in FTC hearing chambers. To resolve these largely engineering problems would have required the full attention and resources of the corporation, but much of the talent—including that of senior executives—was diverted to search out brave new worlds of *Star Wars* technology and acquisitions. "Your star doesn't rise these days by dwelling on the past," a division chief engineer explained. "The total focus is on the future." Roger himself said it best in a magazine interview in January of 1985. "I'm not concerned with what we have now," Roger said, referring to current levels of product and technology. "My concern is with what we will have several years down the road."

An overload of futuristic ideas and programs was taking place. For the only major car program that Roger initiated, the $7 billion midsize FWD GM10 project, new concepts continuously added more complexity, additional "bells and whistles," as the engineers called them. Roger's goal had been to reduce new car development time from five years to three. But he approved GM10 in 1981 and would produce only one car in 1987 and the rest in 1988. That seven-year cycle became the longest, and most expensive, in corporate history. "The GM10 has taken longer not because it's such an unusual car. It's not. It's because the GM10 is an all-new way of building a car." Again, Roger was placing the emphasis not on the product but on the production process.

Yet because of the delays, GM experienced a new kind of look-alike problem. The advanced GM10 designs (still not ready for production) looked very much like Ford's Taurus and Sable introduced in 1985, designs that started at Ford two years after Roger had approved the GM10 configurations yet came out a year and a half ahead of GM. That meant extra expense as GM engineers tore into the basic designs to "make GM look different."

F. Alan Smith (no relation), GM's executive vice president of finance, summed up the effects of this period in his 1986 Executive Management Conference report. From 1983, he said, "GM revenues grew more than $21 billion. In effect, we created the equivalent of an entire Chrysler Corporation or Nissan Corporation in two years." So much for the good news. F. Alan had plenty of the other kind:

Back in 1983 GM led the way with the highest operating margins in the industry. We earned almost 2 percentage

points more on each dollar of sales than our domestic
competition and about ½ percentage point more than the
Japanese. By 1985, however, we had changed places with
our competition . . . our domestic competitors were
outperforming us by 3 percentage points—that's a slippage
of 5 points in three years. Even worse, the Japanese have
opened up a 5-point lead over GM. Since we are almost a
$100 billion company, each percentage point of sales
represents $1 billion of lost profit.

   Since 1980 GM has spent $45 billion on the automotive
business. Capital spending appears to be almost inversely
related to our levels of operating profit. And GM's forward
capital spending plans [Roger's strategic plan] are projected
to be $34.7 billion over the period from 1986 through 1989.
. . . For $34.7 billion, given recent market valuations, GM
could have purchased Toyota and Nissan. This would almost
double GM's world market share, increasing our penetration
to over 40 percent of the entire free world. Can we expect
to double our worldwide market share from our spending
program?

   F. Alan went on to compare Ford Motor Company's new
Taurus plant with a like-sized car plant in General Motors. He
noted that Ford needs two thousand, or 63 percent fewer,
hourly and salaried employees for the same production and
that GM spends about $300 million to modernize a plant com-
pared to Ford's $200 million. In essence, F. Alan was saying
that Roger's gamble on high technology was not paying off.
(Since that conference, F. Alan Smith has had a lower profile
in the corporation, and industry watchers no longer consider
him Roger's favorite to be the next GM chairman in 1990.)

   Also, near the end of 1985 GM repeated the cost comparison it had run with the Japanese in 1981. Back then it was
estimated that the Japanese could build a compact car for
$1,800 less than GM could. After $40 billion in technology
investments, the new study showed that nothing had changed.
"The overall conclusion," GM economist Jim Trask said in his
report, "is that the Japanese cost advantage [adjusted for exchange rate fluctuations] has not changed significantly since
1981." GM had improved, but the Japanese had improved just

as much without major technology investments.

In attempting to prove that modest improvements could produce the same results as massive investments, GM's Advanced Engineering people initiated an experiment. They took a 30-year-old stamping press line at a Truck and Bus Division metal fabricating plant in Flint. They first enlisted the full participation of the workers on the press line, then began a series of small, incremental improvements on each of the machines. Without any substantial investment, this old line was able to demonstrate they could go from 180 parts per hour to 540. Per-piece labor costs were cut by 40 percent, changeover time went from 33 hours to 3 hours, and quality ratings went up more than 20 percent. The point, largely lost on the 14th floor, was clearly demonstrated.

Yet there is a postscript to this demonstration project. Union leadership in the demonstration project did not trust management. They agreed to up production rates on the line after the improvements up to 325 parts per hour—substantially below the demonstrated new capability of 540 parts per hour. The result was that when I sent a photographer out to document this dramatic achievement, he had to wait for 20 minutes while the workers were on their break. With the new efficiencies, the people on that line got a 20-minute break every hour in order to hold down productivity to the agreed-upon 325 parts per hour. Far more than demonstrating the potential for incremental improvements, the project epitomized the larger challenge in human relations.

Productivity depends on people. Roger seemed to be too busy to concentrate on this fundamental fact. During the three years that he was riding high in the public press, his image among workers did not improve. This was partly due to GM's traditional gridlock in employee communications. The clearance process for any publication was so cumbersome and fraught with difficulties that corporate editors knew better than to attempt anything candid, as a story would be emasculated before it finished going through clearance. One result of encouraging union workers to participate with management in joint efforts was that union leaders were able to obtain a great deal more information than they ever had access to before. The union promptly shared with its members everything it learned. This created a curious situation in which GM plant supervisors and salaried staffers were picking up the union publications whenever possible to find out what their own corporate publications were unable to tell them. Roger, however, did not stress internal communications and spent remarkably little time selling his vision.

The overall consensus was that GM executives were too busy getting theirs to care about rewarding the people who were actually doing the work. As the employees saw it, productivity and total sales volume were going up dramatically. They had made major concessions since 1982 to help the corporation get back on its feet. Now they felt they deserved to share in the windfall profits. Roger continued to dwell on the unconscionably high wages of American manufacturing workers, a theme that not only was hurting employee morale but was generally not true. The hourly compensation of American manufacturing workers rose less than 1 percent a year from 1981 through 1986 (adjusted for inflation), while their productivity rose an average of more than 4 percent a year during this period. And in the auto industry as a whole the productivity rise was about 6 percent a year. In essence, the workers were improving their contributions without reward.

In 1984 both money and job security became such strong issues that a union strike was inevitable. Canadian workers were especially upset because under the centralized thinking at GM the corporation was attempting to superimpose the U.S. contracts in their country. Canada is much further down the road toward socialism than the United States, and the Canadians had no need for many of the benefits the Americans offered. Canada did not have quality problems and saw the situation far differently from their American counterparts. (I visited GM's Canadian operations on three different occasions and was repeatedly surprised each time by the workers' antagonism or utter indifference to the U.S. parent. Dropping names of the chairman or president did no good, as the average factory worker claimed not to know who they were.) All of this led to a strike in Canada that fostered closings at interlocking plants in the states.

Roger's response was to scold the union as if they were disobedient children after the strike was over and a new contract was in place. In a *Ward's Auto World* interview Roger was asked if profit sharing would be significant, considering GM's record profits in 1984. Roger said that because of the strikes, "They're not going to get anywhere near what they would have gotten."

"But won't that be considered a breach of your promise to reward the people who helped GM recover?" the reporter asked.

"That guy [union member] can look right into the mirror if he wants to know what happened to profit sharing."

Profit sharing for 1984 was $328, while workers had been led to expect $1,000 during contract talks a few months earlier. Meanwhile, Roger distributed $304 million among his less than 6,000 bonus-level executives that year—an *average* of over $50,000 each. In 1985, the workers got $384 in profit sharing, while Ford Motor Company, with far lower profits, gave its workers $1,200 in profit-sharing checks. During the same year Roger's salary and bonuses amounted to $1,899,917—just under $2 million. And he split nearly $219 million among the bonus-eligible executives.

For 1986 the workers did not receive a penny in profit sharing, while the executive bonuses topped $169 million. Roger's income hit $1.95 million for the year. In Flint, union members took up a collection of pennies to send to Roger as an extra bonus in protest of the lack of equitable profit sharing. At an average contribution of $.03 each, they collected about $10 in pennies to send to Roger. "We got Roger instead of profit sharing," an Ohio employee said.

In a series of tours of eight "friendly" plants designed to quiet the growing employee anger, Roger was presented a T-shirt imprinted "Up Your Assets with Profit Sharing." Roger turned red but held his temper. He felt the tour was a success because the employees were polite and shook hands with him. "It's another example of Roger not understanding human nature," Doug Fraser said. "Any big-name person coming through a plant would get his hand shaken so the guy could go home at night and say, 'Honey, guess who I shook hands with at the plant today?' That's not any indication that they respect you or your actions.''

Roger was, as always, surprised at the workers' depth of feelings over profit sharing. "The people at GM have received their profit sharing every day in paychecks as we've gone out and spent big money to keep them working," Roger said. At the 1986 management conference he expressed his view that big rewards for top executives were necessary to keep good people, while the rank-and-file GM employees were grossly overpaid. He topped it off by explaining the huge bonuses to a journalist, saying: "We think one of the things that has made General Motors great is that our people are highly motivated. When the company does well, they do well. And when the company does poorly, they don't do very well." Evidently that applied solely to the management elite and not to the other three-quarters of a million GM people.

Customers are also people. Responding to them was a matter not so much of forward product planning and strategic concepts but of "feeling" your way through. In many ways, the car business is not a mathematical science but an art form in which mass tastes carry the day. As Tom Murphy, former GM chairman, told me: "Until we put a car on the street, we really don't know how the public will react. We have all kinds of consumer-buying clinics, but they can never figure it. The Corvair, for instance, we saw as a family car. The public thought of it as a sporty car. We had to react and modify it for sporty buyers because the public told us to. Or take the first [Cadillac] Seville. I didn't feel it was deserving of much respect. The second Seville was a far better car all around, but the public liked the first one better. It became a classic. How do you figure it?" One way, of course, is to be responsive to the public by having a people-sensitive marketing team that knows how to listen and respond. Roger, however, saw marketing as something a good finance man could pick up quickly. So he named Robert T. O'Connell, a lifelong finance man, to be the vice president in charge of marketing. In academia, it would be the equivalent of placing the campus accountant in charge of psychology and liberal arts. Yet the O'Connell appointment was typical of many appointments of financial men to areas in which they were completely inexperienced.

"Bob O'Connell came to me and asked for some basic text-books on marketing," says Tom Adams, former chairman of Campbell Ewald advertising agency. "He didn't ask for the job, but wanted to do it right. . . . It was pathetic to watch him reading sophomore textbooks as VP of marketing." O'Connell seemed like an especially ill-conceived choice for a psychologically based position. He was pure finance staff, hard-driven and insensitive to the people around him. I sat in his office on a number of occasions in which he called in his underlings and demanded the impossible. O'Connell was a political animal, who had his fingers in everyone's pie; for the executive assistants reported to John Mischi, who reported directly, and practically hourly, to O'Connell. Whenever O'Connell got a chance to review anyone's speech or presentation, he would attempt to put some example in it from his own list of committee work. His ambitions were as obvious as his examples were inappropriate.

O'Connell's primary contribution as marketing vice president was not to improve on the quality of ads or to provide design staff with real-world feedback. No, O'Connell launched a massive assault on advertising rates through the GM Media Council. What counted was not so much the reach and impact of a publication or television buy as whether the media would cooperate in cutting prices below the standard rate cards. Media sources that refused to play ball were chopped. One such publication was the *Wall Street Journal*, which expressed deep concerns that GM was attempting to turn media buying into a commodity business. As *Wall Street Journal* marketing vice president Bernard Flanagan said in an *Advertising Age* interview, "It [GM's approach] just cheapens editorial content of a medium and leads to its ultimate death for lack of content."

Finance thinking was responsible for the most costly and eventually disastrous marketing directions of the 1980s—the move to centralized programs focusing on interest rate deals. Traditionally, the dealers were given significant allowances to conduct their own marketing efforts, with advertising expertise provided by GM when needed. This, in effect, carried

Sloan's decentralization concept right down to the show-room, the assumption being that the dealer knew his market best and was the best person to decide when a special sale—discounts, rebates, or quiet individual bartering—worked best. With a dealer empire of ten thousand in which every operator was an independent businessperson, the variety of creative selling programs that came out of the dealer world was impressive. There were, of course, always the handful of dealers who would skim the cream, pocket the company pro-motion dollars, and let normal floor traffic sell at as close to sticker price as possible; but the vast majority of dealers used every penny of the company's promotion allowances—and more—to pump up their volumes. Roger's financially domi-nated team saw this as "out of control" and "inefficient." So GM shifted to national promotions, and the biggest gimmick of all was, predictably, finance rates.

Each year from 1982 on, GM raised car prices by anywhere from $250 to $700, then used low-interest finance rates to overcome the inevitable sticker shock. GM was the initiator of virtually every interest rate cut, which inevitably drew Ford, Chrysler, and American Motors into the rate wars. GM kept upping the ante—from 12.9 to 11.9, to 10.9 to 9.9, to 7.7, to 7.9, 6.9, 3.9, 2.9, and finally to an all-time low of 1.9 percent financing on new cars on a two-year contract. The competi-tion had to one-up that, getting to the ultimate low of a zero-interest loan offered by a desperate American Motors in 1986.

"What's really happening," a Ford marketing man said, "is that GM has been unable to predict the market and control inventories, so it is forcing us to match lot-clearing financing when we're on top of our inventories and don't need it. The whole market is suffering through GM's inability to define production rates."

Interest rates did keep GM sales alive, but it was the quality of life one would expect on an artificial lung and heart sup-port system. Whenever GM unplugged the marketing body from the artificial supports, the market stopped pumping on its own. Each time GM waited as long as it felt it could to see if cars and trucks would again sell without the low-rate incen-tives, and each time it was GM whose sales suffered the most.

Without basic price cuts, traditional local incentives, or exciting product offerings, it looked like GM had permanently hooked itself to the artificial supports. Why buy now when you had to wait only a few weeks to get the same cars at lower rates? GM inventories rose each time it tried to get out of the support trap, and ultimately it would give in and come out with an even lower rate than before. It was a vicious cycle, far worse than the traditional roller coaster of market demand.

How much the finance supports actually helped GM's faltering penetration is not known. Many say they did more harm than good. They were immensely expensive efforts, costing billions of dollars directly out of the profit column. The rates moved sales ahead out of the normal selling season. If you had a finance rate sale in June, you could guarantee that sales would plummet in September when the rates were removed. If the rates were used to pick up the midwinter sales slump, then spring sales would be a disaster. In a mature market with 30-plus manufacturers competing, there is, after all, only a finite number of cars and trucks that can be sold in any given year. It was like having a blanket that didn't cover you adequately, so you cut off a corner here and there and sewed the patch back on elsewhere. The size of the market blanket would not change despite the cutting and tailoring. Worse, it was the final step in centralization, removing even the dealer from influencing his own business. Roger's probably unconscious vesting of control in a centralized financial staff was complete.

"We're not selling cars anymore, " a Cleveland Chevrolet dealer told me. "We're selling financing."

In late 1985 Roger's era of heroic recognition came to an abrupt end. And it started with a television ad produced by Young & Rubicam for Ford Motor Company. The film spot starts off with a distinguished couple coming out of a fancy restaurant, and the valet runs to get the man's black Cadillac. The valet comes back with a black Buick. No, that's not it. Then the valet comes back with a black Oldsmobile, and there's total confusion over which car is the Cadillac, which the Buick, and which the Olds. Amid the confusion, another distinguished couple comes out and asks the valet for their

Lincoln, which, of course, does not look like the mess of GM luxury cars. The message is that if you want to "distinguish yourself from the crowd," then you ought to buy a Lincoln. Overnight, the television ad focused public attention on GM's look-alike dilemma, which had been known but largely ignored inside of GM since 1980. Sales of GM's luxury models, already down, fell further. Ford and Chrysler each had a wide range of stylish entries. GM's market share was eroding. The company that had 49 percent of the market when Roger took command in 1980 went to 39.1 percent in 1984, 40.3 percent in '85, 38.4 percent in '86, and would dip to 36.5 percent in '87. Ford and Chrysler, with their emphasis on new models, were picking up the market share GM was losing. *Fortune* magazine became one of the first to ask the growing question:

"Is GM so preoccupied with its spectacular plans for the year 2000 that it's neglecting to build the right cars in the here and now?"

The Ford ad served only to draw public attention to the giant, and once attention was focused, it was apparent that GM was in trouble. It was an internally bloated company that had seen its breakeven point rise by 30 percent from 1980 to 1984 while costs and employment numbers were running haywire. Even Roger's robots were rebelling with more downtime and repairs than performance. Roger's response was to find a new group to blame. This time it was middle managers. He began calling them "the frozen middle." The workers were on board (Roger admitted to his senior executives), and, of course, his 14th-floor team was doing its job; therefore, the problem had to be with Mr. In-between. At a management conference reviewing the failures of 1985, Roger said:

"We haven't gotten our middle management people going with us. . . . My real concern is the middle managers who are receiving our messages—but just don't want to go along, either in terms of their own efforts or in passing the messages along to their subordinate managers. . . . If our middle and lower-level managers aren't with us, they're against us."

I was sitting in a meeting with several executives when someone said Roger was going to use his new frozen middle theme. A group vice president known for his leadership qualities just shook his head. "Jesus Christ, is he going to alienate everyone?" Public Relations did warn Roger about the proposed theme, but he had made up his mind. The speech, as expected, angered one of his last groups of allies in the company.

"If we're frozen," a materials manager told me, "who was it that left us out in the cold?"

Roger would begin 1986 with pockets full of problems— plummeting profits, few internal allies, rebellious robots, falling GM stock prices, and a public image that was beginning to rust through the thin veneer. "I have great faith in electronics," Roger said. "We're going to be all that we can be. We are going to be an electronics company as well as an automotive company." Roger would stick with his plan. "The other companies are going to have to do the same things we're doing," Roger insisted, "if they want to be around in the 21st century."

As the critics began to appear, Roger came out with a new corporate image campaign—"The GM Odyssey: Science, Not Fiction," a far-out series of television ads depicting GM as a futuristic, high-tech culture with satellites, robots, and all. This was Roger's brainchild, and it earned him *Advertising Age*'s Adman of the Year award. The theme signaled a corporate image shift away from a reputation of the most concerned and precise manufacturer to that of a corporation dedicated to pure, far-out futurism.

"I'm done with 'sweating the details,' " Roger said. "Now I want to move on to the 21st century."

6
Buying a Legend

*"We must not introduce into our culture
contaminants which may cause our heritage to
become confused."*

Attila the Hun

Ross Perot, GM's billionaire board member, got excited about the Saturn Project. When the project was elevated to separate corporation status, Ross suggested a kickoff dinner for the team. He also said there should be no head table for the chairman and him to sit at and that union people should be included and should mingle at tables with the executives. Roger accepted all of this but nearly dropped the telephone receiver when Ross mentioned that he had bought 500 copies of *Leadership Secrets of Attila the Hun* and planned to distribute them at the dinner. Roger said nothing, yet he was concerned that Attila, "the scourge of God," might upset the union people (who already thought of Ross's EDS's entry into General Motors as a barbarian invasion). Instead of expressing reservations to Ross directly, Roger turned to his public relations man, Jack McNulty, to "see what you can do about this." Jack broached the subject to Ross on the way from the airport to the kickoff dinner. "Have you read it?" Ross asked. Jack had not. "I thought the Saturn guys would enjoy seeing that some of their ideas aren't new. They've got good senses of humor, but if Roger doesn't like it, it's not that im-

141

portant." It was probably the last time Ross would acquiesce to an indirect request from Roger.

Roger remembers the Attila the Hun incident as an embarrassment narrowly averted. Jack McNulty is fond of telling the story (though he's forgotten the details and calls it the "Genghis Khan" book) because it makes Ross look a bit bizarre. Neither Jack nor Roger read the book. That's unfortunate, for it contains some fascinating insights into the art of leadership. The book, written by Dr. Wess Roberts, a Utah psychologist and human resources expert, presents the sayings of Attila, the man who united the far-flung Hungarian tribes into an empire. Attila is described as "a mighty king in the land of the Huns whose goodness and wisdom had no equal." Attila's might was such that he could easily have sacked Rome, but he showed mercy when Pope Leo I met Attila on the road and persuaded him to turn back. Attila was a master image builder, developing "the scourge of God" concept, wearing crude animal skins and pretending to eat raw meat, all to frighten his foes. Yet to his own people there was another image of strong commonality, of not putting himself above his people in dress or manner and of absolute loyalty to his subordinates. "Seek first the good of your people," Attila said.

Henry Ross Perot was, in many respects, a down-home version of Attila the Hun with a touch of Davy Crockett and P. T. Barnum thrown in. Had Roger read the book on Attila before he bought—or thought he bought—Ross's leadership, he might have understood that a devastating cultural clash was inevitable.

"Ross is a GM kind of guy," Roger said after their first meeting. While no one is sure what he meant by that, it was clear Roger had been thoroughly smitten by the Texan's charm. Superficially, the two men have much in common. They are both small men, Roger at 5'8" and Ross at 5'6". Neither was attractive physically. Ross has cauliflower ears and a broken nose, though he has penetrating blue eyes. Both men are blessed with boundless energy and an absolute constitutional need for a continuous influx of new ideas and challenges. Both speak so fast at times that they lose syntax; sometimes too fast for listeners to absorb their words. Both are impatient men who have no tolerance whatever for red tape and rigmarole. Both are conservative men whose belief in entrepreneurship is sacrosanct. Both are self-disciplinarians and firm believers in the work ethic. Neither is fond of ostentatious displays of either power or wealth. And most important, both Roger and Ross are representatives of their own corporate cultures—which is why their numerous similarities would inevitably be irrelevant.

In 1984 Roger felt his culture was in trouble. His efforts to bring new people into the corporation at the high levels and his insistence on using outside consultants on every major project were evidence that he had little confidence that the GM culture he had inherited was viable. Also, Roger's planned thrust into the 21st century was in jeopardy because of GM's still decentralized computer operations. The computer was to be the heart of Roger's plans. GM had lots of computer power, more than a hundred mainframes and tens of thousands of stand-alone systems. And GM had a wealth of computer expertise as industry leader in computer-aided design and computer-aided manufacturing. GM, in fact, had more computer power than any organization short of the U.S. government. It spent $3 to $4 billion each year on internal computer and data processing operations and contracted with more than two thousand software supplier companies as well. Yet there was no centralized control. Widely varied systems in different divisions and from one staff to another made a corporatewide system impossible. For seven years GM had been trying to get its data processing act together. GM even created a centralized division—General Motors Information Systems and Communications Activity (GMISCA), but it was never given enough power to override divisional budgeting, and the corporation's systems remained in disarray. In addition, data processing outside of General Motors was characterized by low labor rates. Roger saw a way of getting the act together while dealing with his pet peeve of labor costs in one decisive move. It was characteristic Roger Smith thinking. As with Frigidaire and Terex in the 1970s, and GM Assembly Division and Fisher Body in '84, he chose to take the quick way out of a management problem. If he couldn't guide GMISCA, he'd simply get rid of it and the ten thousand GM computer people. He could buy an outside computer services company and hand over all GM computer business and people. Roger needed a company like Perot's Electronic Data Systems.

Once Roger met Ross and saw his elite work force and commando tactics, Roger decided he also needed Ross. Without carefully examining what management techniques were actually involved or considering whether they could be transferred, Roger became convinced that the EDS culture could not only merge with GM's, but that it could permeate and prevail. "Perot's style fits right in with what we're trying to do at General Motors," Roger said, and "EDS has the kind of entrepreneurial spirit that we need to develop in GM."

Once again, Roger did the unprecedented. He bought EDS at the top-dollar price of $2.55 billion and endowed it with special contractual rights of independence that no other GM division or subsidiary had ever been given. He not only guaranteed Ross control of EDS, but offered him a seat on the GM Board of Directors. Traditionally, when GM bought a subsidiary and wanted its CEO, it would bring the individual onto the central staff of the parent corporation, not leave the person to run his original company as if nothing had changed. That, in fact, is how Alfred P. Sloan, Jr., came to GM. Billy Durant bought up Sloan's company, Hyatt Bearings, and brought him to the central office because he recognized Sloan's management skills.

Roger didn't want Ross to join the team as much as he wanted him to define the team culture for him. Roger purposely let the implication persist that EDS would become the dominant culture and even delighted in the spreading rumors that he had brought Ross into the corporation to become the next chairman.

"I've got to keep telling people that I don't want your job," Ross told Roger.

"Don't bother," Roger said. "You don't understand. That shakes a lot of people up around here, and they need shaking up."

So the stories, none of them discouraged in any way by Roger or GM public relations, proclaimed Ross Perot as the "man who will save General Motors." Ross's EDS would be, the media said, "GM's brains and nervous system." The Texan would "change GM into a young, dynamic company." Few media observers questioned the absurdity of a subsidiary of fewer than 14,000 people dominating a 75-year-old culture of 3 million people.

Roger thought he needed Ross, yet from the first time they met it was obvious that the need was not mutual. Ross, at 53 years old, had created a culture and a public persona that gave him more than everything he had ever wanted. "I had no interest at all in selling my company," Ross said. "I had $100 million in cash and 46 percent of EDS stock [worth over a billion dollars then]. EDS was growing at 20 percent and more a year. Why did I need them?" He might also have added that by 1984 Ross Perot was already being heralded as "the greatest Texan since Sam Houston," and groups were forming to urge Ross to run for president of the United States. What could Roger possibly offer him?

Moreover, what could Roger actually buy? EDS was more of a personality cult than a culture. A cult centered around a man of legendary accomplishment and compassion. Ross likes to call the stories about him "half myths," yet even without embellishment he had accomplished more before he met Roger than most men could in several lifetimes. The former IBM salesman had invested $1,000 in 1962 to start Electronic Data Systems, a computer services company that, within 20 years, made him one of the richest men in America. Now Roger had made him even wealthier.

When a reporter once asked him if he preferred being referred to as a billionaire or a millionaire, he snapped back: "Call me Ross." It was the common touch that Roger also strived for, but the difference was that it wore like a comfortable old suit on the billionaire Texan. The son of a Texarkana cotton broker and horse trader, Ross displays none of the trappings of immense wealth. His large but unpretentious home has no live-in maids, his cars have no chauffeurs, and his children have no live-in nannies. Ross does his own shopping, frequently at K Mart, Sears, and J. C. Penney, and buys expensive suits off the rack. He drove a six-year-old car around town

before joining GM and ate most of his meals in commonplace
diners where he mixed with the customers like the "good ol'
boy" that he was. In interviewing him, I was struck by his
constant awareness that he was a common man. "If the ball
had bounced just a little differently," he said, "I'd be working
in that factory." Ross always refers to his wealth as "being hit
with a golden horseshoe."

By the time he met Roger, Ross had lost interest in the day-
to-day administration of EDS, turning it over to his close friend
and EDS president Mort Meyerson and getting involved only to
front major clients as the company's chairman and top salesman. The company was too well established and running too
flawlessly under Meyerson to keep Ross's attention. Ross had
no patience with anything less than grand and heroic themes.
He devoted himself to causes. Over the years his causes have
been so numerous, in fact, that he has given away more money
than Roger Smith can possibly earn during his 10 years as GM's
chairman.

Ross's causes are legendary. ("Not legend," Ross says,
"myths.") A few involve just money, like $15 million for a rare
book collection donated to the University of Texas, another $1
million each year to the Boy Scouts, $100,000 a year to the
Salvation Army, and $10 million to build the new Symphony
Orchestra which Perot insisted be named in honor of his
friend Mort Meyerson. He spent $1.5 million to buy one of the
four original copies of the Magna Carta and loaned it to the
National Archives. And he supported a Catholic school for
disadvantaged children in Dallas (Ross himself is a Presby-
terian).

But none of Ross's philanthropies involve his personally doing what he seems best at—taking on challenges that would
stifle St. Jude. Trying to bring back the prisoners of war still
missing inside of Vietnam has been one of his crusades since
1969, when he spent $2 million to fly a planeload of Christmas
presents to Hanoi. He didn't get his items through to the
POWs, but Ross garnered world attention by standing in front
of the North Vietnamese Embassy, protesting with a bullhorn
in hand. He has financed more than 20 expeditions to free
POWs since then and has spent countless millions more ($1

million on newspaper ads to draw attention to the cause). And, most recently, he has been in the news again when Col. Oliver North revealed that Ross had put up $1 million to pay for the release of hostages in Lebanon. As it turned out, Ross has been a quiet banker for any hostage release effort—covert or overt—for the past 15 years. He was as quick to bankroll Jesse Jackson's hostage release trip to Lebanon as he would have been to support a Jesse James effort to bring the hostages out by force.

Ross tackled the entire Texas school system, spending $2 million and hiring the state's best lobbyists so the other side couldn't retain them. His goal was to slaughter the sacred cow of high school sports and replace it with new legislation that puts basic education first. He would not budge an inch on the legislation he wanted—it had to be "no pass—no play" or nothing. Ross led a similar campaign in Texas to educate young people against street drugs and tighten state enforcement, taking on organized crime as directly as he had taken on the athletes. But by far the most publicized Ross Perot venture was his organization of a commando force of EDS employees to rescue two employees from an Iranian prison. The effort was successful and became the subject of a bestselling book, *On Wings of Eagles* by novelist Ken Follett. Some 40 million Americans would watch an enactment of his daring exploit in a special mini-series on national television.

In crusade after crusade Ross has shown that, once he defines a goal, he goes after it with the tenacity of a bulldog, even if it is as seemingly unresolvable as the POW challenge. Some have called him the "Button-down Rambo," a man who loves grand causes, a billionaire Don Quixote. In trying to explain once why he sent U.S. Marine Colonel Ollie North $1 million in cash for a hostage deal on the strength of a single 3:00 A.M. phone call, Ross said, "What would you do if you were sitting on a pile of money that didn't mean much to you and you got a chance to help some Americans?" While money for philanthropic acts "doesn't mean much" to Ross, he is careful with money when it comes to his personal life. The memories of his Great Depression youth stick with him.

Like Roger, Ross attributes who and what he is to his parents. "We're all what we were taught to be," he says. Ross learned his generosity from his mother. She always fed the hobos who stopped almost daily at their modest home. Once a hobo explained that Mrs. Perot was being hit regularly for food because there was a hobo mark on the curb in front of her house. "Do you want me to wash it off?" Ross asked. "No, leave it there," she said. "That was the greatest lesson in the world," Ross says.

From his father, Ross learned to work and how to sell. He broke horses for his father at a dollar a head and broke his nose twice in the process. Ross became a "day trader," meaning that he could buy and sell horses as long as he had none left at the end of the day. "Dad wouldn't let me take them home," he says. Another story from his youth told of how at age 12 (sometimes the story has him at 8 or 10) Ross went to the local newspaper to try to get a route. It was the Depression and there were none. So he made a deal to build his own route in the nearby black slum of New Town. The newspaper had concluded that blacks couldn't read and would have no need for papers. Ross proved them wrong, building a large route and delivering his papers on horseback each morning. Then his father became ill, and Ross had to leave for a few days to visit him in Shreveport. "New Town was considered dangerous, so no one would relieve me," he says. Ross went from house to house explaining the situation. They asked him to save the papers and deliver them when he got back, and they'd pay him. That incident, Ross says, had a major impact on his life. "It gave me a sensitivity and concern for people who had the deck stacked against them," he says.

Ross may seem too good to be true, but among all who know him I could find no one (outside of General Motors) who doesn't say Ross has always been a straight arrow and super salesman. Ross does not smoke or drink and never has. He made the Scout handbook his personal code of conduct, and he says, "The biggest day of my life was when I became an Eagle Scout." Like Roger, Ross is a devoted family man. He has been married for 30 years and has five children, all of them involved in Ross's businesses and clearly dedicated to their father.

Unlike Roger, Ross doesn't operate on logic alone. "Life's a spider web, not a corporate flow chart," he says. He was only a mediocre student—graduated 454th of 925 in his class at Annapolis. Another much-publicized Perot myth is that he was voted by his classmates as the best all-around midshipman and life president of the class. The myths keep popping up. He is anything but introspective, and sophisticates would call the man simplistic and downright schmaltzy. Ross has always been able to appeal to fundamental human emotions and surround himself with symbols that stir underlying feelings for friends, family, country, and God. His favorite painter is (who else?) Norman Rockwell. "Rockwell painted what I strived to be," he said. Paintings, statues, and flags that symbolize his image surround him. During the hostage crisis in Iran, Ross lined his corporate driveway with 53 American flags, one for each hostage. Symbols are never subtle with Ross. As writer David Remnick said of Ross after an extensive interview, "Abstractions do not become him."

Ross resists any image building that sets him apart from the common man. The "H" in H. Ross Perot, for example, irritates him. "I never once signed my name with an H.—that sounds pretentious. It's just Ross but the press created this H. Ross thing on their own. More myths.

"To lead people," Ross told me, "you've got to do a lot of symbolic things. Your personal integrity is most important." Ross is very much aware of the importance of a leadership image. In 1984, for example, a Dallas business publication ran an article that was critical of EDS's handling of Medicare contracts. Ross sent two EDSers to the magazine's office to offer to buy the entire print run of the issue. Ken Follett, Ross's biographer, tells about the time when he was researching Ross in Dallas and casually said to someone that "when telling a funny story, Ross will cheerfully alter the facts to make it funnier." Ross called Follett immediately and told him in no uncertain terms that he wasn't going to have someone spreading the word around Dallas that he exaggerates. Ross doesn't mind exaggeration, however, as long as the essence of the story is truthful. After reviewing the movie about his Iranian exploits, several people pointed out that there were inaccuracies in it. "It's just a docu-drama," Ross said. "That's just a little TV flair there."

From the navy, Ross went to IBM, where he became a star salesman. Each year he became better, and in his last year with IBM he achieved his yearly sales quota in the first three weeks of January. When they awarded him with a desk job, Ross quit, but not before creating another myth about the event. "I was getting a haircut reading a copy of *Reader's Digest* when I read the quote from Thoreau: 'The mass of men lead lives of quiet desperation.' " That's when he says he decided to start his own business. Ross realized that many people were buying computers but did not know how to run them successfully. There was a need for a company that could translate the manuals into operating performance and make complex systems perform as they were designed to. EDS was thus conceived, not as a company of high-tech innovators, but as standardizers, a crew that could establish a status quo and keep it going.

It was the right direction for Ross, a man who lives by his own set of strict rules. One small instance convinced me of just how firm those rules are. I wrote to Ross telling him about this book and requesting an interview. A week later I followed up the letter with a call. "Oh, yes, we got your letter," his secretary said, "but you sent it to Mr. Perot's home address. You'll have to send the letter to his office address." That confused me.

"Now wait a minute," I said. "He's got the letter, but I have to send him another one? Why?"

"Because," she said, "Ross never answers letters sent to his house."

Never deviating from his own standards, Ross defined exactly what his company would be like while the entire staff was still small enough to fit around the kitchen table. He set everything down in a code of standards, which defined precisely how the EDS employee would look, act, and feel. There would be strict appearance and dress codes: short hair, no beards, no mustaches, no slacks for women. Drinking alcohol at lunch meant immediate dismissal, and cohabitation was forbidden. In case the rules missed something, there was the all-purpose ethical code, which stated, "Your character, integrity, and behavior, both on and off the job, determine the image of EDS in the community. Therefore, your standards of conduct *must*, at all times, be above reproach." Central to his standards book was his personal honesty: "We will conduct our business in the center of the field of ethical behavior—not along the sidelines skirting the boundaries."

Picking the right people was central to his new company's concept. "Eagles don't flock; you have to find them one at a time" was his recruiting motto. An applicant's résumé of Ivy League degree and Social Register background did not impress him. Ross typically hired the best candidates from smaller schools, often Vietnam veterans with distinguished war records. They were young men and women with a string of life successes and a strong will to achieve. "They have to be people who love to win," Ross says. And if EDS couldn't find such people, "then hire people who can't stand to lose." It was not a matter of forcing round pegs into square holes but of finding square pegs at the outset. Ross was borrowing chapter and verse from the U.S. Marine Corps ad campaign of "a few good men." He would emphasize the toughness of the job, the long hours and high expectations, and challenge the recruit to be one of the few and the proud. The headquarters Ross built in Dallas was a heavily guarded affair with barbed-wire fences and a half-mile driveway through a nine-hole golf course (a defensible, open perimeter). As Tom Peters, coauthor of *In Search of Excellence*, once remarked, "They [EDS] are like the Marine Corps. Heck, they *are* the Marine Corps."

Ross attacked massive jobs by putting his people in what looked like SWAT teams. One of the company's first jobs, for example, was to set up the software for an entire state Medicare system. They set up bunks at the job site before Thanksgiving and did not come out until they had the system designed at Christmas. To be part of EDS was to be a member of an exclusive fighting corps. They would not do just a portion of a task or set up systems for others but were after the long-term service contracts with fixed prices. Success came rapidly. Within 22 years EDS served more than 52,000 customers in 50 states and foreign countries. It entered the Medicare and Medicaid business and became the largest processor of health claims in the world. It entered the bank processing business and became the largest, with more than 600 major banks. It entered the credit union business and became the largest processor there. It began to bid on government contracts and quickly found itself with 2,600 people for the government work alone. One of the contracts, setting up a data processing network for the U.S. Army, was the largest contract in the history of the computer services industry.

Ross showed how shrewd a businessman he was in 1968, when he went public with EDS stock. He capitalized EDS so that 12 million shares with a par value of $.20 each were in existence. He determined to limit the sale to 650,000 shares and shopped for a long time before he could find an underwriter that would guarantee a handsome return. R. W. Presspich and Co. bought the lot at $16.50 a share. By the close of trading on the first day, EDS was selling for $23 a share. Ross's retained shares upped his net worth by $200 million in one day. And, of course, Ross topped it off with a homey story of how he really didn't want to go public, but his employees did, so he had reluctantly gone along. Since Ross had always lavishly awarded outstanding employee performance with stock, more new millionaires have been created within EDS in the last ten years than in massive General Motors.

In 1984 as a freelance assignment for Campbell Ewald, I had the opportunity to interview a broad cross section of EDS lieutenants. When these men spoke of Ross, it was with reverence (one man actually choked up attempting to explain what Ross meant to him and his family). Piecing the interviews together provided what might be called "Secrets of Leadership of Perot the EDSer" (Ross did not use Attila's formula, but his own approach is so close that with a few word changes Attila's book could easily be Ross's):

"Morale results from pride in being a Hun. Discipline brings about morale. Chieftains never condone a lack of either morale or discipline. . . . They cause them to happen."—Attila

The first and most obvious aspect of his leadership is instilling a sense of pride in EDS membership. Ross surrounds his people with the symbols of eagles and lavishes praise on them at every opportunity. "The one thing I won't tolerate is one person putting himself above others in EDS. We're all the same and on the same team. We're all labor," Ross says. He thus elevates everyone in the organization to the top level. Ross never allowed private parking spaces or executive dining rooms. He and all of his troops eat in the cafeteria together.

"Never reward a Hun with any recognition for doing less than expected of him. . . . Never reward a Hun for every act completed correctly. Otherwise, he will not act in the absence of your presence or without the certainty of recognition."— Attila

There are no written rewards built into the employee contract at EDS. The downside, of course, is that you have no rights to, or guarantee of, more than the minimal pay for your contributions. The upside is that paternal managers can reward you far more lavishly when you perform well than any contract would allow. At EDS every leader has a bag of cash at his disposal for rewarding outstanding performance. If you have to work late on an important project for a few nights in a row, you would not be surprised to have your wife receive a dozen roses with a note of apology (and praise for your importance to the company). At the end of an important project, your boss might give your family tickets to Hawaii or an envelope full of money or take you and your family out to the theater and dinner (presumably the boss knows your family personally and thus can anticipate what they'd most appreciate). This form of reward is pure Perot. One day early in EDS's struggling days, Ross disappeared from the team effort for most of the day, in itself unusual. Then, when the team members got home that night, their spouses told them Ross had come by and apologized for keeping them away from home so much. He gave each spouse one hundred shares of stock and his personal thank you.

"Chieftains make great personal sacrifices for the good of their Huns. . . . Grant your Huns the benefit of their interest in the welfare of their families."—Attila

Concern for subordinates comes first in Ross's leadership approach. There are nearly as many stories of his family involvement as there were early EDS families. One EDSer told me of how Ross heard indirectly that his son had a learning difficulty. Ross was there immediately to arrange that the boy see the very best educators to work out a learning plan. Another employee had been on the job only a couple of months when his back was broken in a hiking accident. Ross took care of the medical bills and set up an annuity so that the young man would receive support for the rest of his life. Mort Meyerson tells of the time his wife got a bit of Drano in her eye. Local doctors said she would probably lose sight in the eye, but Ross stepped in without being asked, found out who was the best ophthalmologist in the country, and flew her to Johns Hopkins in a rented jet. "Ross saved my wife's sight," Meyerson said. "You can imagine how I feel about Ross after that." The most publicized example of Ross's dedication to his people is when he personally flew to Iran to help in the rescue of two of his employees, even though it meant leaving his mother, who was dying of cancer. She told him it was the right thing to do. After Ross rescued the two executives, his other employees took to kidding him: "You going to rescue me if I get in trouble?"

"Naw," Ross says. "You, I'd let you stay there and rot." No EDSer believed that. They were certain that there was no limit to what Ross would do for his people. And Ross himself reinforced it. "Twenty years from now, if any one of those people need me, I'd go into hell for them, and I know they'd do the same for me. . . . We're family."

Ross had no intention of giving up all this when he was contacted by a New York agent and told that General Motors wanted to buy his company. Ross wasn't interested, but as a good businessman, he figured that he and Mort Meyerson should talk to them anyway—there could be a massive opportunity in it for EDS. When they got to Detroit, Roger took them on a whirlwind tour, flying one of the company helicopters over a number of component and assembly plants and attempting to show the Texans the scope of GM with world maps and film clips. "The sun never sets on General Motors," Ross said, obviously impressed. As he left Detroit, Ross was still convinced GM would become a customer rather than his company's buyer. "You don't have to buy a dairy to get milk. We'll sell you service," Ross told Roger. They parted that day with Roger promising to make an offer and Ross still thinking service contract.

At this point it should be explained that the EDS acquisition was entirely Roger's project. While he led with others like Don Atwood and Howard Kehrl for most high-tech inquiries such as Hughes and Lotus, Roger went after the computer services acquisition on his own. Roger set up a luncheon with John Gutfreund, chairman of Salomon Brothers. As Michael Thomas tells it in *The Nation*, Roger was like "Little Red Riding Hood to the Wolf." Roger made it clear that he wanted to buy a significantly large data processing company. "Investment bankers," Thomas says, "don't keep the city's decorators in clover by telling the likes of Roger Smith to sink his stockholders' excess billions into improving GM's basic business. . . ." Salomon Brothers went looking for a big deal and came up with the idea of an EDS acquisition even though it was not, and never had been, on the block.

A GM senior executive who was close to Roger during this period said, "The idea of bringing in a hero like Perot appealed to Roger's sense of self-importance." Roger, after all, saw himself as an entrepreneur like his father and like Ross. They were kindred eagles. (Ross would later present Roger with a gold watch with the inscription on the face "Storms bring out eagles." It became Roger's most prized possession, and he included a reference to the watch and Ross in his suggested introduction to his speeches for several months thereafter.) From every indication it appears that there was far more involved for Roger than strategic planning and diversification.

Ross, however, was not interested. It was the bankers at Salomon Brothers, from all reports, who came up with a way of making a deal that would be impossible to refuse. First, the EDS offer would guarantee that Ross could retain full control of an independent EDS while gaining the largest nongovernment client in the world. Second, Ross would be challenged personally to help save Detroit and its millions of American jobs. It was the kind of crusade of epic proportions that Ross could not possibly ignore.

"Here Mort and I were. We'd done it all, and there weren't a lot of challenges left ahead of us. Then along comes this challenge. It was the opportunity to save millions of American jobs. It was too exciting to pass up."

Keeping EDS independent, yet bringing it inside, led to a new kind of stock and deal. The "Class E" stock would be in a category of its own, and though EDS would be a wholly owned subsidiary, the Class E stock value and dividends were to be based entirely on EDS—not GM—performance. Class E stock would be held separate from GM stock; in essence, two different sets of shareholders were established. Initially, the New York Stock Exchange threatened to boot GM out rather than accept such an odd common stock arrangement. But the exchange didn't want GM to take its stock outside of the system, so it changed its rules against such special categories of common stock.

Another characteristic of the Class E stock was that GM would issue promissory notes declaring that the stock must appreciate by at least $125 a share in seven years or GM would make good the full price difference. (This was changed to a guaranteed $62.50 per share after an EDS stock split.) That effectively guaranteed an annual compounded rate of return for Class E stock of 16 percent. The offer was nontransferable. This was done to encourage Ross and his crew, most of whom had significant EDS stock holdings, to stay with GM for at least seven years. Historically in high-tech acquisitions there is an immediate brain drain, and the unique seven-year vested increase would prevent it. The guarantee was equally necessary because investors feared that GM could control the value of EDS stock by giving it less profits when times were hard for the parent company. Since 70 percent of EDS's income would quickly come from GM, it was a legitimate fear.

Class E stock with separate stockholders from GM would guarantee that EDS remain an independent company. Roger also guaranteed that Ross would remain chairman and Mort Meyerson president and that Roger would in no way interfere with the way they ran EDS. All GM computer services that EDS would take over—which meant virtually everything—would be billed under fixed-price contracts. As Ross saw it, the guarantee of autonomy was absolute. "Roger Smith understands the uniqueness of EDS's operations," he said, "and has directed that we be able to operate as an independent unit, with strict instructions to leave Mort and me alone to run the company."

Roger, in fact, told Ross, "If anybody shows up in Dallas with a GM procedures manual, I want you to shoot him."

As defined, it was the deal of a lifetime. Ross could keep his company yet pick up $1 billion in cash and 43 percent of the Class E stock. EDS would be handed at least $2.6 billion in new business—about 33 times EDS's current earnings in 1984. EDS would have an entrée to the industrial computer field, where it had yet to make significant inroads. Add to that the personal challenge of helping to beat out the imports and to save jobs, and it was by far the grandest no-lose proposition any businessman had ever been handed on a platter. The deal was signed on June 27, 1984, on the day of Ross's 54th birthday, which was also the 22nd anniversary of the founding of EDS. Roger didn't attend Ross's birthday party, but he certainly provided the cake.

Some astute observers wondered in print about the logic of the acquisition. Many other companies already had made unsuccessful attempts to enter the computer industry. Exxon Corporation, for example, bought up 15 different computer companies at a cost of $500 million yet was unable to break into the office automation business. Minnesota Mining and Manufacturing and Raytheon had both snapped up computer businesses only to watch them flounder. AM International bought 11 computer companies, which resulted in the parent's going into Chapter 11. Others questioned the rationality of a manufacturer, on a five-year product cycle, entering the computer field, which existed on a 12-month cycle. "Other companies have failed," Roger said, "because they got into businesses they had no business in. That isn't the case with GM." Yet the media, by and large, applauded Roger's EDS acquisition as visionary. Privately, the press was delighted to have at last a colorful character at GM. Ross was in the Lee Iacocca category of being outspoken and imaginative in quotes, and it would certainly liven up the dullest corporate act in town. Ross's homespun Texas humor pervaded everything he said. Even clichéd comments like criticizing the

Washington bureaucrats were enlivened with Rossisms like "They couldn't lead a two-car funeral in silent prayer."

Once Ross signed over, Roger wasted no time announcing that EDS would assume responsibility for every piece of computer hardware and software and that 10,000 GM computer people (7,000 in the U.S.) would be transferred immediately from General Motors to EDS. An advance guard of 650 EDS people would come to Detroit to secure the beachhead.

As usual, most of the 10,000 GM transferees learned about the acquisition from the newspapers. They read that EDS had much lower pay rates, fewer guaranteed benefits, and only a minimal retirement program. All of the articles about EDS's stormtroopers, Army bootcamp operating standards, dress codes, and ethics statements devastated morale among the GM transferees. The fear grew, and any significant development entailing computers screeched to a near stop. "Internal bureaucratic problems [within GM]," Ken Riedlinger, the EDS vice president (a former Catholic missionary) who headed up the GM team, said, "delayed our presentation to GM employees from October 18 to November 1. That hurt us." Actually, the limbo was much longer, for the fundamentals of the transfer were known via the GM grapevine in July.

All Riedlinger could do during this critical period was to keep repeating "Trust us." EDS, after all, was a company based on trust in management, not on written procedures and agreements. EDSers came with a history of experience in trusting their leadership. To GM salaried people, who had seen numerous benefits reduced with little explanation during the past two years, "trust us" was not a phrase to which they could relate. The delay in defining a program for transferees was Ross's first experience with GM's bureaucracy, and he could do little. Ross stopped granting interviews for weeks and became extremely defensive.

In the midst of this confusion, EDS began recruiting in Detroit. EDS had already been operating at full capacity when the contract was signed, so there was no way that Ross could spare a large number of people to make the merger work. EDS began running full-page ads to hire new Detroit workers, while the transferees wondered if they would have jobs at all.

EDS would quickly hire some five thousand additional people—many of them right out of college with no professional computer experience whatever. High school business teachers, who might have taught a class using a personal computer, were hired to jump headlong into massive mainframe programs. The EDS ads promised the newcomers that "together we will cross thresholds of countless breakthroughs." EDS hiring became a Detroit joke—"How many EDSers does it take to change a light bulb?"

"No one knows because they're not done hiring yet."

It was, however, a nervous joke, for the ads added to the rumors that GM was going to fire thousands of computer people and replace them with low-paid raw recruits.

One Flint employee was due to retire on February 1 under GM's 30-and-out pension program, but he was to be transferred to EDS on January 1, and EDS had no early retirement program. "I feel like I've been stabbed in the back," he said. The tension during the delay could be felt on every staff. Even for those who were not affected, the horror stories were everywhere, and a "this could be me next" attitude developed. Anti-EDS sentiment grew steadily. "EDS Buster" buttons could be seen on overalls, and derogatory cartoons depicting EDSers appeared on numerous bulletin boards. One I remember especially was a drawing of three "terrorists"—an Arab, an Irishman, and an American in a business suit with an EDS label on his briefcase.

After the uncertainty came the benefit package announcement on November 1. It offered to keep the GM transferees' pay the same and fold in a final COLA payment, but there was little to compensate for the loss of stock vesting, medical, dental, and retirement benefits. A GMAC employee of 24 years figured it out: "In my case it amounts to an $11,500-a-year pay cut, and that doesn't include pensions, which they won't give me enough information to get a handle on." Within weeks GM employees were filing lawsuits to recoup their pensions. A large group of employees filed a class-action suit against GM, claiming that they collectively lost upwards of $500 million in benefits. Some 350 GM Tech Center employees crowded into the United Auto Workers hall and in an outpouring of anger asked the union to represent them. But before the union could organize, the Tech Center group was broken up and scattered around the company.

Riedlinger made matters worse when he sent a letter to all of the new employees telling them there was "no place for a union" in EDS. Those who were considering unionizing, he said in the letter, were "a small number of people. . . . [They] are disgruntled and are apparently motivated by an intention to get even with GM." Within days Riedlinger was swamped with angry responses, and in January he sent another letter apologizing for the first. He admitted that EDS may have come across initially as "arrogant and overbearing or uncaring" but that it wasn't true and that he only hoped they would give him "a fresh start."

Roger was, as you might guess, surprised by all of the anxiety. As he saw it, being transferred to EDS meant an opportunity to be in an all-computer company where an individual's skills would be more appreciated than they would in a service division of a manufacturing company. "In EDS, you have a chance to become chairman," he said, never realizing that few of the ten thousand transferees may have aspired to such heights.

Ross jumped in to quiet the situation and address the threat of unionization. For several months he met with groups of 50 transferees. "Skill is your security," he said. "You want a union, fine. Send me $3 a month and I'll represent you." While Perot's efforts prevented unionization, they did not quell the rising fears.

In fear of continuing lawsuits, Roger agreed to sweeten the pot for transferees. He gave each of them EDS stock worth $14,500, to offset lost benefits. The catch was that they didn't get paid off immediately. Employees who were to receive the stock had to wait 10 years for it to mature. Roger's response to criticism of the stock offer was condescending, at best:

"Sometimes people take cash home and spend it. And then when they get to the time they need it, they say, 'Hey, where's the benefit?' Well, where's the money? Well, they bought a new car, or the daughter got married, or something, and the dough is gone . . . so then what do you do? Well, the guy comes back then and says, 'Hey, GM, look what you did to me.' So, in this case, they earn it over a period of time, and they should have plenty of money so they are literally able to retire in the same way, from either company."

Many said that the new offer was not equivalent to the GM pension, however. A UAW organizer, Maurice Long, said the stock offer was riddled with caveats, conditions, and strings, and the 10-year vesting meant that it fell far short of making up for lost benefits. Others objected to the EDS stock offer that required the transferee to sign an agreement that he waived all rights to sue GM. In retrospect, no amount of money probably could have resolved the anguish. It was more a matter of injured pride and personal hurt that Mother Motors would so casually dismiss them.

One of these employees, Gary Freyer, had 22½ years with GM when he was transferred. "EDS hired industrial psychologists to come to the transfer meetings and try to sell us. Ken Riedlinger had a slick videotape sales pitch. It sounded like a barker's sales pitch. He said we'd be going to the bank with bushel baskets of thousand-dollar bills from the EDS stock. It was much better than benefits."

About this time Ross Perot made a tour of GM facilities to meet his new employees. "I was one of the guys who didn't go out in the hall to meet him," Gary says, "so Perot came in to talk to me. He was all slick salesman, praising me for staying in shape [Gary was a weightlifter and fitness enthusiast]. Perot said they had a special operation, their Health and Fitness Division, that I'd be perfect for." After that I was transferred to that office on the other side of town. The others on that staff treated me like something from Mars. I was given an office, a phone and desk, and physically separated from the others. They said I was supposed to be enthusiastic, but I didn't feel that way. In September I was given a two-hour performance review and told I was 'a fine addition to the health staff.' Then in December I was called in and fired. Out without any overlapping benefits, insurance, severance pay. Nothing. Over twenty years of my life blown away."

Gary, and thousands of others in both GM and EDS, were victims of cultural clash. There was no way that two such divergent cultures could have merged without a great deal of communication to lay down a field of understanding. One critic said it was like "trying to put the Marines into the Social Security bureaucracy."

On the EDS side, there was the assumption—encouraged by Roger—that they were the special force who had been hired to straighten out an inefficient bureaucracy. EDS was not part of General Motors at all (to this day EDS calls GM "our big customer" or "the account"). They were, in fact, set up to see their task as the equivalent of a commando raid at Entebbe. The resistance they encountered was not without casualties. Many of the EDSers who were part of the initial start-up team were personally devastated by the anger and resistance they encountered. Several had nervous breakdowns and were sent to a recovery hospital in California. Their leader, Ken Riedlinger, finally bailed out and took a job at Ford Motor Company, telling his personal friends that the situation was impossible. "Ken poured his soul into it," Ross says. "He told me it wasn't working out. He's a darn good man, and he gave it a good try."

On the GM transferee side, the sense of abandonment remained. Three years after the acquisition, the vast majority of the transferees harbor resentment toward GM and Roger Smith. "If Smith came in here right now," a Dayton, Ohio, transferee told me late in 1987, "I don't think he'd come out alive."

Recently, a group of transferees placed an open letter in the Detroit newspapers to try to gain Roger's attention. The ad summed up the ongoing anxiety. "Why were your data employees selectively discriminated against? Is GM's commitment to some employees to be honored, and not to others?" the open letter asked. "If data employees were treated so fairly, and EDS is such a progressive place to work, why are they more upset today than they were at the beginning? Why did almost a thousand employees take early retirement, or quit outright, rather than transfer to EDS, and why are many more leaving every day? . . . Now is the time to prove that 'people really are your most important asset' (a Roger Smith quote). . . . It's time for General Motors to show all employees that they are a fair and honorable corporation." The open letter was never answered, except in ongoing litigation between employees and GM's legal staff.

GM attempted to bridge the communications gap that was developing through an EDS publication called *In Sync*, a computer term that meant "working together." The transferees, however, called it "in toilet" and refused to read it. Video-tapes, motivational lectures, and one-to-one talks were all tried, without success.

The splicing of cultures was not working, both because of the personality conflicts and due to Roger's assumption that EDS was more of a high-tech company than it actually was. EDSers achieved immediate successes integrating the computer systems for GMAC and in payrolls, because that was the business EDS knew, standardization of paper shuffling. But the Texas company had no experience whatever in manufacturing control systems, robotics, computer-aided design, or computer-aided manufacturing—all GM specialties. To place data processes over what were essentially engineering functions proved disastrous. Dr. Robert Frosch, GM Research Labs' new leader, was one of the first to realize that the EDS people did not have skills equal to the task. Frosch refused to hand over his computer operations to such inexperienced people, especially when his staff had more Ph.D.s in computer sciences in a single department than EDS had in its entire organization. Frosch, fairly new to the company himself, went to the GM Executive Committee and took a firm stand. Howard Kehrl, the vice chairman over all research and development, backed Frosch up, and EDS was kept out of GM Research for more than two years. Other staffs were not so fortunate.

EDS has become known throughout GM as an acronym for "Ever Diminishing Service." Computer uptime in the plants has steadily eroded, with experienced GM computer people complaining of parts orders filled for the wrong equipment and software that doesn't do the job. Equipment has been ordered in large quantities, then left to gather dust in hallways because the EDS people could not figure out who ordered it or what to do with it. Parts suppliers have complained en masse that their factory computer connections have been regularly disrupted, forcing them to miss deadlines and disrupt new Just-in-Time (when-needed) delivery systems. Telephone systems, also operated by EDS, are frequently disrupted. Engineers say that much of the EDS-ordered equipment is excessively complicated and expensive, and they have formed a group among themselves to find ways to "get around" the new structure. In one case, EDS sent 13,300 GM dividend checks to the wrong people, and thousands of GM employees got billings for insurance coverage they didn't request, were dropped from coverage they already had, or found their ex-wives named as beneficiaries while their current wives and children were dropped from the rolls. Old hands said EDS was assigning five and six people to tasks that formerly were accomplished by one GM person. "We used to do this job with 36 people," one transferee said. "Now EDS has 86 people here, and we still can't get the job done."

Handling computer suppliers became a special confusion in the plants. In one Indiana plant EDS selected a small, unknown company because it made the low bid, though experienced GM people said the company would not be able to fulfill the contract. Six months later, the supplier failed to deliver, and EDS was forced to start from scratch with another bidding. In another case, EDS bid on the automation for two new truck plants. GM was expecting a bid of $30 million and received an EDS bid of $150 million.

At the new Fort Wayne truck assembly plant, the most advanced computer-integrated plant in industry history, both EDS and Hughes were employed to set up the computer system. I called a senior engineer at the plant wanting to find a success story for the new subsidiaries. "Do you want the truth or the PR version?" the engineer asked. "The truth is that EDS has been a nightmare. They just don't understand the technology at all. Their method is to move in quick and throw people and money at the problems."

If this didn't square with the success story, it was fundamentally because the GM wing of EDS rapidly became a different culture from its parent in Dallas. Only a few hundred EDSers were mingled with 7,000 GM transferees and 5,000 new hires. And, as with the rest of the GM organization, Roger asked the EDSers to take on numerous exotic projects that drew their attention away from establishing a new culture. EDS was pressed into immediate service for Saturn, Trilby, new joint ventures with Japanese and Korean companies, and the factory of the future. EDS was also assigned projects that no one needed, such as a new automated business package to sell to GM dealers, even though virtually every dealer already had completely satisfactory software supplied by Reynolds & Reynolds and Automatic Data Processing.

The old EDS culture remained in Dallas to keep its 3,200 other accounts operating, work that would account for about 30 percent of the company's total business. Ross Perot stayed in Dallas, coming into Detroit only occasionally for board meetings and to commiserate with EDSers on the many problems developing. But the GM-EDS culture did not have the built-in reverence for its charismatic leader, and the stories of his paternalism seemed more and more mythical as the horror stories replaced them. GM paid $2.55 billion for a culture that was lost in the chaos of cultural shock waves.

Culture shock was universal. Even Ross and his top executives were victims of the differences. When Ross joined GM, he did what any direct person from his culture would have done. He invited the top two hundred executives, in groups of eight to ten, into his home for casual dinners and get-acquainted sessions. "Mort Meyerson went to Detroit and stayed in a hotel for months without getting one invitation into anyone's home," Ross said. "I called a lot of GM people and tried to get them to welcome him. Finally, they took him out to dinner at a country club, and that was it." Ross did not understand that the GM elite was neither direct nor open, especially not with one another. They were competitors for the next rung up the ladder, not comrades-in-arms.

Ross also did not seem to understand that he was being set up, consciously or unconsciously, by Roger to emphasize the differences in their cultures. "I always got the feeling with Roger," Ross says, "that with me he knew he was talking to the guy who knew how to get things done. It was later that I learned this was only talk." He brought Ross in at the highest level and sold him on the competitive dilemma as an open challenge for him to launch a personal crusade.

Ross quickly went into action. He placed a Norman Rockwell picture in his outer office. It was *Coming Home*, depicting a marine returning from World War II telling his friends about the victories. "I put that there for my GM visitors," Ross said. "It's to remind them that we used to whip the Japanese right regularly, and if we ever decide we want to do it again in the car business, we can." At his first GM Board of Directors meeting, Ross declared that he was going to be the spokesman for the employees, the dealers, and the customers. And of EDS's arrival, Ross said, "We are bringing GM from a mature company to a young, exciting company. . . . We will be the brains and nervous system of General Motors."

Ross went around visiting dealerships in "Saturday clothes" anonymously to see about service himself and to "get to know the guys in the trenches." And unannounced, he visited a GM plant in Arlington, Texas. That shook up the GM central office, which was on the phone to the plant every fifteen minutes during the visit, asking, "What's he doing now?" Ross was, in fact, having a down-home-style lunch with the workers on the factory floor.

As Ross saw it, his task was to be the gadfly. His open criticism of GM was, at first, a direct reflection of Roger's own largely inarticulated feelings. He spoke of the only competition as the internal rivalry among GM divisions before the Japanese product invasion. "Fellows, that's intramural sports," Ross said. "You don't even tackle there, you just touch the guy. . . . Now the Japanese have shown us they're competing professionally . . . we've got to compete professionally with them."

From the beginning Ross could not understand the smallness of GM's visions. In a public policy committee meeting, for example, Jack McNulty remembers Ross suggesting that GM not fool around with small tasks but take on a reform of the entire U.S. educational system. Ross had, after all, reformed Texas education, and "it only cost a couple of million," he told the committee. "GM could reform all of American education with just a couple of billion, but it would be money well spent." Ross calls this "another myth." He says a reporter asked him after a board meeting what it would cost to reform America's educational system. "I told him it cost me $2 million in Texas, which is one of the bigger states, so $100 million for all 50 states could do the job. I never suggested GM pay for it."

Another shock to Ross and EDS was that "hands off" did not mean what Roger had originally said. The first indication that Roger wanted to renege on his deal and direct EDS operations from Detroit came over the issue of EDS executive stock benefits. "Roger came down to Dallas and tried to get the board to change our compensation," Ross said. "He didn't like the fact that a lot of EDSers could make more money than he could through stock." Other EDSers in that meeting were surprised by Roger's insistence and stunned when he went into a temper tantrum. "His face turned beet red," an EDSer said, "and he started foaming at the mouth. It was unbelievable."

Ross says of the incident: "I took Roger aside and told him he couldn't be chairman if he was going to act like that." Ross did not back off on his compensation system, reminded him of their deal, and sent Roger home.

From then on, Ross said, "There was a continuous stream of trivia." GM auditors and personnel people visited Dallas frequently. "If a guy comes down and just wants us to fill out forms, then we don't do it," he says. "We give him a hot meal, pat him on the back and say, 'No, we're not going to do this,' and that's it." Ross interpreted Roger's promise of noninterference to mean exactly that—independence. Roger, as you would expect, was surprised that EDS didn't blend into GM policies and procedures. "Independence does not mean indifference," he said. The issue of GM auditors became central. EDS had its own independent auditors, and Ross refused to let the GM teams in the door. This went on for more than a year until Ross finally relented, but not before Roger had branded him with the worst title anyone could acquire in GM—"not a team player."

"Sure, he finally gave in on the auditors," Roger told me, "but what would it be next?"

Roger's unique Class E stock proved to be one of the biggest wedges between EDS and GM consolidation. EDS management had a responsibility from the start to be a profitable self-standing company and serve its separate Class E shareholders. Since a significant amount of EDS stock was in the hands of its own

people, the built-in goal was not to make GM cars more eco-
nomically, but to make EDS more profitable. Early in the transition GM division, plant, and office managers began complaining about overcharging and overspending. EDS was given
a blank check to bring in "whatever it took" to get the computer service job done. "In the past," James Brownlie, an EDS
vice president over the C-P-C operation, said, "things just
didn't get done [in plants] because of corporate constraints,
head-count restrictions, and limited budgets. Now EDS is
profit motivated to get them done. . . . As a supplier, we can
bring in everything needed outside of the plant's operating
budget." EDS, not the individual operation, was given the authority to decide how much of what was needed.

GM insiders say the EDS overcharging amounted to more
that $1 billion in the first year alone. Yet there is no way of
actually knowing how much overcharging—if any—actually
took place. GM, after all, did not have any centralized accounting of computer services before EDS was brought in. Riedlinger says that the first thing EDS had to do was structure a
computer services organizational chart to actually locate the
diverse operations and outside service costs. And much of
what EDS was asked to do had never been done before in GM,
so there were no definable guidelines to follow. In essence,
EDS had to tell GM management what it was telling the transferees—"trust me." It was not a phrase they were comfortable
with either.

Roger had promised, in writing and in person, that EDS
would receive long-term, fixed-price contracts. Initially they
would start with cost-plus billing, which amounted to 9.5 to
10 percent profits but would move as quickly as possible to
fixed-price contracts with 12.5 percent profit margins (EDS
typically received 14 to 19 percent profit margins on non-GM
work). Yet GM began backing off from that promise before the
ink had dried. Two years into the acquisition less than 10
percent of the GM work had received fixed-price contracts.
There were more than twelve hundred unresolved individual
contracts between the two companies. This was, of course,
the work of finance staff that had opposed the fixed-price
contracts from the beginning. In 1985 GM's profits were slip-

ping badly, even though total revenues were climbing. The corporation was going into a cost-cutting mode, and there was a great deal of resentment among finance people that EDS was not being forced to share GM's hardships. Heel dragging on the fixed-price contracts was a way of reducing EDS's potential profits.

"GM doesn't honor its contracts," Ross told me. "That was the biggest shock of all to me." He was referring to the promise of autonomy, of EDS control over auditing, and of the long-term contracts. "Poor ol' Roger makes promises, but he forgets." Publicly, Ross and Roger continued to say pleasant things about one another for the first turbulent year, but the relationship was rapidly deteriorating. Elmer Johnson, GM vice president and corporate counsel, said Ross's dislike for Roger began to surface within six months of the EDS purchase. That was a period when Ross was steadily losing faith in GM's sincerity, watching his own EDS people become casualties in the struggle to change the giant, while thousands of people who were not of the EDS culture were being forced into his ranks.

Ross personally reviewed every one of the lawsuits against EDS and GM that came from the transferees and spoke to most of the plaintiffs in person or by phone. When I spoke to him about the transferees, his rapid speech pattern slowed to a somber caution. He spoke awkwardly about what had happened to the transferees, and his concern seemed genuine. "EDS is a harsh culture," Ross said. "It's not for everybody and never was supposed to be."

Yet there was little at the time that he could do about it. The frustration and lack of control Ross must have experienced during that first year was not unlike that of those caught in the chaos within GM. Ross, however, was too much of a fighter to acquiesce. "A team player at GM is one who will march over the cliff," he said. "Not me."

In March 1986 Ross sent a letter to Roger that contained an ultimatum. Things had to change. Ross gave Roger four choices. First, Ross proposed, we can begin to work together in good faith, but there has to be a written agreement of how that is to work. Second, Ross said, he was no longer willing to bend and compromise on the original agreement. Either GM lives up to it or we must take it to the board. Third, GM can try to terminate me, but with an understanding of the length and severity of the fight ahead. Fourth, GM can buy me out, but, Ross emphasized in the letter, "in my judgment this would be a serious mistake for General Motors." Ross met with Elmer Johnson, Roger's corporate lawyer, to discuss the options. Here there are two stories of the meeting—Elmer's, wherein Perot made it clear that if GM bought Ross out it would be all or nothing, and Ross's, wherein he continued to emphasize that a buyout was a dumb idea and that he just wanted GM to live up to its promises. "Elmer makes a lot of that May meeting," Ross says, "but it was nothing at all. Elmer made no offers, and when he left we stood around scratching our heads wondering why he'd visited at all."

The meeting produced no immediate results, for it was abundantly clear that Ross could not bargain from a position of strength. Even though Ross was the largest single stockholder in General Motors—owning more stock than the entire GM Board of Directors combined—he actually had less than 1 percent of the total voting stock. Pressuring GM was, in Ross's words, "like trying to put your arms around the Atlantic Ocean." Ross was not in control. And if there is one thing a horse trader learns, it is that the person you're bargaining with must be more interested in the deal than you are.

At this point, it's time to stop and ask yourself some commonsense questions. Knowing Ross Perot's background, would you honestly expect him to acquiesce and become a GM board rubberstamp member? Would you expect Ross Perot to ignore the fact that his EDSers were being slaughtered in Detroit in what, in most EDSers' minds, amounted to an ambush? Would you expect Ross to ignore the fact that GM was avoiding its contractual promises? Was it logical to assume that Ross would accept GM management directives when he was promised that there would be no interference with his policies, and leadership? Roger did not recognize the obvious. Publicly, Roger said, "Ross is critical, but he's helpful critical. . . . He's worked through the system. . . . He doesn't come to the [board] meetings in purple suits or anything. . . . He's working his buns off to help us." From all indications, Roger meant it. He continued to envision Ross as a kindred spirit, an entrepreneur, like himself, among bureaucrats. Roger saw no impending confrontations.

And yet this conflict too, could have been foreseen by reading Dr. Wess Roberts's book on Attila's leadership secrets, for on page 59, Attila warns:

"Never threaten the security or esteem of another . . . unless you are prepared to deal with its consequences."

7
A Loose Cannon

*"Human beings, particularly American human
beings, have a tremendous capacity for screwing
things up . . . and they feel perfectly justified in
doing so."*

Roger Smith

A free day at Disneyland where you can meet Mickey
Mouse, Daffy Duck, Goofy, and the GM executive
team—that's what Roger gave all 181,000 of his new
Hughes Aircraft employees for a 1986 New Year's present.
Roger spent upwards of $2.5 million to rent the entire theme
park for a day, and tens of thousands more on giveaway concessions and cotton candy for the kids. Roger heartily approved the party, but had to send his regrets for not attending.
He was too busy back in Detroit justifying his own high-tech
Magic Kingdom to Wall Street, convincing employees they had
to make sacrifices to save their jobs, and planning an executive conference to tell his managers they were spending too
much money on nonessentials.

Yet Disneyland seemed like the perfect place for Roger to
launch 1986. For me, it crystallized the Fantasyland image and
contradictory messages Roger was emitting. I remember one
day in particular when I was writing Disneyland remarks for
Don Atwood (now vice chairman), incorporating all of the
hyperboles and promises we had used with the EDS acquisition. At the same time, I was working on a speech for Roger in

173

which he would boast of the $47 billion he had spent so far on high technology (more like $60 billion if you fold in acquisitions and joint ventures). On the same day, I was reading in newspaper clips of more speculation on where Roger was going to spend the next billion or two. Some said he was bidding on American Express (untrue) and others that he was making bids on a British luxury sports car company (true). That afternoon I attended a public relations staff meeting in which we were told that GM was in serious financial trouble and that there would be no hiring, no research money or travel funds available. Alvie Smith (no relation), the astute head of employee communications, added a challenge to the writers: "The employees don't believe how serious our competitive situation is," Alvie said. "I hope you'll all think of ways to communicate how serious the problems are."

I thought of the Disneyland script waiting on my computer, the newspaper clips speculating on Roger's next splurge, and I said: "Hmmm, I wonder why they don't believe us?" To my surprise, everyone in the meeting immediately understood my sarcasm and laughed with me. But for a group of professional communicators, it was a tense laugh born of sheer frustration.

The first half of 1986 was a boom time for American industry. The economy was in its fourth successive year of dramatic growth. The Japanese peril was being turned away in Washington. President Reagan's G-5 communiqué had succeeded in getting the top five trading countries to adjust currency rates. In essence, that meant the dollar would drop in relation to the yen, making American goods cheaper abroad and, more important, making Japanese goods more expensive here. The falling dollar had already upped Japan's costs by 35 percent, which was more than the cost differential between an American and a Japanese car. With the dollar down and the economy up, Roger's prediction of an outstanding 16.5-million-vehicle sales year was plausible. Indeed, Ford and Chrysler were gaining market share, and their stocks were doubling in value. General Motors was not participating in the boom. In fact, the price per share of GM stock was actually slipping downward, passed in mid-year by Ford, with only half of the giant's size and resources. And each time Roger boasted of major capital investments in technology, with another $10.5 billion slated for purchases in 1986, his stock went down both on Wall Street and in the eyes of his people.

From products to promotions to plants and productivity, Roger's 21st-century corporation was coming apart at every seam. On the product side, the half-decade-old look-alike problem was showing up in lackluster consumer interest. Despite 175 models, GM had remarkably little that excited the market. Ford had the new Taurus and Sable. Chrysler had the new Sundance and Shadow. Hyundai, a new Korean car that knocked GM of Canada out of first place in Canada's sales in 1985, came to the United States in 1986 with an updated model called the Excel. At the bottom of the market, the Yugoslavians were moving in with an old-fashioned economy car—the $3,995 Yugo. At the top of the market, Mercedes, Audi, and Volvo were infringing on the highest-profit segment. And even the Japanese didn't have the decency to bow out after we hit them with the devaluated dollar. The Japanese were holding the line on prices remarkably well, making major cuts in their overhead (at one company, all executives took a 10 percent pay cut) in order to keep the plants operating. And in spite of a 50 percent drop in the dollar/yen exchange rate, they upped sticker prices by only 20 percent. This fact particularly annoyed Roger: "Japan decided it would rather pay that [the exchange rate loss] than pay unemployment to their people." (The Japanese evidently didn't understand the rules of the game: that you raise prices and lay off people to gain profitability.)

In May 1986 Roger raised prices on the vast majority of GM cars and trucks by 3 percent. He added another 3 percent price hike in September. The auto press and Wall Street criticized the price hikes as shortsighted. Here was an excellent opportunity to regain the lost market share simply by holding or cutting prices slightly, making the differential between an American and a Japanese car so great that the buyers would buy American as an economy move. Yet Roger was in a bind. His high-tech spending had forced GM costs entirely out of the competitive market. In 1980, for example, an average GM car cost $300 less to build than a Ford and $320 less than a

Chrysler. By 1986, GM's costs were $300 higher per car than Ford's or Chrysler's. That's an increase of $600 to $620 per car in six years. Roger simply did not feel he could afford to cut prices at current cost levels. Ironically, he could not cut production, either. The higher costs had forced the breakeven point up so high that anything less than full-out production meant potential losses. What Roger neglected to factor into his high-tech strategic equation was that when sales declined he couldn't lay off the steel-collar workers as he had the blue-collar people. The fixed costs of high-technology demanded continuous utilization.

To keep the cars moving out the door, GM came up with a new deal for dealers. A new dealer floor plan inventory program gave the dealers special breaks if they stocked up. "I guess they figured that just having more metal on the lot would mean we'd have to move it," a Houston dealer said. "But it doesn't work that way in a crowded market." Inventories continued to climb. A 9.9 percent low-interest loan program was a dud, followed by a not much more effective 6.9 percent low-interest loan. The modest incentives did not clear the lots, and Roger began closing plants in April. Four major plants, and shift reductions at a half-dozen others, put nine thousand employees on indefinite layoffs.

Cost overruns for high-tech orders were beginning to pile up. The Fairfax asssembly plant (Kansas City, Kansas), for example, went from a projected cost of $75 million to over $1 billion. Roger had planned to hold capital expenditures to $10 billion in light of GM's diminishing income, but he ended up spending $11.7 billion.

With the new plant there was a higher order of computer-based technology and a commensurate number of new problems associated with it. Vision robots in Flint, which were supposed to line up windshields and insert them, were smashing glass. A robot designed to apply glue for carpeting in a Pontiac plant seemed to prefer to spit the goo on assemblers' shoes and on cement floors. An inspection robot at Delco in Kokomo, Indiana, was so inaccurate that it had to be taken off the line and a half-dozen humanoids with hand gauges put in its place. In a Detroit-area plant, a midnight worker had fun misprogramming the automated guided vehicles and sent them scurrying all over the body shop like berserk dodge 'em cars.

The Hamtramck plant, Roger's most advanced high-tech showpiece, was several months late in starting up production in 1986. The plant was critically important because it was building GM's most complex new car line—the E-Ks, all highly similar luxury front-wheel-drive cars. Hamtramck had 260 robots, 50 automated guided vehicles, and a body shop where robots did 97 percent of all the welding. Laser cameras were to check openings to provide perfect fits on every dimension. To Roger, Hamtramck epitomized the difference between the Japanese manufacturing strategy and his own high-tech strategy. In a July interview with the *Fortune* magazine board of editors, Roger said:

> You see they [the Japanese] are making literally a very narrow range of simple products that's not complex at all. . . . In the Detroit Hamtramck plant we're running an Oldsmobile Toronado, a Buick Riviera, an Eldorado, and a Seville down the same line. Now why? Because the computer that we've got is smart enough to say, "Uh-oh, here comes an Eldorado," and knows where to go in and make 117 welds, and the next one comes down and the computer says, "Oh, my God, that's a four-door Seville." The computer actually takes the side framing, sets it aside, brings the other side framing up, and does all the welding for that Seville. Now the Japanese cannot do that. They tend to run a much simpler production system than we do, and in some respects you get a quality edge when you don't have to have the complexity. That's why it is so important that we upgrade our technology so that we can do that [what the Japanese are doing in terms of high quality].

But the smart machines were flunking their IQ tests. The small computer box attached to each body to signal each order's vital statistics frequently gave cockeyed instructions, ordering up the wrong bumpers, the wrong trim, the wrong welds, or the wrong paint, sending instructions to the next robot, which was too simpleminded to notice the errors. The paint robots were particularly cantankerous, slopping gobs of paint on one car, then not enough on the next. The Hamtramck plant manager had to send the worse cases to the 70-year-old Cadillac plant across town for repainting. Anything less than horrid was shipped to the dealers, creating situations in which a buyer received his $25,000 car with a paint job that looked like it had been applied by an orangutan. On a two-hour visit once I witnessed production shut down on three separate occasions. The third breakdown took so long to fix that I finally had to abandon the tour and get back to The Building (to write a speech praising high technology, of course). Overall, the plant was a nightmare, so much so that the highly respected plant manager, Earl Harper, decided to retire five years early rather than fight it another day.

The Hamtramck plant—a $600 million labyrinth more than twice as expensive as anything Ford, Chrysler, or Toyota had—operated at only 50 percent production on its best days. And it succeeded in embarrassing GM by turning out luxury cars with worse quality ratings than the Chevettes. Fortunately for the consuming public, the E-K cars all looked so much alike that they were in very low demand. The plant could remain on a single shift and continue to wrestle with its problems indefinitely.

Yet GM president Jim McDonald told the people at the Hamtramck Rotary Club in May that "the problems that popped up weren't really all that much worse—or different—from the problems at other new plants." That was true. Throughout GM, the manufacturing operations were, as one production superintendent put it, "a nightmare every hour of the day." In sharp contrast, a new Mazda Motors plant, which opened the same year just 25 miles away, cost one-fourth as much as the Hamtramck plant and would produce as many new cars, at higher quality, with fifteen hundred fewer employees in the plant. Technology was not, as Roger had hoped, reducing GM's labor burden automatically. He would end up with more people, more robots, and more problems than any company in the industry.

Throwing money at problems was not having the desired effect. At Hydra-matic Division, for example, the eight new transmissions for the front-wheel-drive cars were a major source of trouble. In 1983, one out of every 10 transmissions required warranty repairs during the first few months of ownership. GM's answer was to install a new division manager, Tom Zimmer, a traditional hard-liner, who, I found through experience, was feared even by his personal staff. Zimmer was given a huge chunk of money, $23.6 million, for a new design and development center in Ypsilanti, Michigan, and a new test facility at the Milford (Michigan) Proving Grounds. The result was an improvement in quality—to 5.7 warranty claims per 100 vehicles in 1986. After millions spent, nearly six of every hundred car buyers would have transmission problems. This was heralded as "a major accomplishment" within the corporation.

The technology troubles led to a shortfall in divisional budget predictions that would add up to a $5 billion shortfall for the '86 model year. The result was that early on Roger was forced to borrow $1.2 billion to continue to finance his capital spending. The annual interest rate on that loan cost GM $100 million a year. Roger's little green box was finally depleted, down to just $1.3 billion of operating capital by June. For a $100 billion company, that was like running the national defense out of a petty-cash cigar box.

Publicly, Roger was admitting that there were "some start-up problems" in some of the plants, and yes, "the problems began when we brought in the advanced automation." Roger, however, was convinced the catastrophes were strictly the result of inadequate training. "We miscalculated how much training would be needed," he explained. At the same time the executives were making speeches that GM had become "the largest private educational institution in the world" and that "the average employee receives more than six weeks of training, and a typical skilled tradesman gets six months of training, before the first new product moves down an assembly line." Roger said that GM would place far more emphasis on training, but saying it did not make it so. At GM, training was one of the last aspects of corporate life still left to the individual divisions and staffs. I had tried for two full years to pinpoint where the training was taking place and how much of it was conducted so that I could make some gee-whiz statements in speeches. But there was no central staff keeping a score-card, and every attempt to simply identify activities led no-where. In an era of unprecedented technology influx, it was astonishing that no one could say how many instructors GM had or how many classroom hours and corporate dollars were going into the effort, let alone whether the curriculums were adequate. That did not change with the admission of the problem.

The technology troubles did not turn Roger from his high-tech course. He was convinced that the technology was right, but the organization was wrong. They were simply resisting positive change down through the ranks. Roger would stay the course but was willing to agree reluctantly to slow down the pace a little to gain some control over the new processes. This resulted in massive cancellations on GM equipment orders. Hamtramck didn't get the robot wheel and tire installers it had ordered. Many other plants had to cut back on their technol-ogy plans. A $2.4 million computer-vision contract was can-celed with Robotic Vision Systems, and additional millions were cut from other orders. The biggest loser was Roger's new robot subsidiary, GMF Robotics. The company, a fifty-fifty joint venture with Japan's Fanuc Co., had about 70 percent of its business committed to General Motors orders. A 30 per-cent cutback in orders meant massive GMF Robotics layoffs. Yet the entire automation industry suffered from the GM re-treat. "GM went from a shop-'til-you-drop mode to Scrooge when it came to getting robots," a Snyder Machine Tool exec-utive said. "GM's cutbacks alone brought the industry down by at least 5 percent."

The anticipated profit shortfalls had to be made up some-where. Overseas operations were the most attractive flesh to cut. Despite major investments in Europe and elsewhere, the overseas operations were not paying their own way. This was partly the result of years of neglect, when overseas assign-ments were GM's Siberia. To be given an overseas job meant that you had just been ushered off the fast track. Staffed by angry, malcontent executives, GM was unable to compete suc-cessfully against more world-oriented companies like Ford.

Roger, to his credit, had attempted early on to take a more assertive role in the worldwide market. He placed Bob Stempel, the man who had turned truck and bus operations around, in charge of overseas with orders to "get tough." The strategy was to concentrate on significant markets like Europe and to sell off anything that wasn't paying its way. With the shortfalls in 1986, that meant selling or closing down operations in the Philippines, Greece, Uruguay, Ecuador, and South Africa and looking for ways to get out of much of the business in Great Britain and Australia.

"GM can no longer be all things to all people," Roger was saying as he withdrew the corporation from entire segments of the transportation market. Roger sold the bus business to Greyhound, which would transfer assembly to a cheap labor plant in New Mexico. A joint venture with Volvo effectively got GM out of the heavy truck manufacturing business. Volvo/White products would dominate, and GM would contribute its extensive dealer network. Roger even agreed to give up on the low-priced car market, allowing Saturn to shift targets up into the $10,000 price range.

Ongoing product programs were cut back as well. The much publicized Saturn Corporation was literally cut in half. Instead of starting with two assembly lines for the new car, there would be one. Instead of 6,000 employees, there would be 3,000. And GM10, the biggest project ever, saw the number of start-up plants cut from seven to four. And finally, a plastic sports car project, the long overdue replacement of the eleven-year-old Camaro and Firebird, was canceled entirely.

What was more significant was not the advance programs that were being cut, but the needed car programs that were not being initiated. For example, GM dealers were clamoring for a four-door version of the Blazer to sell in this fast-growing sport-utility segment. Numerous letters requesting the vehicle had been written to Roger, and there was even a delegation of a dozen top dealers who came to Detroit to plead for this vehicle. Roger said he had reviewed the request, and it was simply too expensive, considering the size of the market segment.

Roger's pleas of "too expensive" did not go over well with

the dealers, since the next week it was announced that Roger was making another grand acquisition. He was purchasing Group Lotus, a British racing car and engineering company, for $20 million. Roger said he was buying the company because of its performance engineering talent base, citing Lotus's advanced work in active (computer-based) ride systems and composite bodies. General Motors Research Laboratories, however, already had demonstrated highly advanced work in both areas. And at the heart of the active ride system was an on-board computer to adjust the suspension to wheel movements. "I can't believe anyone would go to Britain to buy computer knowledge," a GMR computer scientist said. Roger also got Lotus's car production—handmade sports cars including the Lotus Etna, selling at $110,000 each. Dealers countered that they could sell a lot more four-door Blazers for GM than millionaire two-seater imports.

Whether Lotus was a good investment is not nearly as relevant as the timing of the acquisition. When you are in the midst of massive internal staff reductions and program cutbacks, an acquisition like Lotus should reasonably come with a lot of advance explanation to the management ranks. Roger saw no need to explain the contradiction of simultaneous cutbacks and acquisitions.

All companies, of course, get into trouble at times, especially if their leaders set a course that is new and daring. James O'Toole, a business analyst who studied the most progressive companies in America for four years, concluded that downturns are the norm (the half-life of success for companies praised in *In Search of Excellence*, for example, was only six months). "A truer test of a company's greatness," O'Toole says, "is how its managers behave during bad times." Do they take the high road and stick to their lofty commitments to serve employees and customers alike, or do they revert to the low road of quick, and often dirty, survival tactics? The perception within General Motors—encouraged by a dearth of credible communications—was that Roger was reverting to the low road. That may not have been a true perception, but, as before, it was the way in which Roger initiated change—not the change itself—that undercut his own goals.

Reducing salaried costs during the downturn was a case in point. "Meritocracy" was one of Roger's espoused goals. His idea was to create a new system in which employee rewards were based on actual performance and not preordained through union-inspired incremental raises. So Roger eliminated COLA for salaried people, putting in its place a merit-pay structure. The only catch was that COLA pay would have amounted to an 8.5 percent wage increase for salaried people in 1986, while Roger established the maximum merit pay increase at 5.5 percent. This meant that the typical increase would have to be around 3 percent, with some employees receiving no merit increases and others getting the top 5.5 percent. Even the most outstanding performance would not earn the income the individual would have received under the old COLA pay structure. Had Roger gone to his salaried people and explained the internal cost problems and that, for survival, everyone would have to make a slight sacrifice, he probably would have received widespread support. Like the profit-sharing agreement that did not share profits with employees, the merit system that did not reward merit added to Roger's widening credibility gap.

Again, my personal experience with Roger and his closest executives convinced me that there was no intention to mislead. Decisions were based on immediate situational demands, with little or no thought given to the impact on sensitive—and sensitized—constituencies. For example, about this time Roger approved a major change in the performance review structure that demoralized his rank-and-file salaried people still more. The performance review process, evaluations of each employee's work every three months, had become meaningless. The vast majority of the employees received "superior" or "outstanding" ratings. In a period in which heads were to be chopped, it was necessary to have a more meaningful way of separating the goats from the lambs. Roger's solution, however, was both illogical and insensitive. The new policy was that each department manager had to grade his or her employees on a curve—the bell curve with as many *E*s as *A*s, and most falling into the *C* range. In essence, if I were the head of a department of super-bright scientists at GM Research, I'd have to designate half of my people as being average or below and tell them they would not be eligible for even a token pay increase. If a manager had done a credible job up until that point, and had eliminated the inept long before, he would have nothing but high performers. The assumption was that every department had losers. When I asked Roger about this, he said, "These are just guidelines. The manager doesn't have to follow them." Unfortunately, most of the department managers I spoke with assumed that the written word from the 14th floor was a mandate.

As a communicator, I became concerned that these management decisions were going to encourage the wrong people to leave GM. Common sense told me that those individuals with the most limited abilities would feel they had to tolerate even an unjust reward system. Those with abilities and options— even the nonsuperstars—would go elsewhere. In a management proposal asking that we deal with the growing problem, I remember quoting Woody Allen, who said: "After the battle, casualties were limited. Limited mostly to those who could still walk." I pushed this proposal and was told that I should talk to Elmer Johnson, the executive vice president of personnel and other staff functions and one of Roger's closest insiders (Roger would later promote Elmer, with four years inside GM, to the board and executive committee, one step away from the chairmanship). But Elmer's only solution was pure old-style Sloan elitism. "We've got to identify and promote the high achievers," Elmer told me, "at any cost. . . . Get them out of the system and keep them moving up. . . . If we can promote them several steps at a time, we ought to do it." I remember mumbling some reference to *Brave New World*, which Elmer either did not hear or chose not to hear. My concern that a massive corporation could not function with all Alphas went nowhere.

Insensitivity, not ill intent, was the norm. For example, there was a time in '86 when Roger inadvertently hurt his closest union ally. Don Ephlin, head of the UAW's GM unit, was a progressive leader who realized that his union jobs depended on helping GM become world competitive. Ephlin worked hard at setting aside the long-standing adversarial relationship between union and management, initiating numerous joint union-management programs on everything from quality and productivity to the quality of work life. The hardliners, headed by UAW president Owen Bieber, did not trust GM's "reforms." In '86, Ephlin was coming up on a tough election. Roger made it clear that no one in General Motors was to do or say anything that might embarrass Don Ephlin and cost him the union election. Roger, in fact, was willing to jeopardize one union's relationship and his quality image to support Ephlin.

The two highest-quality, and generally recognized as most efficient, plants in General Motors at the time were both in Moraine, Ohio. The Moraine truck plant produced the popular small pickup, the S truck. It had the highest quality ratings in General Motors for any assembly plant for three years in a row. The highest-quality engine plant distinction went to the Moraine diesel plant. The workers were enthusiastic GM supporters who even went out in their communities to talk up their products and sell trucks and diesel-powered cars for the company. They had only one critical flaw—the workers were not represented by the UAW. When Roger sold off Frigidaire in 1979, the International Union of Electrical Workers represented the displaced employees. So, by agreement, the jobs created when the two new vehicle plants opened in Moraine went to the IUE. This organization, with 178,000 General Motors union members largely in component divisions, was noted in the corporation for its cooperativeness. Such unique IUE agreements as two-tiered wages and pay-for-knowledge helped Packard Electric Division and others become cost competitive. Yet giving auto jobs to a rival union was a major bone of contention with the UAW.

In 1986, the IUE Moraine employees were snubbed by the corporation. The Moraine S truck plant, with far higher quality than its sister S truck plant in Shreveport, Louisiana, was kept to a single shift, while its sister UAW plant got a second shift. Worse, the Moraine diesel plant had fallen on hard times. With the return of cheap gasoline, the demand for diesel-powered cars disappeared, and with it three-fourths of the jobs at the Moraine plant. In the GM tradition of internal competition, plants bid against one another on the basis of their cost, quality, and delivery time. In theory, the best bidder—internal or external—gets the additional work. Moraine employees bid on numerous pieces of additional GM business. They were the highest-quality, lowest-cost bidder on a number of jobs. Yet they were not given any additional work. In preparing an IUE speech for Jim McDonald, I was intent on finding out why quality wasn't receiving recognition and reward in Moraine, Ohio. The head of one of the two divisions involved told me flat out: "GM won't give them any work because they're with the wrong union." I pursued this with Al Warren, GM's vice president of industrial relations staff. Al said, "Drop it. We can't make any promises to the IUE until after the UAW election. We just can't take a chance on embarrassing Don Ephlin." (A year after the election, the Moraine plants were finally rewarded—but it meant two years of unemployment for thousands of solid workers in the interim.)

Sacrificing the livelihoods of several thousand outstanding employees so as not to embarrass an ally like Ephlin might be seen as politically astute. But Roger negated whatever benefit this sacrifice may have had by shooting his ally in the foot on another issue. A few days before the national union meeting, Roger approved a news release that announced a major increase in outsourced work to Mexico. GM was already importing some 500,000 V-6 engines and 20,000 El Camino pickup trucks from the Mexican plants at the time. The announcement concluded that several thousand new jobs would be created in the non-UAW plants south of the border, from which engines would be shipped back into the United States, obviously costing UAW jobs. The poorly timed announcement produced a renewed militancy in the union leadership and threatened Ephlin's reelection. He won reelection only after an uphill battle. "It's hard to cooperate with the right hand," Ephlin said, "when the left hand is doing things like handing out work to Mexico."

Examples of truly enlightened union cooperation were popping up all over GM, yet Roger continued to irritate relationships by dwelling on the exorbitant wages GM's union employees were receiving. When a reporter pointed out that with the dollar devaluation a strong case could be made that American labor was now less expensive than Japanese, Roger countered:

"You don't have to go to Japan to get Japanese labor costs. There are plenty of $8.50-an-hour UAW plants right here in Detroit. I could throw a rock from my office and probably hit one of them. It's that small companies are given different wage rates than the big auto companies. . . . I wish we could do that here, but that's never going to happen. So we've got a lot more of the labor-intensive stuff going to Mexican plants now."

Roger was clearly fixed on wages long after they ceased to be a primary issue of competitiveness. To place Roger's stress on wages in historical perspective, it was clearly counter to the philosophy that built the American auto industry. In 1914, Henry Ford established the $5 day when most companies were paying $1 a day. He justified his generosity by saying, "The best wages are not the lowest wages, but the wages that can be reasonably sustained. It is right that the worker shares in the fruits of his labors." In 1916, even with wages that were three times higher than at General Motors, Ford was able to produce the lowest-priced car in the world and outsell GM two to one. Granted, a half century changed the competitive situation, but it did not change human nature. To be told repeatedly that you are not worth your wage is certain to have a devastating effect on morale and inevitably on productivity.

Worse, the connection Roger made frequently between technological improvements and the number of high-paid jobs they would eliminate was hurting his cause. During the recession from 1980 through '83, the vast majority of workers became convinced that new technologies were necessary to become competitive and save jobs. Employees rushed to volunteer for training on every new piece of equipment. I remember asking a plant superintendent in Adrian, Michigan, if the new technology was viewed as a threat. "You've got to be kidding," he said. "Our people are out there competing to get the technology. They know that the more of it they get and learn, the more secure this plant will be." Yet as Roger's rhetoric continued, more and more people in and outside of the plants came to the inevitable conclusion that Roger was spending money not to save jobs, but to do away with as many of them as possible. Auto analyst Maryann Keller summed up the general perception of Roger's high-tech thrust in a May interview with the *Wall Street Journal*. "The goal of all the technology push," she said, "has been to get rid of hourly workers. GM thought in terms of automation rather than replacing the current system with a better system."

Again, my own experience with the top research, engineering, and manufacturing leaders in General Motors did not validate Keller's perception. While Roger's high-tech green light certainly led to excesses, the vast majority of GM's executives believed that new systems would mean greater sales and eventually lead to more and better jobs. The organization was thinking in terms of the Third Wave of job creation, while Roger was thinking, and talking, in terms of the Fourth Wave of automatons and peopleless plants. And, as always, the CEO's words—not the insights of vice presidents, directors, and managers—received the lion's share of attention. Yet there was no malice aforethought on Roger's part. He was just insensitive to what impact the honest expression of his elitist viewpoint might have. I had a personal lesson of just how removed Roger was from any sense of communications or public relations with the 1986 Executive Management Conference.

Traditionally, the Executive Management Conference is held every three years. The top GM executives from the world organization, and from every staff, gather at the posh Greenbrier resort in West Virginia to hear the state-of-the-corporation messages. Roger decided to take personal charge of this year's conference. To underscore the corporation's diminished resources, he decided to hold the conference on a single day at the GM Tech Center in Warren, Michigan. Roger decided who was to speak but gave them no specific guidance concerning the conference's theme and what he hoped to gain from the event. The executives tentatively began developing their presentations. Then, just two weeks before the conference date, the senior executives for whom I was writing called me independently to ask who was being invited to the conference. They had heard rumors on the 14th floor that it wasn't going to be the traditional all-corporation audience.

Roger had hand-picked the guest list, and it was already in the process of being mailed when I caught up to it. I was amazed that the list was comprised almost entirely of North American manufacturing executives and managers of larger plants. There was only a token representation from engineering and marketing staffs and virtually no overseas executives. What the list said in no uncertain terms was that Roger considered his problems to be centered on manufacturing alone. He had given them targets, and they had fallen short. So he was calling the manufacturing people in to chastise them. When I told my two executives, they were stunned. It meant tearing up what we had already developed in order to address more directly the narrowly defined audience. I spread the word to other speech writers, and the slated speakers worked on refocusing their talks. Roger made the decision to single out a lone segment unilaterally. The executives I was writing for were both located on the 14th floor a few yards from Roger's door. They could have opened their doors and yelled to one another. Yet Roger was not yelling, or even whispering, his plans, and the executives obviously did not feel comfortable enough to ask directly.

The management conference went as expected. Roger and his top executives spent their podium time largely justifying their recent decisions and laying the blame everywhere but on their own doorsteps. The manufacturing people were scolded and sent home. A follow-up inquiry by a public relations director revealed general displeasure with the conference. The managers felt that a large part of the problems that kept them from meeting their goals originated on the 14th floor. They remained largely unconvinced that the high-tech route was realistic, and many were alienated by having been singled out for censure.

One event at the conference did attract corporatewide notice. Jim McDonald, the popular GM president, spoke of the fact that quality had actually been going down in recent months, despite his six-year drive to make quality GM's number-one operating priority. Jim was GM's quality guru, often saying "Quality has to come first; if we don't have that, then nothing else will matter in the long run." A great deal had been done to improve quality since 1981. A vice president of quality, an easygoing executive named Ed Czapor, had been named to head the effort. At Jim's suggestion, the vast majority of GM's top executives went on a full-week training course at Phil Crosby's Quality College in Winter Park, Florida. Then Roger agreed to spend a few million dollars to buy into Crosby's operation and establish a quality school in Detroit where GM people from all levels were pushed through the intense course. The basic Crosby thesis was that quality is free. If you do all of the right things to achieve first-time quality, then you will save so much in reducing scrap, rework, and inventory that the effort will actually save you money. Given all of this and more, quality was falling in most plants in early '86. At the conference, Jim stunned the organization with one blunt sentence:

"I'd like to say I'm proud of being part of this management team, but right now I can't."

You would have to know the man to realize just how high on the Richter scale his simple vote of no confidence measured. Jim was the perpetual optimist in the corporation—not lavish in praise or censure, but always positive. In internal conferences in which he and Roger appeared together, you could always expect Roger to make the tough, often angry response, while Jim would follow it up with the good-news side of the same thought. There was no meanness in his makeup, no sarcasm or vindictiveness in his words. Superficially, he was just a pleasant guy who was easy to like. Actually, Jim was a deeply internal man who had known personal tragedy in his life and who, while friendly with all, was close to none. He once told an associate, "My wife is the only friend I have." Yet people trusted Jim and accepted that anything Jim said would be straightforward and honest. At GM, for Jim to criticize you like that was tantamount to having your mother say she was disappointed in you. It hurt.

Jim was frustrated. In his mind he had done all the right things to make quality the top priority, yet the organization was not responding. There were, however, a lot of factors that he could not control. First and foremost is that Jim was president, not chairman. One of the first rules of achieving quality

in an organization, Phil Crosby taught, was for the chief executive officer of the company to become its primary advocate.
Roger said the right words, but he did not say them often or
place primary stress on them. For example, while Jim McDonald and the top 90 GM executives went through the Crosby
Quality School, Roger elected not to attend. "I've got to weigh
the priorities of my time," he explained. From the beginning,
Roger talked about quality only in terms of the "first 50
miles"—the fit and finish that affected only the initial sale. He
did not emphasize the long-term problems that had pushed
GM's warranty costs up to $350 per car, the industry high.
Quality was Jim's assignment, not Roger's. Yet the entire organization was watching and waiting to see what Roger was
going to do about quality. Every one of those managers had
lived through several regimes and heard all of the quality su-
perlatives before, but when it came down to the daily operation, cost and quick delivery always won out.

About that time, mid-1986, I visited GM's Competitive Assessment Center at the GM Tech Center. There all the competitive cars, as well as GM's, were brought in and stripped down
for minute comparison. I asked why GM's quality was not rising compared to the imports and barely holding its own
against Ford and Chrysler.

"Do you see anyone stopping production or closing down
plants like Hamtramck because of quality?" an assessment
manager asked. "No, and the people that I get through here
from the plants haven't seen it happen, either."

Jim McDonald once focused the problem for me when he
said, "For the longest time, everyone seemed to be waiting for
the 14th floor to do something. I didn't understand what they
were waiting for, at first. Then it dawned on me they were
waiting to see if we really meant it. They were waiting to see if
we were going to walk like we talked." With cost cutting
becoming a priority again in early '86, the organization was
responding to what it thought was Roger's prime directive.
Once again it was putting cost before quality.

A postscript to this episode shows just how much impact a
leader can have. As Jim's speech writer at the time, everywhere I went people were asking me if Jim really meant what

he had said. They were concerned. Jim posed no direct threat to their position or income. In fact, Jim was a lame-duck president with less than a year left before retirement. But he got through to them. These were proud men, and the disappointment expressed by one of their own, a manufacturing guy like Jim who had sat where they were sitting, ate at their pride. It is no fluke that overall quality ratings began to climb again after the management conference. They rose for the next six months, then faltered when extensive emphasis on budget cutting started to take its toll on morale and quality.

By the midpoint of the disastrous 1986 calendar year, Roger was becoming sensitized to his image problems. His long overdue sensitivity proved that he was, after all, primarily a financial man. For while he had generally ignored criticism in the local Detroit press, and from the ranks of his own organization, his attention sharpened when his peers in the financial community began speaking out against him. The financial community was becoming overwhelmingly critical of his 21st-century scheme. Ford and Chrysler were doing so well in '86 that they both initiated stock repurchase programs that further enhanced the value of their common stock to investors. In sharp contrast, the GM lots were overflowing with unsold cars, and Roger was issuing more stock, not less, through his acquisitions; GM stock prices fell below Ford's, and the investment houses were putting "sell" signs on their GM holdings.

At GM's spring meeting with the auto analysts, the stock presentations that Roger and his top executives made were thoroughly rejected. The analysts called Roger's strategic plan "uninformative" and "naive." GM's breakeven point, they said, was up to nearly 5.6 million vehicles—a full 30 percent. That meant GM would have to grab about 43 percent of the domestic market just to stay out of the red. Yet they questioned the logic of GM's attempting to hold on to a 45 percent market share in such a crowded market. The problem with GM, they largely concluded, was "nonexistent cost controls" and "poor planning"—the two items they felt that a financial-side CEO should have had most under control. Open discussions of ways to get rid of GM's current leadership ensued.

About 40 percent of GM's stock was held by no more than 65 portfolios, and there was a growing fear that a couple of dozen of the largest portfolio managers might get together and either attempt a hostile takeover of GM or, at the minimum, demand Roger's abdication. Roger apparently decided that he needed job protection, so he entered a multimillion-dollar contract with Gershon Kekst and Co., a New York firm that specializes in helping companies ward off hostile takeovers. GM's legal staff told Roger that the odds of any group of stockholders garnering enough votes to threaten a hostile takeover of such a mammoth company were less than a million to one. And with his compliant board of directors, the odds were even lower that a coup d'état could come from within. But the risk-oriented chairman was not willing to accept such odds. He hired Gershon Kekst.

Immediately, Roger ordered all public relations events, all speeches, internal publications, and stockholder relations materials to be cleared by Gershon Kekst. The first advice that came back to us from Kekst was to play down the high-tech stuff—it doesn't sell cars, and it only reminds Wall Street of GM's excessive spending. The 1986 annual report, carefully massaged by the Kekst team, does not contain a single reference to the 21st-century corporation. The chairman's combined message in the report ends with the new theme:

"Above all, General Motors management is committed to earning a superior return on investments for our stockholders."

The incursion of Kekst into every utterance that went through GM public relations created a great deal of strain on daily operations. There were delays in sending everything to Kekst via GM's New York treasurer's office, a process that added a week to the already cumbersome clearance process. There were also major differences between looking at everything through financial eyes and trying to reflect the manufacturing corporation back in Detroit. And there were stylistic confrontations. One I remember in particular occurred when one of Kekst's young PR people, with the ink still damp on her M.B.A. degree, tried to tell speech writer Allen Perlman how to structure a sentence. Allen is GM's most intellectual speech writer and happens to hold a Ph.D. in linguistics as well. The heat of his response, if not the light, must have warmed her ear for some time to come.

Kekst, however, ruffled far more than some professional feathers. He shifted all focus to New York, at the expense of every other constituency. For example, he encouraged Roger to demonstrate his sincerity in manpower reduction by going public with internal programs. Roger publicly announced that GM was launching major staff cuts (actually, the cuts had been in the works for several months) of 25 percent of its white-collar workers and the closing of 11 plants by 1990. That meant 25,000 salaried people and 29,000 hourly would be let go.

"The plant-closing announcements," Don Ephlin said, "sent absolute terror throughout the corporation. It just wasn't necessary to lump them all together like that. We had known about nine of those plant closings for years. They were old plants that were replaced with new ones. Putting all of the closings together was just done to impress the financial guys, without the least consideration of what effect it would have inside of General Motors."

Nor was the salaried employment reduction as dramatic as it appeared. In the mid-1980s, GM's normal attrition rate was pushing 5 percent a year. In other words, 5 percent of the work force was reduced naturally through resignations, retirements, and deaths. Over the four-year time span announced, that meant that most of the reduction would have taken care of itself if GM simply refrained from hiring replacements. Explained this way, the fear of lost jobs could have been minimized even with the lump-sum announcements. Roger, however, revealed his knack for shooting himself in the foot once again by telling a reporter: "We're still hiring even as we reduce our work force. We need a different kind of person for the future company." One can only imagine how great a sense of security that gave his long-term employees.

Roger's sudden about-face to appease Wall Street created a major rift even on the 14th floor. The conflict was centered on market share. The dominant financial side urged Roger to go all the way and renounce market share as a primary goal. Profitability was more important. The operating-side executives largely felt that GM's future would be determined by whether it could hold on to its markets through this difficult period. To give up on market share would mean reducing capacity, losing some dealerships, and generally downsizing the company's auto industry position. Until Wall Street spoke up, Roger seemed to side with the operations thinking, but that was changing. At the Executive Management Conference Roger responded to a question on market share by saying, "I'm not going to be like the railroads. . . . I don't think the bankruptcy courts care a lot about how big your market share is."

To complete the tale of conflicts, confusion, and alienation during the first half of 1986, we have to return to those folks who were partying it up at Disneyland. As with EDS, Roger promised to keep his hands off Hughes Aircraft's independent operations. Yet within a few months of the Fantasyland beginning, Roger's accountants were making strong recommendations that Hughes's salaried staffs be reduced by several thousand and that salaried employees—many of them leading scientists in their respective fields—be told to work overtime without pay. And while they were at it, they could do away with those company-paid-for donuts at research staff meetings, if you please. Hughes, however, was a highly decentralized organization without a strong central leader like Ross Perot. Not having any preconceived notions about what life would be like in a profit-oriented company, Hughes employees largely expected the worst and acquiesced to GM's mandates.

What started at Disneyland seemed destined for the doldrums. Roger saw a survival-level need to improve his image, yet he was headed in the wrong direction. A 2.9 percent low-interest financing effort to clear nearly a million leftover cars by late summer cost him $3 billion and resulted in a $339 million operating loss for the third quarter. This was the first time in GM's history that it actually lost money on car and truck production during a booming economy in which auto sales were at record levels. *Detroit News* columnist James Higgins said what was on everyone's mind:

"Nobody can be that stupid."

8
Buying Off a Legend

"You [GM managers] don't like the guys on the
factory floor,
you don't like your customers,
you don't even like each other. . . .
Hell, you don't like anyone."

Ross Perot

T he greatest rescue mission in Ross Perot's life will not
be the time he sprang two employees from an Iranian
jail, but when he rescues all of his EDSers through his
single-handed assault on General Motors.

By the summer of 1988 the top EDS executives still held
contractually inside GM will be free to walk away with their
pockets bulging with GM ransom money. They will just as
likely join their leader-in-exile, Ross Perot, to start an all-new
corporation—financed through the most generous buyout
agreement in corporate history. And recognizing Ross's flair
for historical significance, one can even predict the date the
new company will come into existence. If past history means
anything, it could well be on June 27—Ross's 58th birthday,
the 26th anniversary of the original EDS's founding, and the
fourth anniversary of GM's acquisition of EDS.

That Roger would have agreed to the bizarre terms of the
buyout, terms that almost certainly guaranteed the departure
of most of EDS's best people, becomes perfectly logical when
Roger's vulnerability and Ross's superior maneuvering are
considered. By any measure, the buyout was totally lopsided.

"I just kept making obscene demands," Ross told me, "and they [GM] kept agreeing to them." The only aspect of the agreement that Roger was unyielding on was that Ross had to agree not to launch a GM takeover for at least five years—well after Roger's retirement. Beyond this paranoia clause, the buyout was in Ross's favor.

Roger agreed to pay Ross and his top three lieutenants some $750 million—about twice the face value of their stock holdings—for them to bow out of GM. The other three were the key EDS leaders, Mort Meyerson, Tom Walter, and Bill Gayden. Meyerson was Ross's right hand, the man who actually ran EDS during its most successful years and was recognized by the financial analysts for three years running as the Most Outstanding Chief Executive in the computer services industry. Tom Walter was the chief systems engineer of the corporation, the most sophisticated high-tech genius in EDS. And Bill Gayden was the marketing leader who built the international side of the company.

Yet far more important from Ross's perspective, the agreement went much further than these four men. In fact, it amounted to a potential buyout of all the original top EDS leaders. Roger agreed to conditions that could all but negate the benefits of the original $2.5 billion EDS acquisition. The buyout guaranteed that EDS executives would have absolute job security for 13 months. They could not be fired for anything short of moral turpitude. "They'd have to steal something," Ross said. But after 13 months they would receive complete vesting of their EDS stock (which would not have vested under the original acquisition until 1991). Once the stock was vested, this entire elite team had the right, and the resources, to leave GM. Just five months thereafter (June 1988), they would have the right to go to work for Ross and Mort again.

In the agreement, Ross Perot was not restricted in any way from starting up another EDS-like company on a nonprofit basis immediately and in three years converting it to a profit-making business and hiring every one of his original EDS people away from GM.

And just as important for the many EDSers left behind, Ross

got written promises that Roger would finally live up to the original contract. EDS would receive fixed-price, long-term contracts as quickly as they could be worked out. The promise of EDS autonomy was spelled out in the buyout agreement far more clearly than before. In other words, the key issues over which Ross had fought were conceded entirely.

And Roger didn't even buy the satisfaction of forcing Ross out of EDS. The buyout agreement left Ross with perpetual access. He was given the honorary title of "founder" and allowed to keep his office at EDS headquarters in Dallas (though Ross himself eventually decided to move to new offices). And Ross was encouraged to stay involved with EDS, to help the company close major deals in the future, to wander any EDS hallway in the world. For $700 million, Roger did not manage to close a single door to the EDS founder. "I will continue to work with the EDS people doing all the things I have been doing," Ross said immediately after the agreement was signed.

Ross made it very clear to Roger that, buyout or not, EDSers were still his people. "I feel a tremendous obligation to our people to provide them security in the event that something goes wrong [in GM]," Ross says. "I don't want to be in a position where EDS people are left in jeopardy. I owe them too much. As I see it, I've got a couple of options. One, and I told Roger this, if they don't treat EDS right, I'll go back and start a union. I'll make John L. Lewis [the great labor organizer] look like a choirboy. The other option is to start a new EDS. Believe it or not, the agreement doesn't prevent this. . . . I can't believe they could have been so dumb as to write the contract that way. . . . But I will do whatever it takes to provide opportunities for my people. . . . I'm not through with my business career. Hell, I'm only 56 years old. I intend to work until they carry me off in a box. . . . Everyone has a purpose in life; mine is to create jobs.

"If any one of the people who are building EDS ever needed me, I'd be there. I mean, there's no question in my mind that if I were ever in India and needed somebody at EDS to help me out, they'd show up. They know that. I know that. There's no formal agreement at all. We might decide to do something together," Ross stresses. "Or we might decide we're not having fun together and do something independently. It would be very relaxed and informal. That's the way our relationship has always been; it's very close."

In 1987, I talked to a number of EDS managers who felt that GM had not lived up to its promises, and several confided that if Ross Perot could be persuaded to initiate a new EDS, they would join him. Given Ross's personal management style, the loyalty is still strong among the original Texas crew.

"Ross insisted on provisions to protect us," said an EDS manager at B-O-C Group. "I think he felt that we never would have been able to force GM to live up to its promise of fixed-price contracts without his doing what he did. So, what I'm saying is that while we felt abandoned at first, many of us understand he had our welfare in mind through it all. He did what he had to do. . . . Yes, when I get my stock in a couple of months, I'll do what is best for my family then. GM still has a chance to earn my loyalty, but I frankly don't see them doing much, and there isn't a whole hell of a lot of trust left."

In essence, if the EDS people return to Ross Perot, or simply abandon what looks like a sinking ship when their stock vests, GM will be left with the 10,000 computer services people that it already had before the 1984 acquisition and 7,000 or so new recruits, yet with none of the EDS entrepreneurial culture that Roger paid so handsomely to acquire. Not only will the top EDSers vest out, but many below them will leave for the obvious reason that it is no longer the commando outfit they enlisted in. "Many of us came here because of what EDS stood for," a one-year EDS man told me. "It isn't the same now, and I'm sure a lot of us are going to get out as soon as we can."

When Roger bought EDS, he said, "If we hadn't found it, I guess we would have bought a college somewhere in Iowa and started our own. We needed an entrepreneurial company that had the youth and enthusiasm to do the job." Roger added later, "We looked at a lot of different companies, and we decided on EDS because of its strong leadership. We need the EDS spirit as much as their skills." In the end, Roger would get neither the leadership nor the spirit.

"If there is one thing your book should do," Roger told me,

"it is to dispel the notion that I bought Ross out to silence him." Roger insists that the Perot buyout was intended to eliminate a divisive force inside the corporation that was interfering with achieving corporate goals. Jack McNulty, Roger's PR chief, inadvertently contradicts this, saying, "Management's reputation was at stake." Yet if there is any lingering question about why Roger agreed to the buyout, a single provision in the agreement contains the answer.

As with Roger's earlier efforts to squelch stockholders from expressing themselves at annual meetings, Roger attempted to silence Perot with a gag clause in the agreement. The provision called for a cash penalty of up to $7.5 million if either party spoke out publicly and critically against the other. Perot, with a $3 billion-plus net worth, found the gag provision amusing. "Don't ask me anything that will cost me too much to answer," Ross says, punctuating it with a laugh. But Ross has not let it deter him in the least. "I'm going to say what I think and do what I would always do anyway," Ross says, and his record of outspoken statements since the buyout proves that the "silencer" provision was, once again, a misunderstanding of the man.

Insiders on the GM legal staff say that Roger had full knowledge of and involvement in the buyout agreement. But Roger, after much public embarrassment over his gag clause, said:

"The lawyers prepared the agreement, and they put that in there. I didn't really pay any attention to it." Does that mean he didn't even read the buyout agreement? "Well it was 15 pages long, and I trusted the lawyers." (Roger was evidently pleased with his lawyer, Elmer Johnson; for just a few months after Johnson wrote the Perot buyout, Roger promoted him onto the board.)

Whoever was responsible for the gag clause, it once again revealed a dearth of public relations insight. To enforce the clause and try to collect $7.5 million after a Ross Perot statement would only focus more media attention on Ross's criticisms. Even to suggest invoking the penalty would initiate a new round of GM bashing in the media, a group that happens to believe in open expression. After numerous Perot comments since then, the provision has not been invoked.

The bigger question, of course, is why Roger is so frightened of what Ross might say that he would agree to what amounted to unconditional surrender. To understand Roger's vulnerability, it is necessary to go back to mid-1986 and witness the events as they unfolded.

In May, when Roger received Ross's ultimatums by letter, it should have been obvious to him that it was only the beginning. Ross had suggested, among other things, that they buy him out. Roger had sent his attorney, and, after an uneventful meeting, the assumption was that the crisis was over. Yet even a cursory knowledge of Ross Perot's background should have told Roger more was to come. Here was a man who had proven he was fiercely loyal to his EDSers, a man who saw money only as a means to greater ends and whose tenacity was proven on the grandest scale. Ross could not sell out in May because the best he could have done at that time was to cut a deal to save himself. That wasn't good enough.

Ross denies staying to develop a rescue plan for his people, nor will he admit to planning any tactics. Yet, conscious or not, the strategic genius of his moves is self-evident.

Until mid-1986 Ross had been outspoken, but in ways that were clearly complimentary to Roger's own perspective. Ross kidded about companies saying they needed a level playing field, referring to Japan's self-serving trade tactics. "The playing field has never been level," Ross said. "It wasn't a field at all when we started EDS. It was a cliff." Roger agreed. He said what he had heard GM leaders say. Alex Mair, the outspoken vice president of technical staffs said that GM had been too prosperous for too long and had lost the competitive spirit. "GM had no effective competition," Ross echoed. "It owned the bats, the balls, both teams, the dugouts, the stadium, and the lights. It's hard to lose that way." Roger agreed.

"Ross is trying to encourage us along the lines of what we want to do," Roger said. "I don't think he's criticizing us. He doesn't point at us and say, 'You're doing a lousy job,' or anything. Ross is working his buns off for us."

Many inside GM disagreed that Ross had the corporation's best interest at heart. They pointed out that while people like GM vice president Alex Mair were outspoken about GM flaws,

Mair's comments were restricted to internal audiences and always ended with a charge of specifics for GM actions. Ross was public and, therefore, could hurt GM's already pathetic corporate image.

"If Ross really wanted to help," Howard Kehrl said, "he could have concentrated on solving the internal EDS problems. At least he could have made specific suggestions that we could do something about. All he gave us at the board meetings were generalizations."

Roger, however, made it clear that he believed in Ross Perot and didn't want to initiate a confrontation. Publicly, he continued to praise Ross. "Ross is one of us," Roger said. "We are all trying to change the corporation."

During this time, the Texas gadfly was buzzing freely around the company. He visited plants, development labs, styling studios, test tracks, and accounting offices. And he used his down-home charm to encourage people to speak their minds. "I've been with GM for 24 years," an Arlington, Texas, plant employee said, "and I've seen mostly arrogance from executives. Ross is a real change." Ross revealed his natural affinity for the working people, living as he did closer to their lifestyles than that of GM's executives. He refused to accept a free company car and instead traded in his 1979 Chevy for a new Oldsmobile, bargaining over price at the dealership like everyone else. He would often go to dealerships without identifying himself to check on service and just to talk with the mechanics. And Ross was in regular contact with his EDSers who were operating—or attempting to—in every plant and office in the corporation. With his ability to put people at ease and get them to talk freely, Ross gained a thorough overview of the corporation and an appreciation for the tremendous frustration so many felt.

After all attempts—including two reorganizations of the GM EDS crew—failed to resolve the EDS contractual problems (still at less than 10 percent of fixed-price contracts), Ross stepped up his public attacks. "You want to know how to teach an elephant to tap-dance?" he asked. "You find the soft spots and start poking." In late July Ross got out his prod. In an interview with the *Wall Street Journal*, and on several less formal occasions, he made thinly veiled attacks on Roger's spending spree.

"We [GM] are spending billions to develop new cars. This isn't a moon shot; it's just a car," Ross said.

"Brains and wits will beat capital all the time. . . .

"Our [GM's] solution is to go out and buy new uniforms. The team looks good, but it still can't play."

.And he jabbed at Roger's tendency to blame the workers. "GM has failed to tap the potential of its people," Ross said. "In America we tend to blame the workers, but the workers don't design the cars, or sell them, or set up the standards. American workers are the salt of the earth, and they could beat anyone if they were given half a chance."

Ross's outbursts started the press speculating once again that he was campaigning for Roger's job. Roger had let such rumors persist back when the chair was not a hot seat, but now that he was under criticism from Wall Street and the media, the press speculation became a personal threat. Still, Roger made it clear that no one was to confront Ross.

"He's impatient," Roger said, "but he's impatient for the things we are." Later someone said that Roger was practicing "good dog diplomacy"—saying "good dog" publicly while he was looking for a stick to beat Ross with. That was simply not the case. As unbelievable as it may seem, Roger continued to admire the Texas folk hero and to throw flowers at him even while Ross was hurling bricks in his direction. There was almost a childlike adoration for the man who, in so many ways, exemplified Roger's father. And Roger's admiration was mixed with a degree of fear. "I don't want to antagonize him," Roger told those who urged him to fight back.

In the Public Relations Department there were discussions about what we should do about Ross Perot. It would be a messy proposition to attempt to vote out the largest stockholder. Public debate was out of the question considering Ross's skills and Roger's lack thereof. And someone, not knowing about the ultimatum letter, even suggested a buyout. I said that would be a bad idea. President Lyndon Johnson, Jack McNulty's former boss, had a similar problem with J. Edgar Hoover. When someone asked Johnson why he didn't fire

Hoover, he said: "I'd rather have him on the inside of the tent pissing out, than on the outside of the tent pissing in."

True to GM form, in these discussions no one suggested that Roger be asked to call Ross and tell him to tone down the criticism. Roger was not that direct. "I disagree with Roger in front of others, and Roger likes it," Ross said. "I disagree with Roger in front of the board, and Roger likes it. I'll be the only board member to vote against something, and Roger actually likes it."

"Not once did anyone call me and suggest I was hurting General Motors," Ross said. "There is also an ethics committee in GM, and they didn't talk to me, either. There wasn't a whole lot of openness or honesty there."

While Ross was looking for soft spots publicly, his partner, Mort Meyerson, was attempting another way out of an unpleasant situation for EDSers. Mort had stepped out from the EDS presidency and served as vice chairman of new business ventures and acquisitions. In this new capacity he came up with a strategy. EDS had been working with AT&T for a number of years, and in 1985 they entered a joint venture to establish a worldwide telecommunications network. The relationship between AT&T and EDS was exceptionally cordial. Meyerson got Roger's permission to explore some options with AT&T. In the talks, Meyerson suggested a number of deals, including the complete buyout of EDS by AT&T, but that was never a serious goal. Meyerson's plan was to get GM to sell 25 percent of its EDS stock to AT&T, keep 25 percent for itself, and go public with the other 50 percent. Ross and the EDS employees could buy additional shares of the public offerings. In this way, Ross and company could regain control of EDS while keeping two of the biggest clients—GM and AT&T—around.

"Mort tried the idea out on us first," Ross said. "We [at EDS] all got excited about it. We were very supportive of Mort's idea. I took it to Roger, who agreed, Roger got the board's blessing, then appointed Don Atwood and other team members to negotiate. It was not an end run around GM."

Yet the deal was not falling into place. AT&T was not enthusiastic because, without the GM long-term contracts con-

firmed, there was no way of appraising the actual value of EDS
stock. Still the talks went on until Meyerson took his idea to
Roger for approval.

"There wasn't anything in that for GM," Roger said. "Sure, it
would give EDS control, but what was in it for us? No, we
never had any intention of selling EDS, no matter what anyone
says."

When the story of the AT&T talks broke in the *Wall Street
Journal*, EDS and AT&T both confirmed them. Roger, however, denied it. "We have never had EDS on the block," he
insisted. "EDS is too important to our future." The press criticized Roger for not being honest about the talks, but, in fact,
Roger saw it as a nonevent. He'd heard a few ideas about joint
ventures kicked around by Mort Meyerson, and nothing came
of them. Roger had no idea what the hoopla was all about.

With the AT&T deal blocked, Ross stepped up his public
attacks on GM. Only this time the rubber tips were removed
from the barbs. In two major interviews with *Ward's Auto
World* and *Business Week*, and in several other publications,
Ross hit GM hard:

> Detroit used to be the car capital, but they treated people
> very poorly. So the people organized and created unions and
> reacted against what they saw were caretaker owners.
>
> • • •
>
> The first EDSer to see a snake kills it. At GM, first thing
> you do is organize a committee on snakes. Then you bring in
> a consultant who knows a lot about snakes . . . then you talk
> about it for a year.
>
> • • •
>
> GM should stop massive amounts of capital spending.
> Instead, find out from those down in the ranks their ideas
> for competing effectively . . . they know.
>
> • • •
>
> Roger said Saturn would be paperless, so the first thing I
> did was to call and put my order in for the first car. After
> they realized I wasn't kidding, they said, "We'll send you an
> order form." I said, "You can't. Saturn is paperless."
>
> • • •
>
> Let's say there is a problem with the brakes. They will send
> one bright, highly motivated staff person, probably a

financial type, out to check on the brake problem. He talks
with an accountant, who talks to someone in long-range
planning, and finally they form a committee to talk to some
poor devil working on brakes who knows what the hell to
do.

• • •

This place cries out for engineers with greasy hands who
know how to make cars to be making the policy and
motivating every member of the GM team.

• • •

What it takes to be successful [in GM] has nothing to do
with making better products . . . it has to do with following
the procedures, understanding the politics . . . understanding
the power structure.

• • •

If we did not have such a thing as an airplane today, we
would probably create something the size of NASA to make
one. . . . It's a good thing the Wright Brothers didn't know
any better.

• • •

It's not technology. GM must treat employees with dignity
and respect.

• • •

They're going from personnel philosophies that are so
archaic, they're no longer relevant to modern ways to deal
with people.

• • •

It costs $140,000 a year to heat one [executive] parking
garage. I'd shut that thing down; it has nothing to do with
making cars.

Roger's sense of humor was straining, but he kept up the
supportive front initially. Roger said, "The other day I was
talking to Ross, and he was saying, 'I have to make a speech or
something to tell everyone I don't want the chairmanship.'
And I said: 'Well, Ross, I don't know if we need another
speech.' "
Ross probed deeper. "Just a trip to the 14th floor is depress-
ing. That's a time warp. . . . Get rid of the 14th floor. Get rid of
the private dining rooms and chauffeured limos and heated
garages. Get rid of everything that separates people." Ross

laughs about the reaction when he finally hit the sensitive spot. "They went nuts when I criticized their chauffeurs and executive dining rooms," he said.

Roger's temper finally surfaced. "Ross has an office that makes mine look like shanty town," he said. "You want to see executive perks, you visit Toyota's dining room. It's a palace with a waiter behind every chair." And, "Ross doesn't have a very deep knowledge of this industry. With fifteen thousand parts and regulations on everything, it's a complicated business. You can't just skim across this pond." As for Ross's suggestions, Roger said, "Look at reorganization and Saturn. We did those things long before we knew how to spell 'Ross Perot.' "

Ross's reaction was tongue in cheek: "I was surprised, I guess, that he [Roger] would aim criticism at me personally. I'm not mad. I'll just stand on my prior statements that I consider Roger to be one of the smartest and most creative businessmen I have met."

During this period of open confrontation, I was calling around the company to research speeches, and I made a point of asking what the executives and middle managers thought of Ross Perot's barbs. Since EDS was the butt of continuous jokes, and Ross was the commander-in-chief of this incursive force, I expected angry responses from the proud GMers. I found just the opposite. GM people continued to complain about EDS, while praising Ross Perot's outspoken comments. Ross was saying publicly what GM employees were telling each other privately. In Ross, they were hearing direct feedback of their comments to him, and they were delighted that they were finally being aired.

Ross was fast becoming a folk hero inside of GM and, to GM's dealer and supplier contingencies, a serious threat to Roger's faltering leadership. The appearance of unanimity on the 14th floor had always been sacrosanct. Conflict meant a lack of control, something Roger was not in a position to endure. With Wall Street already questioning his ability to get things done, and Gershon Kekst whispering warnings in his ear, Roger was beginning to understand the broader implications of Ross's thrust.

While the verbal volleys were gaining center stage, Ross found two other spots to drive barbs into. First, Roger had decided that the corporation was not going to pay profit sharing for 1986, yet he would insist that his executives receive their bonuses. There was already a great deal of controversy on the 14th floor over this issue. The more people-sensitive executives urged that Roger forget the bonuses or approve a symbolic executive pay cut of, say 10 percent, to let the employees know the executives were sharing in the company's misfortunes. Roger insisted on the bonuses and knew he could easily get the board to approve them on December 1. Ross, however, was certain to vocally oppose the move. Ross was already hinting in that direction with statements like:

"In a war, you feed the troops, then you feed the officers because the troops fight and the officers plan. . . . It's hard to fight when you're hungry." Ross would certainly be an embarrassment on the bonus issue.

The second front was even more frightening. Ross let the word out that he would launch a frontal attack to make GM live up to its contractual agreements. He requested to speak before GM's Fairness Committee (an oversight committee), where he planned to accuse Roger directly of reneging. Also, Ross says:

"I talked to my lawyers, and I was getting ready to file a shareholder suit. They were violating securities regulations, and I had an obligation to protect my stockholders."

There was an even larger soft spot that Roger needed to protect. This was the one year in which Roger could not afford to have an inside critic exposing GM's machinations. For Roger had painted GM into a financial corner with his spending and was unable to get the organization to make cuts fast and deep enough. The third-quarter losses were much worse than most suspected. David Healy of Drexel, Burnham, and Lambert, a respected New York investment banking firm, concluded that GM was playing with numbers. In an article entitled "The Case of the Missing Thirteen Billion Dollars," Healy wrote, "Our suspicion is that the company inflated its third quarter operating profit to avoid reporting a net loss for the period, and 'paid back' the borrowed earnings in the fourth quarter." That, however, was not the brightest of ideas, since the fourth quarter, after the low-financing incentives were removed, was a disaster. GM sales dropped by 10 percent, while Ford sales increased by 26.6 percent and Chrysler's went up by 12.8 percent. By November, when the buyout came up, GM was down to a paltry 33.8 percent market share—a half-century low.

The worst, however, was yet to come. For Roger had done what seemed to be the impossible. GM would pass the $100 billion revenue mark in 1986 yet actually make no money. Roger did post a net income of $2.945 billion for the year, but that was largely the result of some extremely innovative accounting. In a thorough analysis of General Motors for 1986, David Healy concluded that the corporation's financial statements were "an accounting course in themselves." There were numerous nonrecurring charges, loans from one division to another, LIFO (last-in-first-out) inventory gains, foreign tax credits, and two major changes in pension accounting procedures, to name just the high points.

"GM seems to have reached something of an accounting high-water mark," Healy wrote, "by claiming an apparent $4 billion total U.S. loss on its tax returns and simultaneously showing an $87 million pretax U.S. profit in its stockholder report."

Roger took full advantage of new financial accounting standards to retroactively redefine the first nine months of 1986, which had the effect of removing $640 million from the cost of goods sold and adding $330 million to net earnings. Healy called this GM's "repeal of schoolhouse arithmetic." And he concluded that it, and other sharp-pencil actions, allowed GM financial staff to improve corporate earnings by 24 percent above actual earnings.

Roger took money out of his left pocket and put it in his right pocket to improve the overall impression of profitability. General Motors Acceptance Corporation, GM's wholly owned and completely internal finance operation, was hit up for $5.5 billion in long-term loans. This was described in the third-quarter report as being totally balanced against current receivables and was said to be "already paid off." In fact, the debt would continue indefinitely. But this accounting method did add $5.5 billion from receivables to current assets. Healy reported that, without this accounting shift, GM would have been in the red on working capital in the third and fourth quarter of '86.

The most important accounting task was to continue to pay dividends. GM had not missed a dividend in nearly 70 years, and Roger certainly didn't want to be the first chairman to break the string. So the shifting of funds and creative accounting allowed Roger to meet an internal test of working capital that allowed the dividend payments. Not to have made a dividend payment, though that certainly would have been realistic given the circumstances, was too great an admission of GM's financial troubles. "Some of us," one GMAC finance man said, "felt that it was our fault that we failed to convince people that GM was in deep financial trouble." You have to admit you've got a problem if you want others to be concerned. But the 14th floor overruled us."

In looking at Roger's situation in late November of 1986, it was obvious that he would have agreed to any terms to get the loose cannon off his deck. Each time Ross would speak out against GM, you could close your eyes and hear GM and EDS stock click down another notch. Roger's survival as chairman depended on giving Wall Street some good news. To do so, he had to make the most embarrassing year in GM corporate history somehow look good. That kind of creative reporting would not be possible with the vocal Mr. Perot shouting the truth from the decks.

Ross may have suspected he had yet another front working for him at the time—Roger's growing paranoia that a hostile takeover was imminent. Gershon Kekst and Roger's own legal staffers were warning about the possibility of a takeover. Roger agreed that Ross was the only billionaire around who had the power and daring to pull off a stock acquisition. There was a sense of urgency as senior executives visualized their entire fast-track careers being cut off at the top should Ross Perot somehow gain the chair. Finally, a rumor circulated on the 14th floor that Drexel, Burnham, and Lambert, an investment firm known for takeover bids, was working with Ross

Perot to gain control of the giant auto company. James Evans, a GM outside board member, and two GM corporate lawyers were sent to Drexel, Burnham to confront the firm and make it clear GM would not relinquish control without a fight. "A Drexel, Burnham executive told me this story much later," Ross says. "He said no one at Drexel, Burnham knew what the GM guys were talking about, and they got a good laugh out of the visit afterward." Yet Ross Perot did not want GM and had often said so. During Ross's many outspoken interviews he never once threatened a takeover, and there is no indication that he conferred with Drexel, Burnham or other firms about such a possibility. Yet Roger's advisors had conjured up a take-over bogeyman to loom over the 14th floor.

At this point, two stories about what happened next emerge. Elmer Johnson, GM's corporate lawyer, says that Ross's lawyer, Tom Luce, called him and said Ross was ready to sell his remaining holding in EDS. Luce says, "That's not true. Elmer Johnson called me and asked if Ross would consider a buyout." It really doesn't matter who asked for the dance, since the significant point was that it was clear Ross Perot was in the position to "call the tune." One of the basic business lessons Ross had learned from day trading horses as a boy was that the one who needs the sale most is going to pay the price.

Ross had relied on Roger's sensitivity and had timed his moves precisely. He knew just where and when to put the burr under Roger's saddle to get the desired reaction. If the effort was not intentional, as Ross claims, then it was one remarkable example of intuitive business maneuvering. Ross was not a simple, outspoken rube. While his speaking patterns gave the impression of off-the-cuff commentaries, Ross Perot was not one to blabber without appreciation for the consequences. He had built his fortune and legendary populist image through careful expression. "He's not reckless," Roger had said of Ross in 1984. "He's very calculating, very intelligent. When he does something, he knows he's going to make it work."

Nor was Ross insensitive to the impact of conflict on a cor-poration's fortunes. Within EDS, speaking up against the orga-nization was a fireable offense. Many of the GM transferees were let go because they criticized the company. "They had the wrong attitude," an EDS manager said. "That hurts our business." Ross knew precisely what he was doing.

The timing of the buyout was important, both to exert maximum pressure and because of the Tax Reform Act of 1986. Had Ross waited until after December 31, he would have lost as much as $100 million because of the tax law changes, one GM accountant calculated. So when Luce called GM during the first week in November, he told Elmer that Roger had one chance only to buy Ross out. It had to be at the December 1 board meeting or not at all.

There was no time to bicker. Roger agreed to be more than generous. In all, he gave Ross nearly $62.50 per share times his 11.3 million shares. It broke down to $33 per share for the stock and $28.90 per share from the contingent note attached to each GM Class E stock. The contingent note guaranteed all Class E stockholders returns of $62.50 per share by 1990. In other words, if Class E stock sold for $45 in 1990, GM was contractually bound to give each stockholder another $17.50. The buyout simply paid Ross off in full—five years ahead of the agreement.

"This is probably the best deal we ever made," Roger said. "We paid about $51 a share after taxes and get the value of the stock. I don't mean to minimize $700 million, but I think we can raise that by reselling the stock." To buy the stock at $51 and resell it for $26—the price of the stock immediately after the buyout—didn't seem to many to be much of a bargain. Roger, however, said that the buyout was important because "if the EDS people thought we were being unfair to their leader, we would lose their goodwill." (A GMISCA transferee pointed to the estimates that GM was currently spending about $10 million just to fight employee lawsuits and said wryly: "The only 'employee goodwill' he cares about is a 'good will and testament' for the thousands of employees he's trying to do in.")

"I really thought the board would tell Roger he was out of his mind. It was the dumbest business deal I ever heard of," Ross says. "I found during the negotiations that they'd agree to anything on the business side no matter how ridiculous, but they were very tight on anything that had to do with criticism or taking over GM. The antitakeover provisions were very strong. I had to commit to not making any effort to take over General Motors for five years," Ross said, pausing to laugh. "I was happy to do that because I had no interest in taking over General Motors."

Roger had worked to consummate the buyout. He had called each board member in advance of the December 1 board meeting to be certain they would vote his way. The entire decision was arranged before the board meeting, which, with virtually no discussion, led to a unanimous vote.

There were some glitches when moving that fast. One aspect of the buyout that seemed to be overlooked until the last minute was what to do with EDS now. A quick decision was made to lump it into a new business unit comprised of all GM high-tech operations—including the recently formed Hughes Electronics Corporation (Hughes Aircraft, Delco Electronics, and defense operations), electronics components divisions, plus EDS. That would put EDS back into a more conventional position—without board representation and reporting to Executive Vice President Don Atwood, well below and away from Roger on the organizational chart. The only problem was that no one bothered to work out any of the details or even to call Don Atwood's public relations director before the announcement. The new business unit wasn't even a name yet, a fact that further impressed the media about GM's lack of internal organization. Roger's innocuous announcement didn't help matters. "The new unit," Roger said, "will promote even greater synergy among the operations and will enhance the development and implementation of advanced technology systems."

Yet with all that effort, the buyout resulted in about one hour of peace for Roger Smith. That's how long Ross waited after the contract was signed to issue a public statement:

> At a time when General Motors is closing 11 plants, putting 30,000 people out of work, cutting back on capital expenditures, losing market share, and having problems with profitability, I have just received $700 million from General Motors in exchange for my Class E stock and notes.

I cannot accept this money without first giving General Motors directors another chance to consider this decision. This money will be held in escrow until December 15 in order to give the General Motors directors time to review this matter and the events that led to this decision. If the General Motors directors conclude that this transaction of December 1 is not in the best interest of General Motors and the Class E stockholders, I will work with the GM directors to rescind this transaction.

Roger was in a meeting in the treasurer's office in New York when he was handed a copy of Ross's press statement. His face turned crimson, and he exploded. Within minutes he was pulling Elmer Johnson out of a meeting. "What the hell is going on?" Roger demanded. Elmer didn't know. As Roger paced, fumed, and cussed, Elmer called Luce in Dallas. According to Elmer, Ross's lawyer was equally surprised.

At the same time, Ross was holding a press conference in Dallas. And, as always, Ross was casual and in command. When a reporter asked if all this was happening just to get rid of him, Ross lightened up his audience by saying:

"I would hope not. My philosophy is 'to know me is to love me.' "

Ross told the reporters that he had asked that the buyout offer be made public for a full week before consummation, but Roger wanted an immediate buyout. Ross said his next-best alternative was to put the money in an escrow account, to let the world see just how bad GM's management was, and give the board of directors a chance to represent the corporation's best interests.

"I felt an obligation to make sure that the people who own the company, not the people who run it, knew what was going on," Ross said. "I could not make it a matter of public record until the contract was executed.

"The issue is not whether I'm off the board. Fellas, $700 million will buy you a brand-spanking-new, state-of-the-art, world-class car plant—and the several thousand jobs that go with it. Now that's what I'm concerned about—the highest and best use of the money."

"The entire buyout agreement," Ross said, "was only a way of getting everything out in the open." He had realized that the behind-closed-doors efforts to negotiate contractual disputes, and the indirectness of GM's management style, would never be resolved without confrontation.

"I just looked at all the facts," Ross said. "I talked to all my associates, and finally we, you know, we spent a lot of time saying, 'What is the highest and best use of our time?' Right. One thing, we do business historically all day, every day. That's the way we created all these jobs. That's the way we built this company. And so I think there was a very strong feeling if you get into something like this, it just drags on and drags on and drags on. And when you look at all the factors and concerns and what have you, then, it's very important to get this issue squarely on the table. Let everybody take a close look at it . . . see if it's the best course of action.

"I don't see this as a battle between individuals. What happens to me is not nearly as important as what happens to eight hundred thousand jobs at GM. Three million people get a paycheck because there is a General Motors. Keep in mind that what is happening to me here today is not nearly as significant as what losing your job in a closed plant is to the person who loves his job. Right? . . . I won't exactly end up down at the public shelter tonight."

In the news conference, Ross made it abundantly clear who he thought was to blame for GM's competitive problems:

"The favorite thing to do in this country is to dump on labor," Ross said, "and that's absolutely rotten and unfair. . . . If we've got a losing team, what do you do right away? You put in new leaders, right? You've got to have a quarterback who can throw and win.

"The companies that are moving up treat people as full partners. You treat them with dignity and respect. Everybody is a full player on the team; everybody has real trust back and forth both ways. See, if you don't trust me, and I don't trust you, a big part of our energy gets lost right there. Right? Because, I'm wondering what you are going to do to me next. I wanted to clean all that out fast [at GM]. That doesn't cost anything. That's just changing how you do business."

"Jesus Christ," a senior GM PR director said in a hastily called meeting, "if you can't shut someone up with a three-quarter-billion-dollar payoff, what will it take?" Ross's maneuver had Roger demanding some new ideas. "What will we do now?" he asked all of his advisors. Gershon Kekst suggested some tough counter language, but Roger didn't feel comfortable with that. It wasn't his nature to enter direct confrontations, and he felt it would only be demeaning to GM and the chairmanship. Roger did manage to get a board member to publicly announce that the decision to buy Ross out was unanimous and there would be no reconsideration, but that didn't reduce speculation significantly. Most observers, not understanding Roger's control over his board, fully expected the directors to respond to Ross's challenge, and when they didn't, journalists started calling it "Roger's politburo." As Ronald Glantz of the San Francisco-based Montgomery Securities said:

"I'm disappointed that Roger Smith is so determined to have a rubber-stamp board that he'll pay almost a billion dollars to screw up EDS."

Once again, Roger's inability to understand the depth or complexity of human relations caught him unprepared. He fully expected Ross to take his money and crawl into the woodwork. And he miscalculated public response, figuring that after taking a few days of heat for the buyout he could put it behind him. He had never been more mistaken.

The buyout made Ross Perot a martyr of sorts. He was perceived as having spoken up for the common man—as having spoken the truth—and been squelched by a paranoid GM chairman. Ross was suddenly referred to as the man who could have been GM's salvation. That he had spent the vast majority of his time in Dallas, and had made only a handful of management proposals during his GM board tenure, went unnoticed. What would GM do without its helpful critic? Or, as one columnist put it:

"If you remove the grain of sand, do you still get the pearl?"

The cries of outrage came from all directions. Maryann Keller said: "If the price of harmony is also conformity, then you lose the uniqueness of EDS—and all that money was wasted." An EDSer wrote to *Ward's Auto World* saying "Ross Perot certainly has a better track record than GM's 14th floor at building a successful company. His ideas should be given a try." And Texas oil financier T. Boone Pickens said: "GM's attempt to silence the most outspoken advocate of constructive change at the company is a severe blow. . . . The best acquisition GM has made in my lifetime is Ross Perot."

The praise for Ross was accompanied with censure for Roger. *The New York Times* started an article on Roger with the statement that "Few executives in recent years have been longer on vision and more plagued by reality." The investment community was up in arms, and so was the public. Letters to the editor in both Detroit newspapers were running about 90 percent pro-Perot, and a significant number of the respondents were outraged GM employees. Leo Bednarkiewicz, a Detroit-area GMer, summed up many opinions in his letter to the *Free Press*, saying:

"There's no money to reward good performance, no funds for replacing necessary work items, and forget about profit sharing. But presto, almost a billion dollars appears immediately. No wonder bean counters such as Smith make Harry Houdini look like a rank amateur when it comes to creating illusions."

Roger's first reaction was to lie low and wait for the wave of consternation to wash over and back out. Unfortunately, he had one small problem with that. Roger, as a Detroit Economic Club member, had invited Ross to speak on December 8—precisely one week after the buyout. And Roger had agreed to introduce Ross. The Economic Club was Detroit's premier business forum, a luncheon gathering where U.S. presidents, CEOs, and the world business leaders spoke to typical crowds of two thousand or more. Here was Roger's worst fear realized, a public debate with the Texas super salesman. Roger knew he was overmatched, but he is not a coward. He made up his mind that he would attend and introduce Ross no matter what the consequences.

The Roger-Ross luncheon became a national media event. Requests for Economic Club tickets swelled to more than seventy-two hundred—more people than the record crowd that had come to hear President Ronald Reagan speak there. More than 150 requests for press credentials came in. CNN, NBC, ABC, CBS, the British BBC, and even Canada's French-language stations were setting up cameras. *The New York Times, Business Week, USA Today, Time, People,* and even *Popular Science* had contingents of reporters. Local Detroit media people complained that the national crews were forcing them out. Two dozen television cameras were set up on a special island of risers a hundred feet in front of the podium. Outside at Cobo Hall, site of the luncheon, EDS picketers carried signs saying, "Keep Talking Ross." UAW members carried placards protesting plant closings. "No Payoffs, No Layoffs" and "Fire Roger Smith" were the two most visible signs. A full detachment of Detroit police was on hand for what was typically a prosaic affair of stewed chicken and potbellied, balding businessmen.

"Make it look like business as usual," Roger said. GM was to have only its two regular tables for employees, though GM Photographic did manage to set up an in-house camera.

When the assignment had come down to write Roger's introduction speech, I had quickly volunteered but was told that "you couldn't play it straight enough." Allen Perlman, our most serious speech writer, was drafted for the task. Roger made it clear that he wanted no barbs, no attacks or references whatsoever to the buyout. The introduction was to be cloyingly sweet, with lavish praise for the EDS founder. I suggested that the approach made us look hypocritical, but no one agreed.

"On the night before the speech," Jack McNulty says, "Roger and I were in Washington, D.C. I went over his speech with him in the hotel room. I had accumulated a bunch of really good one-liners to get some shots in at Ross. Roger read them and laughed, but then he turned serious. 'No, I don't want to provoke him,' Roger told me. 'I've got to be on the podium with him, sit next to him, for an hour. I've got them [the one-liners] in my head, but I don't want to use them.'"

When the two men entered the hall that morning, it was like watching gladiators enter the arena. Roger walked erect, but stiffly, unable to hide his self-consciousness. Ross entered in a wave of cheers, confident and cheerfully ready for contention. At the podium, Roger became all business, reading his introductory remarks without expression or eye contact with Ross. He recounted Ross's legendary achievements and ended by describing him as "a simple, generous man with rock-solid principles and bulldog tenacity."

Had Roger been able to turn and talk to Ross directly, he would have realized that Ross had no intention of castigating him that day. "I was in Detroit," Ross later said. "Roger had invited me to be there. There was an appropriate way to handle it." Ross was not placated by the chairman's praise, yet he did not attack Roger directly—at least not by name. His topic was American competitiveness, and his references, to anyone following the Ross-Roger controversy thus far, came through. However, to those who didn't want to hear the message, it sounded like a generic locker room pep talk. Some of the more telling excerpts from Ross's speech:

> Whether we like to admit it or not, today we are losing in the world-competitive battle. . . . We are like the inheritors of great wealth: we are living the good life, we're taking out much, and we're putting back far too little. . . .
>
> Now the thing that just breaks my heart is the best and brightest out of Asia are learning skills that will create jobs. Our best and brightest all want to be Wall Street bankers, consultants, and other things that contribute little to the real worth of this country and contribute very little to creating jobs. . . .
>
> Many of our business leaders grew up in an era where there was little competition. All the competition was within the companies, the big U.S. companies. Not among the companies. . . . It was so bad we had to create intramural sports. . . .
>
> We don't understand our system. The average student gets a college degree and has no understanding of business and the free-enterprise system, but they all understand sports. OK, you've got a losing team. You're the owners. What are you going to do? You're going to replace the quarterback; you're going to replace the coaches.
>
> In business we criticize the players and the lower-level

managers. The average American sits there and says, "Well, yes, that's all right." Now we've got to change that. We are the leaders, and we must provide the leadership. . . .

. . . your entire organization is [should be] driven to win, you are driven to be the best. You work together as a tightly knit, unified team. You waste no energy on nonessentials. You spend all of your energy on product and on the service.

Brains, wits, the creative abilities of American people are an incredible substitute for capital, so you certainly don't have to lose even if that's all you have. The whole success of the company centers around people—not finances.

At EDS we encourage people not to look up to one another because it stifles communications. If we find anybody looking down on anybody else, we fire them because that really hurts the team effort in a company. We have a philosophy in EDS that you can manage inventory, and you can manage things, but you must *lead* people if you hope to tap their full potential. . . . The definition of an EDS leader is one who won't ask anyone, anytime to ever do anything he or she hasn't done before and wouldn't do again in a minute and who would never ask anyone to do anything that was improper or unethical. . . .

In our company [EDS] there's no penalty for honest mistakes. They're like skinned knees on children—they're painful, they're superficial, they heal quickly. We encourage creativity in our people.

I hope it's apparent to all of you that the people in EDS occupy a very special place in my life. Next to my family, they are the very best part of my life. I don't just like the people in EDS—I love the people in EDS. And I suggest that wouldn't be a bad attitude in this great country because, by golly, the people who do the work are easy to love.

The crowd loved Ross's talk, cheering, applauding, and chuckling each time Ross made a point that criticized management. Ross didn't need to be impolite to his host to get his messages across. The *Wall Street Journal* reported: "Clearly, this town was Mr. Perot's for a day."

Throughout Ross's talk, Roger fidgeted, scratched his head, and adjusted his glasses often. He did not laugh at Ross's jokes, clap at his points. Instead, he busied himself with the three-by-five question cards submitted from the audience. As moderator, it was Roger's task to select the questions that Ross would answer after the speech. According to an Economic Club member sitting next to Roger, there were at least 40 questions that dealt with GM. But Roger did not pick a single one of them—passing on only those that were safe, such as "What courses should college students take?"

The only time Roger smiled, a tight-lipped smile, was when Ross was asked if he would consider running for president of the United States with Lee Iacocca as his running mate. Ross said: "Boy, they think they have controversy now. Between the two of us, that'd be one way to get President Reagan off the front page. We'd stir up more trouble than we could ever solve. Poor old Sam Donaldson [NBC reporter] would probably spin out and turn into an ash in 30 days."

In the press interview after the event, the two men continued their civility. Yet Ross would not avoid direct questions, and when the question about executive bonuses at GM was raised, Ross showed his willingness to take the $7.5 million penalty if necessary to maintain his candor:

"At Valley Forge," Ross said, "the troops were fighting barefoot in the snow. If George Washington had been out buying new uniforms with gold braid, it would have been hard to rally the troops."

Roger refused to answer questions with specifics at the press conference, saying, "This is Ross's day." He was absolutely right. A *Ward's Auto World* survey of the Economic Club audience showed that 96 percent of these businesspeople, primarily from the auto industry, agreed with Ross's criticisms of General Motors.

"I have said for years," Ross noted, "that you can give money to the church and expect a 20 percent negative response. Ninety-six percent. That's scary."

9
Saturn Eclipsed

*"I am not the visionary genius they said I was
then, and I'm not the bumbler they say I am now.
And neither is GM."*

Roger Smith

A fter the Texas Rambo left town, there were not enough
pieces left of Roger's credibility to fill a body bag. Every
major constituency—employees, stockholders, customers, and media—joined in picking apart Roger's 21st-cen-
tury corporation vision. By every measure of management
achievement—return on investment, stock prices as an expression of confidence, employee productivity and morale,
market share (without artificial supports)—Roger's leadership had failed. The only aspect of performance that showed
any signs of life was in total revenues, which were at an all-
time high, success enough for Roger to peg executive bonuses
on. "If you can't reward that level of achievement," Roger said,
"then I don't know what." Volume without significant profits,
however, did not impress many. Ralph Nader was yelling that
Roger Smith was bad for General Motors and should be retired. Even some members of the docile board of directors
were privately asking if the best thing Roger could do for
General Motors would be to resign.

In public relations there was a great deal of teeth gnashing
and head scratching to come up with an approach that might

rejuvenate Roger's, and the corporation's, credibility. In a memo to Roger, I suggested a new theme—an admission that these were dark days, but with so many accomplishments behind us, there were better days ahead. Every one of the public relations managers was opposed to the idea. GM did not admit to lows. And they were particularly opposed to my suggestion that the theme be carried in Roger's annual Christmas message to all employees. Roger, however, liked the idea. He gave both thought and attention to the script and obviously practiced the delivery. Roger came to the podium for his Christmas address, looking tired yet as determined as ever:

> For thousands and thousands of years—long before Christianity—gatherings like this took place at this time of year. Families, tribes, and communities came together when days were short and the prolonged darkness made hearts heavy. They came together to reassure themselves that no matter how dark and cold it seemed, the light and warmth would return to life's wondrous cycle. Today, Christmas and Hanukkah continue these ancient festivals of light . . . of hope . . . of renewal. It is a time to banish cynicism—to stop dwelling on the darkest hours—to regain the childlike wonder in the renewal of life.
>
> Here at General Motors, we are going through an unprecedented era of renewal. The darkest days *are* behind us . . . and the light *is* staying longer with each succeeding day. We can take heart in the warmth that is coming. We can be reassured that the seeds we have planted—the seeds that seem to sleep beneath a blanket of snow—soon will break through the surface and blossom for all of us.
>
> You've all seen the headlines that say General Motors is closing plants, laying off thousands of people. What the headlines overlook is that these closings are linked to plant modernizations and new plant construction. This modernization effort is making GM more efficient, more competitive, and, therefore, more capable of serving those people who are our customers and saving jobs for those people who are our employees.

It was time to add up and present the accomplishments, to

count our blessings. (One hourly employee said, "Counting blessings is OK for Roger Smith, but I'm no good at fractions.") Despite the blatant failures, GM had made progress in some areas since 1981. And Roger certainly deserved some credit for a high measure of risk taking. He approved numerous projects that he had little or no faith or interest in. The competitive challenge was immense, yet the solutions were nebulous. Roger approved a bewildering assortment of experimental efforts, some of which were beginning to hold out genuine promise or at least to give some indication of where the organization should be aiming. As three Harvard professors said in their book, *Changing Alliances*, "General Motors is making a big effort . . . and substantial progress . . . in defining how it is to compete as the world's largest automaker."

At this low point in Roger's chairmanship—and before we see how he reacted to the investors' full-scale revolt after Ross Perot left town—it is best to pause and review the record. It was certainly true by the end of 1986 that more of Roger's 21st-century corporation strategies were in place than were left to achieve.

Transition to front-wheel drive was behind them. The vast majority of GM's passenger cars were now being built with the more space- and fuel-efficient transverse-mounted engines, trans-axles, and integral frame and body construction. GM, in fact, now produced more front-wheel-drive cars than any other manufacturer.

A major acquisitions program to diversify into electronics and bring in the talent Roger felt was needed for high-tech products was largely behind GM. The list of projects and acquisitions was long, including equity investments in a half-dozen machine intelligence companies, Hughes Aircraft, Lotus, and the ill-fated EDS acquisition. Saturn initial investment was behind GM. Roger was making it clear that the shopping list was complete—no additional "lulus" would be forthcoming.

Reorganization was largely behind GM, at least in the car and truck groups. (Component divisions were still being moved around in the boxes.) While there was some question lingering about the value of the massive effort, the fact that it was over and most of the new operations were beginning to settle in was indeed a plus.

GM component divisions, a longtime drain on cost competitiveness, were finally being addressed under Roger's leadership. GM's component divisions also went through a minor reorganization, but, even more important, they endured a major period of competitive evaluation. Component operations are on the periphery of the GM world and were traditionally ignored and left to do their own thing. They were—and still are—the last vestiges of decentralization where semiautonomous divisions are run under the Sloan tenets. In all, there are 13 divisions with sales of more than $31 billion. This does not include Delco Electronics, now part of the Hughes-Delco-EDS group. But it does include a host of three-quarter-century-old GM division names such as Fisher Guide, Inland, Rochester Products, New Departure Hyatt, Packard Electric, AC Spark Plug, Harrison, and more. GM's component divisions actually employ more people than Ford and Chrysler combined.

GM was the most vertically integrated of all the car companies, with a full 70 percent of its parts made inside the corporation. Ford, in contrast, made about half of its parts and Chrysler about 30 percent. GM's vertical integration was once its greatest strength. It could make profits off a larger portion of the overall car and retain greater control of costs, quality, and delivery than by working with independent outside suppliers. But as world competition grew, vertical integration went from a tremendous strength to a major liability.

With the vast majority of Roger's capital improvement funds going to assembly and stamping plants, the component plants did not share in his high-tech renaissance. While many of these divisions were operating at a loss, little attention was paid to them until 1985. Lloyd Reuss (pronounced "Royce" like the car) was the new head of Chevrolet-Pontiac-Canada Group, and he wanted to do things in new ways. Reuss, a bantam-weight clotheshorse who was always campaigning for the next job up, decided that it was not cost-effective to use GM parts in the next generation of C-P-C vehicles. His engineers ordered competitive bidding with outside suppliers—

nothing new in GM. But Reuss went further, deciding that the vast majority of the parts should come from low-cost, high-quality outsiders. Don Atwood, then overseeing the components divisions, felt that GM's internal resources—both parts and division technical people—should be used. "We've got too large an investment in the component operations to ignore them," Atwood said. "Components are 40 percent of our costs; they have got to be 40 percent of any competitive solution." Atwood and Reuss were at each other for months over the use of component divisions. Roger decided to stay aloof from the hassle, leaving it up to President Jim McDonald to resolve the conflict with an executive fiat. Jim, however, did not feel he had a clear enough picture of each component's competitive position to make the decision. Jim also believed in decentralization and the division's right to choose its parts from the best possible source. The tension became so great that Don Atwood went away for the weekend in a huff, saying that he wasn't going to rehearse his remarks for the '86 Management Conference on the following Monday. Don, a team player at heart, changed his mind on Sunday night, and with an all-night script rewrite and slide production effort, we were prepared for the big show.

To get a handle on just how competitive the component operations actually were, outside consultants were called in to run competitive analyses of each GM part and component compared to both domestic and foreign competitors. The result was what many called the "traffic-light strategy." Components designated as green were world class in cost and quality and would be kept. Yellow components were marginal and could be brought up to green with some work and investment. Red components—about 13 percent of the total—were found not to be cost competitive and plant facilities would be either sold or phased out to buy the same products outside GM. The money saved from eliminating red components could thus be invested into bringing the yellow components up to all-go green.

Many competitive success stories came out of the component division challenge. In plants where work and jobs were threatened, managers joined forces with the union members to find ways to survive. Employees agreed to eliminate job classifications that were limiting flexibility. Some plants wrote new agreements eliminating many of their own benefits. They worked with design engineers to modify parts for ease of manufacture. The unions even pointed out where some jobs were not needed and how to make others more efficient.

"Our labor rates were three times as high as our competitors' in the wiring harness business," says Elmer Reese, Packard Electric general manager. "We developed a number of strategies with the union's full involvement." One of the strategies was a unique, multitiered wage agreement. Under the agreement, newly hired employees receive 55 percent of regular union wages and benefits. They receive modest increases for 10 years until parity with senior workers is reached. And with the union's full participation, Packard outsourced much of its labor-intensive assembly work to facilities in Mexico. The result is that Packard's blended wage rates today average $10 an hour. "Packard Electric is still in the wiring business," Reese said, "and over twelve thousand Americans still have jobs."

GM's Mexican strategy, what I like to call its "Emanuel" labor policy, had grown dramatically. Under Roger's chairmanship, GM had become the largest single private employer in Mexico. Plants operated in Reynosa, Matamoros, and Juarez, with a full-scale car assembly in Ramos Arizpe. There were 35,000 GM employees in Mexico by the spring of 1987, and Roger announced that GM would double that number and build midsize Chevrolet Celebrities, Buick Centuries, and Olds Cutlass Cieras to ship back into the United States. Outsourcing to Mexico became overwhelmingly attractive when pesos were devalued in 1982, giving employers a 50 percent break over the already low wage structure. The average GM worker in Mexico makes about $1.22 an hour—benefits included. That's about $20 an hour below their UAW counterparts. Outsourcing, obviously, is a major bone of contention with the UAW. "GM hasn't tried hard enough to be competitive here," Ephlin says. "Outsourcing to Mexico amounts to exploitation." As long as Roger's Emanuel labor policy restricted itself to farming out tedious handwork to save the more sophisticated work for U.S. workers, there was not a great deal of opposition. But when Roger announced full-scale car production south of the border, it was clear the strategy had taken a more disconcerting turn.

The component divisions have had a number of advantages in making some dramatic turnarounds. Having been left out of the high-tech quest, most are not burdened by horrendous fixed costs. As employees of free-standing businesses, the workers have a far clearer understanding of the relationship between their work and product successes. "Everything they make can be purchased elsewhere," Jim McDonald frequently reminded them, "so none of them have a right to exist unless they are world class in cost and quality." As GM vice president John Debbink, head of Power Products components group, says, borrowing from Samuel Johnson, "The certainty of being hanged two weeks hence does wonders to concentrate the mind."

There were some tragedies in the component group as well. The trim plant in Elyria, Ohio, for example, was deemed non-cost competitive. Roger decided to sell it in a sweetheart deal in which the new owners would be guaranteed the same levels of GM trim business. In other words, just get rid of the high-cost UAW rates for us, and we'll cut you in on the operation. The union leaders at Elyria balked at first; their quality ratings were high, and they did not feel that they should receive less income than the GM assembly plant down the road. Then realizing that their economic future was at stake, the Elyria workers offered major concessions to improve productivity. But the decision had been made; Elyria would be sold.

Of all the one-time expenses that were behind GM, the largest was assembly and stamping plant modernizations. With $42 billion invested, high-tech manufacturing in GM was reality in 79 percent of all assembly plants. And that figure approaches 100 percent with the yet unpublicized closings of additional plants by 1991.

It's interesting to note that there had been so much modernization, so rapidly, that remarkably few people were able even to maintain the scorecard. In 1986, for example, the

annual report had one set of numbers on plant modernizations, the Public Relations Department and speech writing
were using a different set, and Government Relations had yet a
third conflicting set of numbers. It was so confusing that I
finally went to Jim McDonald and asked him to define what
had been changed. That no one below the president of the
corporation knew the scope of the modernizations is a testa-
ment to the size, and confusion, of the overall effort.

In all, 40 GM plants had been built or received extensive
modernization since Roger took command five years earlier.
There were eight all-new assembly plants—Fort Wayne, Indiana; Orion and Hamtramck, Michigan; Wentzville, Missouri;
Shreveport, Louisiana; Bowling Green, Kentucky; and Moraine
and Fairfax, Ohio. The 19 modernized assembly plants
stretched from Tarrytown, New York, to Oklahoma City, and
from Janesville, Texas, to Oshawa, Canada. While three stamping plants got the largest chunks of high-tech equipment
(Mansfield, Marion, and Parma, all in Ohio), virtually every
GM stamping facility was updated.

Roger had announced the closing of 11 plants that had not
been modernized, which left only 6 low-tech assembly plants
in GM's North American operation. They are plants in Van
Nuys, California; Arlington, Texas; Lakewood, Georgia; Lordstown Van, Warren, Ohio; Scarborough Van, Ontario, Canada;
and Flint Line #2, in Michigan. These are the plants most likely
to be closed in the event of any downturn in the economy or
further erosion of GM's market share. It is worth noting that
all of them have had aggressive local unions. In deciding
where to invest for plant modernization, GM makes it clear
that the monies will go to the plants with the fewest union
problems.

That the initial cost of modernization was behind GM was
good news. "These are one-time costs that will not be repeated." Roger says. Then he contradicts this by adding: "We
are learning so much at Saginaw [the peopleless factory of the
future] that we're going to have to tear up even the new plants
like Orion to get the advantage of the new technologies. You
ought to see it; it's really something."

Roger was sticking to hardware, yet the corporation was

learning about the humanware side of the manufacturing equation at a phenomenal rate. This, I believe, is the unsung achievement of this tumultuous era, that the children learned more than their corporate parent. If Roger was stuck on high technology, an ever-increasing majority of his managers and engineers were learning—from painful example—that even an average employee, if trained and committed, was more cost-effective than an entire army of mechanical men.

They were learning from another one of Roger's unorthodox joint ventures, NUMMI (New United Motors Manufacturing Inc), the 50-50 car-making project with Toyota in Fremont, California. NUMMI was, at once, an embarrassment for Roger and the greatest single "deal" of his chairmanship.

The joint venture cost GM $20 million plus an old, closed-down plant. For that $20 million, GM got a plant that turned out 940 cars for Chevrolet a day with the lowest costs and highest quality in the corporation and with the most involved and satisfied work force. Absenteeism—a billion-dollar-a-year performance problem in GM—was only 2 to 3 percent at NUMMI, a fraction of the absences at the vast majority of GM plants. NUMMI produces 25 percent more cars per hour than GM has been able to do, with one-third the floor space. Toyota was able to achieve—with low technology—what Roger had not been able to do in a single plant despite a $42 billion investment in five years. That was embarrassing. Roger does not volunteer comments about NUMMI and is less than animated when he refers to its achievements. He saves his raves for high-tech plants and, of course, for his Saginaw "factory of the future."

NUMMI was set up as the ultimate test of whether the Japanese emphasis on people could actually work with American union employees. The old Fremont Plant, closed in 1981, was the worst-case scenario. Fistfights on the assembly line were common. Absenteeism was at 20 percent, on-the-job drunkenness was commonplace, sabotage was common, and the union had more than eight hundred unresolved grievances (written complaints against management) pending when the gates finally closed. Tony DeJesus, a UAW leader at the plant, said that the management-worker relationship had boiled down to "constant preparation and training as to how to fight with each other." If Japanese management could work here, it could work anywhere. Yet neither side was confident going in. After a full two years Roger said, "The jury is still out on NUMMI." Kan Higashi, Toyota's NUMMI president, said: "In Japan, we had really strong rumors about the UAW, that they were very confrontational."

Today, the Fremont UAW workers have a motto: "Nothing but the best." If you stop one of the employees on the assembly line, you are more than likely to get a self-righteous lecture on quality. Drop a piece of paper on the spotless floor, and the next person to come along will quickly scoop it up. Get anywhere near a car going down the line, and the visitor will get yelled at to put on a shop coat, as your belt buckle could inadvertently scratch the paint. Yet these are the very same people—in fact, many who were considered the worst—from the rebellious GM days.

"Trust is most important," Higashi says. "It has to start with the management. You cannot expect people to trust you while you are doing nothing for people. You have to give first."

Respect begins by giving each individual the dignity of being an equal in importance to the common task. Or, to put it in Ross Perot's words, "You've got to get rid of all the things that separate people." At NUMMI, there are no assigned parking spaces, no executive dining rooms, and not even a separate area in the cafeteria for managers. There are only four levels of management, yet they are hard to pick out, as everyone dresses much alike. There are no demeaning time clocks. Pride and peer pressure keep everyone on time. When you come in, your arrival time is marked on the big board for all to see. If the plant manager is five minutes late, everyone knows it all day long. Yet no one would point it out; that would be too critical. Just knowing that everyone knows is enough. "The individual must set his own standards," Higashi says, with the understanding that those standards will be drawn from the identity of being part of the group.

UAW president Owen Bieber said in touring the plant, "I was most struck that there is hardly any management here at all." In NUMMI jargon, "There are no managers, no supervisors, only team members." Everyone in the plant, from assemblers to senior managers, works in small four- to seven-member teams. The team leaders, some 250 of them who are chosen out of the ranks, were sent to Japan for several weeks to learn their tasks. They, however, are not supervisors in the sense that they tell others what to do. Each team leader must know the tasks of every team member, and he must act more as an older brother to pass along knowledge. All decisions are made by the total team, with the leader acting as facilitator in a democratic process. Ideas on how to do each job better are discussed by the team, and if they agree, then the idea is submitted for management approval—also decided by teams of workers and managers together. The teams have the real power. And yes, any team member can pull the cord and stop the assembly line at the first sign of a problem or flaw in the product. The team is a basic "family unit" with personal identity, pride, and internal pressure not to disappoint others.

One thing that most impressed me, and many others who have worked with the Japanese, is that they see the entire process—from mining the raw material to servicing the car 10 years later, as a flow. Just-in-time, or *Kanban*, is part of this concept.

Pieces are built when needed and delivered only at the precise moment when they are required in the assembly process. In GM plants, just-in-time has been largely misrepresented as a no-inventory delivery system, but it is more than that in the Japanese approach; it is part of a continuous flow, an artistic motion that one strives to achieve. Every motion should be flowing and natural, like a ballet. If a worker has to bend awkwardly to do his job, then the symmetry of his motion is disturbed, and he will tire. A 50,000-pound machine must be moved three inches in order to facilitate the individual's body motions. "One should never have to fight the car to build it," the NUMMI trainer explains. "If you must hold nine bolts in one hand and fumble with an air wrench in the other, that is clumsy and wasteful." One understands that the sin of awkwardness, of assembly in fits of effort, is as much aesthetic fault as it is a flaw in the quest for efficiency. The entire system is pure oriental poetry that emphasizes the beauty of the process of life, the grace of 10,000 stalks of rice bending in unison in the winds.

In one respect, this emphasis on consistency is a return to the early days of the auto industry when Henry Ford insisted on keeping cars identical so as not to disrupt the production flow. That was when he said, "You can have any color car you want, as long as it is black." The Toyota system is not quite that simplistic, but it is close. Only one model vehicle comes down the line, and no more than 10 percent variation in orders is allowed per week. Most features that are considered extra-cost options are included in the basic car to keep manufacturing consistent. Options are built in batches. The idea is that, if cars come down the line with random option orders, the system is made awkward. One car has more options and is difficult to build. The next has fewer and changes the pace. The next is more difficult again.

A process is not designed under this system with a machine in mind. Just the opposite, a human being first must master the process and define the motion, and only then can a machine be considered to imitate the more rudimentary tasks. Robots are not preferred over people. Toyota, for example, does not use robots to paint cars. The advanced paint technology is present, including positive-pressure booths to seal out dirt, and water flowing under floors to absorb dust, but a human does the actual painting. Toyota feels that robots remove the personal concern for the task. They cannot, for example, react to a nearly imperceptible piece of lint on the body or a fine scratch from the grinding wheel. While some high-tech machines are employed in preliminary stages, individuals are much preferred for the more important tasks.

NUMMI appeared to be a loser at first. It seemed to be having an extremely difficult time working out relationships with suppliers. It would reject an entire order if a single part was found to vary from the defined standard. It did not set a Job One production date, then swing into full production in a month in traditional American fashion. Instead, it followed a slow process of refinement. The first shift did not reach full production for nearly a year, and Toyota refused to put on a second shift until the first was turning out perfect products.

Yet with each car that actually was shipped, GM engineers gained more respect. The vehicles were near perfection, required virtually no dealer preps and repairs, and warranty costs on these cars were less than a third of GM's average $350 per vehicle. Once convinced, GM managers began clamoring for the opportunity to put their engineers into the NUMMI plant to learn the system. More than twenty-five hundred GM people spent time in the plant, then fanned out through the corporation to preach the new doctrine.

Yet there was a very real question of what they had learned. Individual techniques, like just-in-time, were seized and duplicated in home plants with only modest results. Team decision making became a GM fad that backfired when managers continued to dominate the decisions and dictate what problems the teams should address. In watching all of this, Higashi told a *Wall Street Journal* reporter that he was "afraid that the GM upper management doesn't understand the basic concept."

The basic concept Roger was missing was that all of the parts of the Japanese system were based on an assumption alien to the GM culture. The assumption was that people—not productivity, not even profitability—are what business is all about. Toyota, and the most successful Japanese companies, commit to lifetime employment. This means that the individual is not a commodity, but a permanent asset. Toyota does not hesitate to invest great amounts in training—the average worker at NUMMI, for example, received six hundred hours of training before the plant started up. NUMMI thought nothing of sending an assembly line worker halfway around the globe for a three-week training course in NUMMI's sister plant in Toyota City. And when sales slumped in 1986 for small cars, and NUMMI needed fewer people, they used the slow time not to lay off workers, but to send them to more schools, to gain more skills. As Peter Drucker explains in *Managing in Turbulent Times*, in their system "the right of the employee to his job takes precedence over everything and everybody else." This is a far different concept of management responsibility, which can be seen from the fact that the Japanese auto companies and their suppliers own equity in one another and commit the well-being of one to the entire group. "The holder of such shares," Drucker says, "is not a bit interested in the dividend; he is concerned with the orders for steel he receives from the auto manufacturer." In other words, he invests in order to create and maintain jobs. That's a long way from Roger's transferring ten thousand computer people out of GM to reduce costs, or from his Emanuel labor strategy to eliminate expensive American workers. The basic assumption—the worker's trust that management has his well-being in mind—is missing, and without that, the full benefits of NUMMI remain out of reach.

Yet much was learned from NUMMI. More than twenty-five thousand GM managers and engineers spent time learning there. Those who carried the NUMMI gospel spread a degree of respect for the individual and recognition of the tangible benefits of cooperation. And with even partial emulation, improvements were appearing. The GM25 Project, for example, benefited from the lessons of NUMMI.

GM25 was the code name of the Chevrolet Corsica/Beretta car project. Corsica, a four-door family car, and Beretta, a sporty two-door, had distinctive outer skins yet identical drive trains. They were designed to be a Chevrolet exclusive, to help that division regain some of the market share it lost when GM decided to clone its models in all other divisions. The Corsica and Beretta were actually the first cars to appear that were begun and delivered under Roger's leadership. Coming to market at a time when Roger's image was low, they were centerpieces for his new table.

Corsica/Beretta was a $1.8 billion car project—the largest in the history of the industry. The plants that produced them would be high-tech. Linden, New Jersey, and Wilmington, Delaware—the two plants involved—each got 275 computer-controlled robots to do painting, welding, and material handling chores. Both got the most advanced automated guidance vehicles (AGVs) in their body shops, and Linden could boast of having the first machine vision system in the corporation that did its job in a full-production environment. The vision system, located at the end of the weld line, had 90 optical sensors (cameras), and inspected 150 welds in 30 seconds. Roger could point with pride at the high technology. Yet the technology was not as extensive as originally planned. "We looked at the technology as it was being used in other plants," says Linden plant manager Dale Snyder. "We said 'no' to a lot of the stuff that was available."

Corsica and Beretta's greatest accomplishments were more in the NUMMI human areas than in gadgetry and smart technology. It was the first beginning-to-end example of synchronous manufacturing (also called *parallel* or *simultaneous engineering*), in which all of the specialties were brought together in the earliest stages—design and manufacturing engineers, suppliers, machine manufacturers, purchasing, marketing, and finance. This team approach replaced the traditional sequential process of the design engineer doing his thing, then sliding the blueprints under the door to the manufacturing engineer, who handed them off eventually to plant management. While still on the engineering and management level, it was a major step toward broadening participation.

Much was done to assure unprecedented cooperation. A single manager, for example, was placed in charge of all four of the plants that would have a hand in producing the Corsica/ Beretta—assembly plants in Linden, New Jersey, and Wilmington, Delaware, and stamping plants in Parma and Marion, Ohio. The Tonawanda, New York, engine plant, which produced the motors for the new car, was also plugged into the direct link (Tonawanda, incidentally, got $34 million for new diagnostic equipment for the project). Narrowing the span of control prevented much of the traditional plant rivalries and communications glitches.

Corsica/Beretta took a direct lesson from NUMMI. They learned that a slow, more methodical development process would mean a higher-quality car. So they did not rush into production as every new GM product had in the past. Instead of building a few handmade prototypes for testing, they built 17,000 preproduction Corsicas and Berettas. Plant employees were given some of these cars to take home and evaluate. Thousands more went to rental and leasing companies to get some hard-use feedback. A few Chevrolet dealers received preproduction cars, and the GM executive ranks got a number of them for the vehicle evaluation program (I was given a

Corsica to use for three months). In this way hundreds of thousands of actual miles of experience were gained, and discrepancies discovered and fixed, before production. Surprisingly enough, all of this did not stop engineering flaws from reaching the public. The Corsica, for example, had a design problem with the ignition-steering column lock mechanism. In some cases the key would not start the car unless you first jiggled the steering wheel. Instead of fixing the problem, GM attached instructions to the sun visors of the first Corsicas on how to shake the wheel. Some users, myself included, did not think to read the sun visor before attempting to start the car and were subsequently stranded. Yet even with a few errors sliding through, the Corsica and Beretta were considered to have the smoothest manufacturing start-up period in GM corporate history.

Nor were the new plants forced to rush into production before the manufacturing facilities had the bugs worked out. A gradual start-up, as at NUMMI, was allowed. A year into production, neither plant had reached its full production targets. Linden, for example, was at 800 cars a day, considerably short of its 960-unit quota. Gradual start-up produced far higher-quality cars than the old way, and it allowed many of the technology problems to be addressed, thus avoiding much of the embarrassment experienced at Orion and Hamtramck in 1985.

A lot more attention was paid to training employees on new technologies and encouraging their personal involvement. Yet this fell short of the total team approach practiced at NUMMI. Dale Snyder, Linden's plant manager, is one of the bright new fast-trackers who is thoroughly convinced that the NUMMI way works. He's a people-oriented leader who draws waves of respect from men and women on the line as he walks through and has union stewards stopping to pat him on the back as if he were a voting member. "We're beginning to build a relationship with Quality of Worklife Groups [precursor to teams]," Snyder says. "You have to understand that this union has been considered militant in the past and has never ratified a national contract. We have a way to go before teams will be functioning here."

Linden requires 29 employee-hours to build a new car. That's an improvement over the 40 employee-hours it takes elsewhere, yet it falls far short of NUMMI's 23-hours-per-car mark. The difference is even more dramatic when you realize that NUMMI's hours-per-car figures include building the car body on the premises. Linden does not. Using pieces of NUMMI such as just-in-time and buttons for workers to stop the line has not achieved the same levels of productivity or quality as a total team approach. Jim Peters, who has been manager of 10 different GM plants, worked at NUMMI. He explained that "there is no one thing at NUMMI. It is the way the total system works."

And Linden is burdened by the fixed costs of the high technology it has. The robots and manufacturing computers are not reducing the work force and labor costs as much as teamwork alone can. These costs, however, have to show up somewhere; in this case, in the price of the cars. The Corsica sold for $8,995 and the Beretta for $9,555. This gives these two small cars as much as a $750 price disadvantage against Ford's Tempo and Chrysler's Plymouth Reliant, their closest market rivals. Corsica and Beretta were well-designed and well-manufactured cars, but in a market crowded with competitors the price differential was against them. Several months into the new-car launch and a rather extravagant $14 million promotion effort that included giving away 500 cars, the Corsicas and Berettas were gathering dust in dealer showrooms. Roger was forced to offer a $500 rebate to offset their price disadvantage. But more than a year into production, the Corsica and Beretta were not able to achieve their 500,000 sales target, and many analysts believe it is doubtful that the cars will justify their $1.8 billion project price tag. While the Corsica and Beretta were new products that Roger could justifiably brag about, they also contained a lesson in technology versus total team systems, a lesson not lost on the rapidly learning GM middle managers and engineers.

Saturn Corporation is the best example of how the organization was learning in ways that drew it away from Roger's high-tech vision. Saturn Corporation started as a high-tech concept. The name itself came not from the planet but from the aggressive NASA rocket program to put a man on the moon. That seemed appropriate, for in the 1960s the Russians were well ahead of us in space technology. Saturn was just such a come-from-behind and succeed-through-technology program. It was Roger's commitment to beat the Japanese in the entry-level economy car field, which the American automakers had lost so ignobly.

Saturn would be a blank sheet on which GM's best engineers and managers would write the future. It started with three fundamental rules. First, Saturn was to go all the way—employ the most advanced technologies that could be found anywhere in the world. Second, Saturn was to be entirely new. There would be no carryover parts from other cars. Except for a few nuts and bolts and bearings, every part of the Saturn car would be completely new. Nor would any existing machinery or processes be employed or old buildings used. This would be a company that was new in every way, one that used the most advanced concepts to rethink and reinvent every aspect of the automobile. Third, it would be entirely American. Not a single foreign part would be incorporated into the car; not a single foreign worker engaged in manufacturing it. Here was Roger's ultimate experience.

"I really think that Saturn is going to have a big impact not only on the auto industry," Roger said, "but also on a lot of industries, where people are going to sit down and say, 'Hey, maybe what we need to do is start with a clean sheet of paper and see if this is really the way to make a vacuum cleaner. We've been doing it this way; let's get 10 of our engineers and send them off for a year and say, OK, you want to get the dirt off the rug—how do you do it?' "

Roger, however, didn't take a few engineers. He committed 350 of GM's best to Saturn—more than in any car program in history. He gave them a $5 billion promissory note and set them up in a totally separate company—a wholly owned subsidiary. "We wanted Saturn to have the same freedom and entrepreneurial spirit that we had with EDS and Hughes," Roger explained. And, of course, in a subsidiary he would not have to grant the workers the same wages and benefits that the GM employees received. Since there were numerous restrictions in setting up new GM dealerships, Saturn would also allow all-new contracts with new dealers. Saturn dealerships were to be completely separate and distinct. Saturn was to be a "no year" project, meaning that it would come on line when—and only when—everything was in place. But Roger immediately contradicted this in saying, "I intend to drive the first Saturn off the line long before I retire in 1990." In short, the company was to be literally a blank sheet.

Yet Roger began writing his own scenario on the Saturn *tabula rasa* from the very beginning. He drew a picture of Saturn as ultra-high-tech. The buyer would sit down with the salesman at a computer terminal. He would say, "I don't smoke and don't want others smoking in my car," so the salesman would punch in "no ashtrays." He'd say, "I like the car to feel firm in curves and yet give a soft ride on the open highway." The salesman would punch in a tailor-made suspension system. "I live in Florida and have sensitive eyes," he'd say, and the salesman would order up a special tinted windshield. The salesman would show the prospect a wide range of interior and exterior colors on the display screen to select from. While all of this was going on, the computer would be checking the buyer's credit and ordering him insurance on the vehicle. When he pressed the "execute" key, every one of the fifteen thousand parts that would go into his car would be automatically ordered from the right suppliers and computer-directed to arrive at the factory at precisely the right time for assembly. A robot would meet the shipments at the dock and deliver them to the high-tech assembly line. Highly flexible automation meant that a wide range of cars, with an infinite number of personal choice variations, would move down the same line. A four-door station wagon with plastic seats and manual windows would be followed by a two-door coupe with a posh interior, big engine, and all-electric comfort items. Robot quality inspectors would make sure there could never be a defect moving forward through the plant. All of this would be accomplished—from buyer's first choice to delivery—in just two weeks (it now takes six), without a single piece of paper changing hands along the way. Orders, supplier invoices, billings, and even the monthly payments would be handled electronically. This entire scenario was pieced together from a wide range of interviews and speeches where Roger spoke at length about his out-of-this-world project.

When Roger wrote his Saturn vision on the minds of anyone who would listen, he would emphasize that it fit into a far grander American technological revolution. "Electronics is going to change the way every one of us lives," Roger would say. "We've been playing the kid games with the VCRs and little computers that just isn't even a scratch on the surface."

"Of all our many forward product programs, I consider Saturn to be our most important," Roger said in 1984, "because in the long run it will have the most impact on our corporation. The principles of Saturn will be applied across product and divisional lines. In time, we'll 'Saturnize' all GM vehicles— small and large. That means we'll eventually be producing all our products more efficiently, more effectively."

When President Ronald Reagan visited GM's Tech Center in July 1985, Roger took him by the arm and talked him through his Saturn concept, and the president was "Saturnized."

"I was going to come here and suggest—urge—you to be bold," Reagan said, "but I find that you have been bolder than even I was going to suggest. The energy and creativity of your Saturn project confirms my belief that mankind is on the edge of a new era of opportunity and progress—putting technology to work for us—which is what your Saturn project is all about."

Saturn caught the imagination of the American people more than anything else GM could have done. The excitement of high technology was combined with a fighting-back spirit. With very little effort from GM's Public Relations staff, *Saturn* became a household word. Four months after the company was announced, a poll showed that 41 percent of American households recognized the name—higher name recognition than the vice president of the United States usually gets. When Roger announced he was looking for a site for Saturn, a bidding war followed. Thirty state governors visited Detroit to look at the Saturn proposal, and 38 states made proposals. More than a thousand sites were offered, and the data provided on them filled 20 large filing cabinets. Inside and outside of GM, the Saturn crew was wined and dined and celebrated like conquering heroes. Guy Briggs, a Saturn vice president, told me, "We're pulling down the goal posts, popping the champagne corks, having a party in the locker room, *before* we get started on the game."

Once the game of defining the choices got started, it was clear that Saturn was not going the way that Roger had envisioned it. The young, creative staff looked at all of the options. They came up with a number of technical innovations that were shared with GM divisions, such as laser trimming of steel stampings that went to Grand Rapids, numerically controlled metal repairs that went to Parma, and new computer paint applications that went to B-O-C Lansing. But it was more and more clear that a stronger Saturn thrust was in the people management arena. Many of the Saturn engineers had spent time at NUMMI and appreciated what they had seen. And they had involved the UAW as partners in planning from the very inception. In a speech I wrote for Guy Briggs, which became a standard talk for all Saturn executives, the fundamental Saturn approach was summarized. Guy said:

> Let's face it, none of the technology—the robots, the computers, the machine intelligence—none of the processes—none of it is going to make much difference without the right people. It is in the people area that we've been most amiss in the past. The adversarial relationship between management and labor has been the greatest single obstacle between us and consistently high quality. There is a story that epitomizes this conflict—of the union leader and plant manager who had been going at each other for 20 years. Finally, they called a truce. On the first day of the truce they got together for lunch. In fine spirits, the union leader proposed a toast: "Here's wishing you what you're wishing me."
>
> "There you go," the manager said, "starting it again."
>
> Saturn, more than anything else, is an experiment in people management—not in the management of brains and worker brawn, but in total participation, contribution, and commitment of every person involved. Every Saturn employee is going to be a decision maker. Every manager.

Every machine operator. Every skilled tradesperson. Every secretary and maintenance person.

Saturn is based on a single principle—and that principle is that we're all in the same boat; we'd all better row in the same direction. . . . The union is our partner. The UAW is a stakeholder in Saturn and participates in decisions. A UAW advisor is on the Saturn management staff and is part of everything, including the recruitment and selection of our employees. Our Saturn-UAW agreement, which many are calling a model for all industry, is a genuine living document. We're a team, and we're going to work every challenge through with group consensus.

Status is out. It gets in the way of genuine cooperation. Saturn will have no posh offices for executives, no preferential parking or executive dining room. There will be no traditional job descriptions or differentiation between hourly and salaried employees. In fact, Saturn will not have time clocks. Everyone will be paid a salary.

Everyone will work in self-directed teams of from 5 to 15 people. The team will be responsible for 100 percent quality before it goes to the next customer—whether that next customer is the car buyer or the next work team in the process. At Saturn, we will not have a quality director—we'll have six thousand quality directors.

Suppliers may find this surprising. For our work teams are going to do it all—seek resources, keep records, obtain and work with suppliers. Zeroing in and pleasing the decision maker, a traditional game in the supply industry, is going to be different, since every one of our people will be making decisions.

Saturn people are a fixed asset. We're investing heavily in education and training, and we are giving our people every guarantee possible of job security. With genuine job security our employees need no longer fear new technology or process efficiencies. In fact, they can welcome productivity improvements as a means of achieving even greater job security.

We want to build trust—to allow each person to make mistakes. I know that sounds like a contradiction when we are after 100 percent quality, but we believe that the achievement of quality is going to take the creative contribution of every person. Creativity doesn't come when you fear for your job or feel you have to bury your mistakes.

Key to the Saturn approach is participatory management. Just a few of the unorthodox measures include workers deciding on their own production schedules, setting their own rules, visiting suppliers as the GM representative, and having full access to Saturn financial data and GM's computer banks. And there would be other human touches, such as child-care centers on the plant premises, dieticians and legal advisors on staff, and exercise rooms for employees off duty or on breaks.

The Saturn approach would take GM along the lines of NUMMI, and in some respects even further. The Saturn-UAW contract, for example, determined that the worker would receive 80 percent of his earnings in straight-time wages and the other 20 percent from achieving performance goals and profit sharing. And the contract was purposely nonspecific on a wide range of traditional points. The idea was that it would be a living document in which the only thing set in stone was that employees would agree to work together, to find solutions in a democratic manner. Saturn scared the living daylights out of many union leaders, who saw it as another way of manipulating the worker, without giving him any genuine equity in the profits of his labors. They pointed to Roger's profit sharing promises as proof it would never work. Harley Shaikin, M.I.T. business scholar, voiced the overall doubt that GM would ever give its employees any true power. Shaikin says, "Managerial prerogative remains at the core of GM's labor relations strategy."

Saturn was a courageous attempt to regain the critical entry-level market. As Roger said so often, "If you can't build a small car competitively in the U.S., the industry will have trouble building anything." In a very real sense, he was correct. The marketing people tell us that the average person's first car is typically a small economy model. If he or she is satisfied with this first experience, it is likely the customer will stay with the same nameplate for the next, upscale purchase as the family grows and affluence increases. That was the Sloan strategy that built Chevrolet into the largest car division (by sales) in the world (now overtaken by Ford) and fostered lifelong nameplate loyalties. Marketing people warned that, without competing in the entry level, each upscale model would eventually lose its comeback buyers. For Chevrolet at its zenith, that amounted to 70 percent of its business.

Yet Roger gave up the goal. By December of 1986 the decision was made, with Roger's direct involvement, to abandon the goal of building an entry-level car that regained the economy market. Instead, Roger endorsed an upscale concept in cost and luxury, which puts Saturn right in the middle of the pack of cars GM is already producing. It will be little more than a replacement for one or more of the current offerings and will not reduce the number of cars GM is importing from Japan, Korea, and soon from Mexico.

High technology could not easily bridge the advantage the foreign competitors had, so Saturn's high-tech vision was also sacrificed. The Saturn management team suggested that the super high-tech was not going to be feasible by 1990. By all reports of these meetings, Roger was disappointed in these conclusions, but reluctantly agreed to back away from the leading edge. Robot orders were cut extensively; employees would meet the parts at the loading dock. Saturn also sought to reduce overhead by using some existing parts from other car lines and by possibly buying some used machinery from other divisions. Supplier selection has fallen in line with the corporation's norms. And Roger's paperless process will not come true at Saturn, either. In essence, every goal and original tenet was abandoned.

"Our system won't use computers as extensively as we had first thought," says Richard "Skip" LeFauve, the latest Saturn president (there have been three in two years). "It's fair to say Saturn will be less automated than the original concept."

Even the plan for creating all-new Saturn dealerships apart from GM's ten thousand existing ones has been modified; instead, there will be a separate showroom on existing dealership lots, with dealers possibly selling other cars off the same floor. Dealers who rushed in to buy into Saturn franchises are complaining that GM hasn't lived up to the concept's promise. When Roger cut funding of the project in half in late '86 to reduce costs, he also had the winner of the construction site bidding war up in arms. Tennessee won the site selection by providing numerous tax breaks and relocation allowances.

Tennessee governor Ned McWherter announced he would cut the offers in half, including reducing job-training funds from the state by $10 million. And journalists are beginning to compare Saturn to the ill-fated Edsel, the last all-new car line created by a Big Three automaker. One manufacturing executive, recently retired, told me, "Saturn is washed up. It is just another car project now. Roger could save a hell of a lot of money by admitting defeat and canceling it out."

"Saturn is the key to GM's long-term competitiveness and success as a domestic producer," Roger said early on. Today, he makes the same statement, but now about his high-tech Saginaw factory of the future. Of Saturn he says, "It has not been cut back and is still on schedule." Yet I, for one, believe that Roger should have listed Saturn at the top of his accomplishments when he was looking for feathers to display in December 1986. Saturn's Skip LeFauve recently told *Detroit Free Press* auto writer John Spelich how he saw the redirection of Saturn:

"I think it's unfair to say we're not doing what Roger dreamed we would do," Skip said. "Leadership is establishing a vision and encouraging people to get out there and do something. And that's what Roger did for Saturn."

That the "something" that was taking place was a contradiction of Roger's vision was not Skip's point. Roger had stirred innovation in a traditionally staid corporation, and when the innovation did not lead down his own yellow brick road to high technology, he did not force the Saturn deviants back on the straight and narrow path he had defined for the future. The NUMMI and Saturn paths, and variations on this people-oriented theme throughout GM, contradicted Roger's own vision, yet they would leave GM with a far stronger management team than even he realized.

Another major project that had promise for the future was a reduction in the number of models and a clear identity for each car division. The number of models had gotten completely out of hand under Roger's leadership. Part of that was a matter of circumstance. GM had moved faster than its competitors toward smaller, more fuel-efficient front-wheel-drive systems, but the sudden drop in gasoline prices in 1983 and beyond had signaled a return of market demand for big traditional designs. GM was forced to keep old popular models and the new ones, too. They ended up with more than two hundred different models, some of them selling not in the thousands but in the hundreds. Lloyd Reuss pointed out the diminishing returns of model proliferation.

So as the Texas Rambo left, Roger had a defense against his numerous critics. No, he was not the visionary genius they had said he was before, nor had be bungled things as badly as it appeared in December '86. He could point to the great human resources of the corporation and the diversity of paths that had been explored. He had upgraded the corporation's technologies far beyond any other automaker and had allowed (though not participated in) a genuine renaissance in thinking about human relations.

"This isn't the corner drugstore," Roger said. "I don't take your order, then mix the sodas, then run around and make the change. We have a wealth of talent in General Motors."

10
Wooing Wall Street

"If this chairman is not prepared to speak to the owners, then we will get a chairman for GM who is."

Harrison J. Goldin

I'm not running a popularity contest," Roger had said in the past to media assaults, to employees sending pennies in protest, and to managers mumbling against him in the halls. Yet when the one group who could put him out of office finally spoke, Roger's ears perked up like RCA's Nipper pup listening to "His master's voice." He listened, and he did what he was told, dropping his visionary strategic plan like a stolen house slipper.

The shareholders in total, and more specifically the major fund managers and investment analysts, had already shaken Roger with criticism earlier in the year. As Gershon Kekst kept whispering in Roger's ear, the shareholders could use their proxies to push him out, or fund managers could simply boycott GM stock, creating a financial crisis in the company that would serve the same end.

The shareholders asserted themselves after the Ross Perot buyout, but not solely as the consequence of it. Roger had largely ignored the shareholders since his ascension, had canceled the regular stockholder forums held under his predecessor, Tom Murphy, and had minimized input at annual meetings

249

in an era of more, not less, shareholder participation. Because of the numbers of GM shares (319.5 million shares of common stock) and the certainty of dividends for three-quarters of a century, GM shareholders had never expressed themselves. Among portfolio managers, GM stock was treated more like a utility or bond and kept in the rarely touched permanent investment core. Flat GM stock prices and low dividends in the midst of a three-year-long bull market saw GM stock placed on the "hold" or "sell" list by mid-1986. Under Roger's administration, GM stock had gone up less than 50 percent since he took office. At the same time Ford stock had shown an eightfold gain—from $7.62 a share to $57.63—and Chrysler stock had gone from $2.50 a share to $37.75. GM's return on equity was at 10.4 percent, while Ford's was at 25.4 percent. Profit margins dropped during Roger's high-tech quest, from 5 percent in 1983 to 2.9 percent in 1986, while Ford's had risen to 5.4 percent and Chrysler's profit margin was at 6.2 percent. So when shareholders and more formidable portfolio managers rose in response to the Ross Perot buyout, they were expressing much pent-up anxiety over the failure of GM to live up to its investor responsibilities.

The shareholders charged that the buyout was "greenmail" because GM had repurchased Perot's shares at a premium while not making the same offer to all other shareholders. "Give me $62 a share for EDS stock [selling at $25 a share at the time], and I'll go away, too," one stockholder said as he filed suit against the company. Millege A. Hart III, former EDS president, contended that the buyout amounted to the purchase of a corporate directorship, which was against New York state law. He filed suit. Abraham Duman, an Illinois investor, filed suit in Detroit, saying that the buyout was "an enormous waste of corporate assets." Another Illinois investor filed a separate lawsuit in Delaware, claiming it was "a misallocation of resources." The legal actions, however, were of little concern. GM's legal staff had concluded going in that the buyout was not illegal. Under the general category of "business judgment rule," executives and boards have a wide latitude in running their companies. Many of these suits are still pending.

Stockholder resolutions to change GM bylaws, however, were a much more direct slap at Roger's authority. The Wisconsin Investment Board, holding the fourth largest portfolio of GM Class E stock, initiated a resolution that said GM must be prohibited in the future from discriminating against shareholders when buying back stock. Three other investment groups considered cosponsoring the resolution. And a rather eccentric Washington, D.C., investor named Evelyn Y. Davis initiated her own resolution, which would limit stock premium payments in the future to no more than 5 percent above fair-market value. Roger reacted by visiting the Wisconsin Investment Board and explaining his side of the buyout. He resolved to respond to any portfolio management group that wanted an explanation of the buyout. And Roger even called Ms. Davis later and asked her to "please drop the resolution." He was successful with the Wisconsin investors but could not budge the resolute Ms. Davis.

Less than a week after the buyout Harrison J. Goldin gave Roger a call. "I asked Smith if he'd address the Council of Institutional Investors, and he agreed," Goldin said. "I also told him Mr. Perot had agreed to meet with us the same day. Smith gave no indication that he had problems with that."

To understand this situation, you must know who J. Goldin was. He was the comptroller of New York City and was also cochairman and a founder of the Council for Institutional Investors. The council was the most powerful group of investment managers in America. It included 40 pension fund managers who collectively controlled assets of $160 billion—which was 38 percent of all pension assets in America—and had the vote of about 10 percent of all the stock ownership in the country. The companies represented by the council also held six million GM shares and more than a million Class E shares. But, more important, it was led by J. Goldin, who was a crusader on corporate governance and a tough-as-nails investor. Goldin believed pension fund managers had the ability, and social responsibility, to directly influence companies through proxies in ways that help shape and improve the broader social environment. With his New York City pension funds earlier, he had invested in mortgages calculated to increase housing in low-income neighborhoods. He fought proxy battles for corporate health issues and women's rights, used his power to oppose apartheid in South Africa and to force companies in Northern Ireland to end religious discrimination in employment. Here was one of the very few men who had the power, and temperament, to take on a corporation the size of General Motors. To address Goldin and possibly Perot in the same meeting was more than Roger cared to encounter. He decided to send a delegation in his place. The team was comprised of Don Atwood, the articulate head of the new Hughes-Delco-EDS subsidiary; Lester Alberthal, Ross's newly appointed EDS president; Treasurer Leon Krain from the New York office; and, of course, Elmer Johnson, his lawyer and buyout architect. Yet Roger did not bother to inform Goldin that he didn't intend to appear himself.

The council was clearly angered. Many members felt Roger was being deceptive, avoiding the meeting so the group would be unable to come to a conclusion on a stockholder resolution before the deadline. By law, any resolution must be submitted by December 19 in order to be included in the proxy statement for the corporation's May stockholder meeting. Michael Nugent, a member of the council who handles investments for the International Brotherhood of Electrical Workers Pension Fund, said, "He [Roger] gives the impression that he's wandering around, not quite sure of what he's doing, but I'm not so sure." Roger's no-show did look like a tactical maneuver, yet it was actually only a shaken man trying to avoid another devastating confrontation.

J. Goldin was less tentative about Roger's missed appointment. He told me later, "When I learned that Smith wasn't coming, I told Atwood: 'If this chairman is not prepared to meet the owners, then we will get a chairman for GM who is.' Atwood got on the phone to Smith during the first break and said that Smith didn't understand he was expected, but that he'd meet me where and when I requested it. That wasn't as good as meeting with the full council, but it was a start.

"I met with Smith in my office and told him I didn't like the high-handed way he was treating the company's owners," Goldin says. "I told him we were dissatisfied with his company's productivity, market share, products, and everything else. He can't continue to claim deferred results forever.

"A well-run company doesn't have to show quarterly improvements on a regular basis, but when you spend tens of billions of dollars and don't show any improved results, it's time for an accounting. I told him he had to develop a balanced plan and to communicate that plan to his owners. And we [pension fund managers] have the right to decide basic policy questions that are the prerogative of owners. He understood what I was telling him."

When the press asked Roger why he had avoided the initial meeting, he said simply that he had sent "the proper level of management." That didn't go over well with the council members, who felt the CEO was the only proper representative to their group. Finally, in mid-January, Roger met with the full council and then told a reporter:

"There was a misunderstanding. The people we picked to go were *not* the proper level of management, but they were the people who were most closely involved. . . . This is not unusual. For example, with South Africa we get the people in General Motors most familiar with South Africa. We met with Harrison Goldin's people on Ireland—the plant manager from Ireland. We try to get the people who are intimately involved when you're discussing something like that. But when I understood what Harrison was saying, that he wanted me to come to this thing, that's why I came today."

Ross Perot, of course, did not make Roger's explanations of the buyout easy. "I'd like to have a lie detector hooked up to those guys [Roger, Elmer Johnson, et al.] when they are telling that stuff," Ross said. "You'd see the needle go crazy." Ross continued to say that the buyout was "morally wrong," which fanned the flames for shareholder action suits. When the person who receives greenmail openly admits that the action is inappropriate and shameful, that makes it much easier for the lawyers to make a case against the act in court. "I've alerted the stockholders," Ross said, "that if they accept this, then they deserve what they get." Ross offered to meet Roger anywhere for an open debate on the issues. Roger declined, saying, "I have nothing against Ross Perot. I like him and think he is a patriotic and generous American. The issue was corporate governance." Elmer Johnson was playing Roger's hit man during this period, making the tough criticisms of Ross that Roger did not dare utter. "Perot didn't want to realize that he sold his company," Elmer said. "The first time I knew Ross had a conscience was three minutes after he got the money." As for the $7.5 million gag rule, no one brought that up, though both sides were violating the terms. "If it comes to litigation," Ross shrugged, "I'll write them a check."

Roger came to the belated realization, with lots of advice and coaching, that the controversy wasn't going to blow over this time. He made up his mind that this was one battle he'd have to fight himself. Roger disbanded his executive SWAT team and agreed to appear personally before any investment group that wanted him. He even sought out some that had not asked. Roger went on the campaign trail with the investment community, making 22 meetings from coast to coast in less than two months. It was an amazing show of personal will and determination.

The 22 meetings were, to his surprise, centered on GM's overall performance and cost-cutting plans. "Most investors said the Perot thing was over," Roger said. "They didn't want to discuss it." At an internal managers' meeting, Roger said, "I'm absolutely convinced as I go around and talk to the analysts and the other people I see, we'd be right where we are today in our relations with the public had the Perot buyout never occurred. So we can't hang it on that."

In these investor meetings, Roger threw volleys of numbers at the analysts, gave them the specifics on GM's cost-cutting programs and market projections. The analysts and fund managers, however, had sharp pencils of their own. Roger was overwhelmed in these meetings by the thoroughness of their figures and the massive holes in his own projections. One meeting in particular, with the top people at Sanford Bernstein in New York, had Roger coming back to Detroit raving about how right they were and how off-base GM's calculations were. Roger had already decided to have another Executive Management Conference in February and said he wanted to recount the meeting with Sanford Bernstein in minute detail.

When I heard the story of the meeting, I was disturbed that Roger wanted to make it the centerpiece of his presentation. Frankly, it made him look like a rube. That the $2-million-a-year CEO (a finance man himself) heading up the world's largest corporation—with the broadest and best-paid cadre of financial people anywhere—would openly admit that a couple of young analysts in New York had a better handle on GM's costs than he did was astonishing. That night, I actually woke up dreaming of what a fool Roger was going to make of himself before his complete management corps. The next morning I told the head of speech writing that she was going to have to talk Roger out of this. He could make the same points without looking naive. Many others in public relations, and the Gershon Kekst gang, felt the same way. After a number of tactful conversations, which I got back secondhand, Roger was dissuaded from giving the running Sanford Bernstein scenario. In a highly toned-down version, Roger addressed the meetings, saying:

> In our meetings with institutional investors . . . what they are eager to discuss, and insistent upon, is General Motors and its future. Most of these investors that we're seeing right now are big holders of GM stock, and a lot of them have literally bet their reputations and their futures on GM. They are acutely aware of what the so-called auto specialists are saying about GM. And their bosses and their customers are asking them, "Why are you still holding GM stock?" Their questions are sharp. Their questions are incisive. One analyst said GM's costs are out of control, and major restructuring is needed to get the company back in shape. The same analyst [actually from Sanford Bernstein] said, "How could a company with such huge financial resources, well-laid-out and ambitious product and facilities spending programs, and such feeble competitors, mess up so badly?" Another analyst said, "In a reversal that would have been unthinkable five years ago, Chrysler has become the low-cost producer, and GM has become the high-cost producer." And here's another one, and this one really got to me. He said simply, "We recommend the sale of General Motors common stock. In an increasingly competitive automotive marketplace, GM's high-

cost structure has made it particularly vulnerable to a deterioration in its financial and market positions."

Well, in the series of meetings we've had, some institutional investors are frankly telling us that they expect our earnings to drop even more. . . . They say, "Look at your cost structure, your excess capacity, your high breakeven point." They see us, right now, as a highly leveraged, marginal operation, where the loss of a few hundred thousand units either from a lower market or lower market share could drop our earnings significantly.

GM's current capacity, they point out—counting NUMMI, Japanese and Korean imports—is over six million units now. So their simple question is, "What do you do with a one-million-unit excess capacity?" Well, we answer that by telling them about more carefully matching production with sales. And they say, "Yeah, that'll help avoid excess inventories," but they still point out that doesn't address the excess capacity and all the fixed costs that go with it to adversely affect profits. So we tell 'em that we must and will make the necessary adjustments with capital planning to remove these excess costs. And our investors want to know what we're going to do to get back to a lower cost position. And here we have a lot of good things to say. Decreasing capital spending, savings from head-count reductions, plant closings, joint ventures, elimination of noncompetitive operations, and so on. But the investors then say, "Ford and Chrysler are reducing their costs, too, and so are the Japanese, and new lower-cost producers from Korea, Taiwan, and other areas are invading the North American market." And our investors also point out that from the discussions they have with our competition, some of their cost-reduction targets per car are larger than what we're talking about. . . . Our meetings with the investment community have underscored the fact that we have serious problems beyond the cosmetic that we simply have to address. . . .

They're giving us a message out there it just must start to pay off. They're telling us that the time for planting the seeds and cultivating the fields, that's over. They said we gotta start to harvest the crop.

Roger was convinced. Overnight he turned away from his high-tech vision and reverted to a financial man's thinking and

speaking in pure return-on-investment terms. When Roger was first elected chairman, a *Detroit News* reporter said he was "Wall Street's kind of guy." Six years later he was ready to prove it.

For a month after Perot left town there was a scrambling to come up with some good-news items. One such effort was to raise the new-car warranty coverage to six years or 60,000 miles on the power train and six years and 100,000 miles on corrosion protection. That appealed to Roger, since Lee Iacocca had been making hay with commercials on his industry-leading five-year, 50,000-mile warranty. Lee's motto was "We back them better because we build them better." The increased warranty coverage seemed like a good gimmick, mainly because it would cost GM nothing in out-of-pocket money beyond the current coverage for a full three years. By that time, it was hoped, GM's $350-per-car warranty costs might come down. And if they didn't, well, it would be the next chairman's cost item. "It won't cost us much even then," a public relations director who covers warranties explained to me. "There are numerous restrictions on the coverage, and it's limited to the first owner—very few people keep the same car that long." In trying to develop a gee-whiz presentation on the 6-60 coverage, I was told by the legal department that we could not say it was "the most comprehensive coverage in the industry." The Mercedes warranty, for only two years, was comprehensive, while GM's was highly limited. Still, the 6-60 warranty was announced with some fanfare, only to have Chrysler top it the next week with seven-year, 70,000-mile protection. Since Chrysler had far lower costs and was sitting on significant reserves, Roger concluded that an ongoing warranty coverage war would be lost. So the 6-60 did little for Roger's image campaign.

Roger also urged Don Atwood to get some fixed contracts signed with EDS to convince the stockholders that GM was committed to Class E stock profitability. General Motors Acceptance Corporation was the logical signer. GMAC was a financial organization and had been most satisfied with EDS performance with all of its experience in the same genre. A five-year contract for billings was forced through quickly. Roger called the contract a "significant milestone" and said that it "brought the total volume of GM revenues covered by fixed-price contracts to about 15 percent. Eventually, we expect 75 percent of the total GM revenues to EDS to be covered by these fixed-price contracts, and we are well on our way to accomplishing this."

Another fix aimed at impressing the investors was Roger's Stock Buyback Program. Ford and Chrysler had earlier bought back large blocks of outstanding stock, which had the effect, of course, of increasing the value of each outstanding share. Roger announced that GM would spend $5 billion by 1990 buying back as much as 20 percent of GM's common stock. In true Roger Smith hyperbole, it would be "the largest stock buyback ever by a U.S. corporation." The announcement pushed GM stock prices up by nearly $4 on the day the release went out. Yet the more serious investors were not convinced. Ford and Chrysler had accomplished buybacks with surplus profits, but in GM's position it would have to borrow money to get the stock. That would strain GM's already troubled finances and make it even more vulnerable to losses should an economic slowdown occur.

The stock buyback announcement was yet another case of Roger's not considering the psychological impact of the act on the vast majority of his employees. They had recently learned they were not to receive profit sharing, yet the top executives were getting bonuses, Roger had $750 million to buy out Perot, and now he was going to spend another $750 million in 1987 to buy back stock. That would increase the value of GM stock, but who would benefit most? The union members pointed out that Roger's bonus-level executives, who receive massive stock options as part of their benefit package, would be the beneficiaries, not the majority of employees who were in the midst of cost reductions, income cuts, and job eliminations. Once again it was conceived as the selfish act of an insensitive GM elite.

Bonus announcements in January of 1987 hurt Roger's credibility a great deal, especially coming out on the same day that he said GM was prepared to move much of its production overseas if the United Auto Workers were not willing to make cost concessions in the upcoming contract talks that summer. Roger did, however, realize that the bonus announcement was hurting him with the single constituency he was trying to woo. The investment community did not see the bonuses as justified or as proof of cost-cutting sincerity. Roger moved to solve this problem through a new program to eliminate cash bonuses and modify stock incentive plans. "Management's reward will be linked directly to the success of the company's stock," Roger explained (a move that sounded very much like the EDS approach that Roger had so severely criticized in the past). The announcement, however, contained a few loopholes. Over five thousand executives would still receive cash bonuses via the performance achievement plan. Some $60 million was set aside for this cash award plan. And to compensate for the reduction in cash bonuses, key executives would probably get significant pay increases. The new vice president of personnel, Roy Roberts (recently promoted a half-dozen levels at once from plant manager), suggested that Roger, too, would get a raise. "As far as I'm concerned," Roberts said, "you cannot pay Roger Smith too much for the job that he is doing. . . . He is undercompensated."

Cash bonus reduction was not the image enhancer Roger had hoped for. The stock buyback became even more suspect since, with increased stock bonuses, Roger's elite would benefit even more. Fattening the executive performance achievement plan at a time when its salaried counterpart for the rank and file, the merit awards, was being cut, didn't help, nor did the cries about Roger giving himself another raise. But even more relevant, placing a larger emphasis on awards keyed to stock market success put far more emphasis on the short-term, quarterly-return mentality. Roger's thesis had been that there was too much emphasis on quick returns and not nearly enough on corporations investing in their futures. The bonus plan changes contradicted his words and put his executives in the same position that he now found himself in—linking his prosperity, and very survival, to impressing Wall Street.

None of these actions, however, was enough to restore credibility, nor to hide the reality that GM sales continued to fall while inventories crept upward. Gershon Kekst said that something dramatic was needed. GM had to announce a major cost-cutting effort in line with the objectives Roger heard during his 22-stop investor campaign. After much bickering among financial staff, the big statement was created:

"General Motors will reduce costs by $10 billion between now [January of 1987] and 1990."

Here was the kind of dramatic commitment tailored to answering the investment community's tremendous anxieties about a bloated and out-of-control General Motors. Ten billion dollars was a nice round figure that people could remember, and it seemed like a bold new initiative on Roger's part. It was decided that a personal letter would be sent to every stockholder of record giving the specifics of the plan. Gershon Kekst's organization would write the basic letter, then everyone in senior management would review it. Kekst may have had the concepts, but the firm was atrocious in putting together the words. Half the GM speech-writing staff was asked to attempt rewrites. Even Jack McNulty, an outstanding writer in his own right, took a cut at it, then threw up his hands after Kekst changed most of the wording back "to speak in terms shareholders will understand." Clumsy wording prevailed because there simply wasn't time to delay. The letter had to be in the mail in two to three weeks, maximum. There was a sense of urgency here, since the letter had to have its impact well before the May stockholders' meeting, which everyone assumed would be where the first shots might be fired in the anticipated revolt. The letter must disarm the irate investors. The four-page, single-spaced letter tried to explain everything public relations could find that was right with General Motors, in new products, plants, and processes. But the important point was the $10 billion. Forgiving the awkward committee style in the personally signed letter, one section carried the message:

Cost Reduction Program

We have established tough, near-term goals for cost
reduction as well as profit improvement throughout the

Corporation. The impact of implementing our long-term strategies does have a near-term cost. However, we anticipate that our cost improvement plans will take effect quickly and enable us to end 1987 on a positive earnings note.

Cost reductions will be achieved in a number of areas, including the following:

- As a result of efficiency gains made through GM's recent reorganizations and the removal of unnecessary layers of management, GM's worldwide salaried employment will be reduced from its mid-1986 level by 25,000 employees in 1987 and an additional 15,000 employees by the end of 1988. This salaried employment reduction program, being accomplished to the greatest degree possible through attrition and retirements, will result in cost savings of $500 million during 1987, and accelerate to annual savings of $2 billion in 1989 and beyond.
- Also related to improved organizational effectiveness, corporate staff expenses will be reduced each year, resulting in a total annual reduction of $200 million by 1990.
- Divestitures, restructuring and joint ventures recently implemented will improve our profit position beginning in 1987. The most notable divestitures/restructurings are: the sale of General Motors' South African subsidiary, our withdrawal from the European heavy truck business, the planned sale of our North American transit bus operations to Greyhound and the restructuring of GM-Holden's Limited in Australia. The joint ventures between GM and John Deere in diesel engines and between GM and Volvo in heavy-duty trucks will improve GM's profitability in these businesses. We anticipate annual savings of over $200 million starting in 1987 related to these actions.
- As a result of efficiency gains made possible by our new and modernized facilities, we recently announced the closing of 11 assembly and fabricating plants. These closings will result in significant fixed cost reductions. Annual savings will approach $500 million by 1990.
- Going forward, GM's vehicles will be built with the most competitive components and parts. As a result, we are reviewing our current level of vertical integration in order to eliminate uncompetitive component manufacturing

operations. Related cost reductions will total at least $500 million annually by 1990.

In addition to these specific cost reduction plans, GM is committed to annual cost reductions through improved assembly plant efficiencies, more effective supplier relationships, and enhanced product quality and related warranty expense reductions. These and additional ongoing cost reductions, which will be significant, reflect improvements in manufacturing efficiency made possible by our modernized facilities and improved manufacturing processes. In 1986, total annual cost reductions amounted to $2 billion. At every level of the organization—including a large unionized labor force which has gone through an unprecedented retraining program—we are dedicated to making the technology pay off in improved quality and reduced costs. . . .

In 1987, the Corporation anticipates up to $3 billion in further cost reductions. We expect that these cost reductions efforts will accumulate to $10 billion annually by 1990. Based on anticipated market and economic conditions, these cost savings are designed to enhance stockholder value and promote achievement of an after-tax return on stockholder equity of at least 15 percent by 1990. . . .

Roger B. Smith

The $10 billion reduction became the core of a communications blitz to the press and shareholders. It was accompanied by a new promise, summarized in Roger's first-quarter report: "A major element of our strategic redirection is our belief that, in today's competitive environment, maximum profitability may be best achieved at less production capacity than we currently have." In other words, Roger was publicly promising that the corporation was giving up on maintaining its traditional market share. It would make more money by cutting back on production capacities, meaning fewer vehicle sales would be possible in the future.

The $10 billion sounded good, but, like the 11-plant announcement the previous year, there wasn't much in it that could be considered new direction. Some $5.6 billion of the $10 billion improvement, for example, was simply the baseline assumption of improved overall operating performance. It was calculated on a 1.7 percent improvement factor for 1987 and a 1.3 percent improvement each year through 1990. That was a given, without any change in current efforts.

Another $1.6 billion were actions that had been announced as much as a year earlier. They included a billion-dollar savings by eliminating twenty-five thousand salaried employees for *each year* from 1988 onward. Eleven plant closings would start saving money after the cost of layoff awards was amortized in 1989 and beyond. The joint ventures that would save a couple of million more dollars were announced in 1986. C-P-C Group had long since announced a program to cut $1,800 from the cost of each car, and B-O-C committed to $2,200. And the previously announced efforts to do away with unprofitable component plant operations meant another quarter billion dollars of savings already defined.

In essence, $7.2 billion of the impressive $10 billion project was, or should have been to anyone watching, old news (virtually no press picked up on this). The big $10 billion was, in reality, $2.8 billion.

The additional cut, however, was significant. It meant closing three, and possibly five, more assembly plants to save another $100 million in 1990. Another seventeen thousand salaried employees would be cut to get a $400 million savings in 1989. Central Office reductions of $100 million in 1987 and onward were announced. That was a 15 percent budget cut that was so unspecified in the plan that no one could tell me if it included any employment reductions. Another $100 million in '88, $300 million in '89, and $100 million more in '90 would theoretically come from additional cuts in vertical integration—in other words, more outsourcing of parts. And one of the bluest-sky figures of all was $200 million saved beginning in 1988 from warranty cost reductions that had not yet begun to materialize. The newly announced cuts—called by one GM accountant the "Save Roger's Ass Action Plan"—amounted to $2.8 billion. By no means was this a paltry sum for a company that had already committed to cutting down to the marrow, but hardly the startling $10 billion blockbuster it was purported to be.

For the Executive Management Conference in February, Jim McDonald was asked to present the $10 billion package to the executives, since the biggest bits were to be taken out of his operating side. Jim determined to break it down logically into (1) baseline assumptions, (2) previous announcements, and (3) new action plan. The treasurer's office was livid that Jim was showing the strings behind the puppet numbers. And they were even more incensed with the statement in his script that "the $10 billion is conservative. It's doable. In fact, I've got to say that it is the very least you should achieve."

What followed was an attempt at indirect redirection of Jim's speech. I was called in by a number of financial executives to "discuss" the talk. They said Jim was undercutting the impact of the statement, that he shouldn't imply that it was a "piece of cake." Each time I was called in, I told them I'd relate their concerns to the president, which I did. Jim McDonald, however, was a man about to retire, who had built his career on matter-of-fact honesty. He said, "You tell the treasurer's office that if they have a problem to see me. Nobody tells me what to say."

I carried Jim's message back to Bob O'Connell of the treasurer's staff. "You don't understand," O'Connell told me. "This is the way RBS [Roger Smith] wants it."

"Then why doesn't he tell Jim directly?" I asked. After all, they were only a wall apart. O'Connell avoided the question and went on explaining that I had to communicate to McDonald that "cost" and not "quality" was the most important priority for the company now, and Jim had to say that.

Once again, I told Jim what O'Connell and the other financial guys had said, and I added that I was told it came directly from Roger. Jim turned silent for an instant, looked off into space, then looked back at me. "You don't understand what I told you before. *Nobody* tells me what to say."

It's important to understand here that Jim McDonald and Roger are, by their own definitions, personal friends. They belong to the same exclusive hunting lodge in northern Michigan and frequently meet in social and recreational settings. They had lunched together every day they were in The Building. They met each other a dozen times a day in meetings and hall passings. That one friend would not say to the other "What's this crap about . . . ?" is beyond me. As an executive committee member explained to me: "The worst communications in General Motors are on the 14th floor. We just don't communicate or cooperate."

When anyone refers to the 14th floor, of course, they generally mean the executive committee, the so-called "ruling committee of General Motors." While this committee has formal meetings at least once a month, the seven-man team meets informally almost daily. They work no more than a few hundred yards apart and break bread together in the Executive Dining Room on the same floor. In terms of management span of control, the executive committee system looks neat on paper. Each person is the operating executive for a major segment of the total, so a meeting of this small team encompasses the entire senior management of the corporation. Roger chairs the executive committee, followed by the president (F. J. McDonald from 1981 to 1987, R. C. Stempel since mid-1987), who is responsible for the operating side. The president has three men on the executive committee who report to him: the head of North American Passenger Car Operation (now Lloyd Reuss), the head of Truck and Bus and overseas operations combined (an odd combination that Bob Stempel had headed up), and the executive over a hodge-podge of high-tech acquisitions such as Hughes and EDS, combined with the massive component operations (Don Atwood has filled this slot). The executive vice president of finance also sits on the committee (F. Alan Smith), and there is the vice chairman's slot, the most nebulous position of all. At different times in GM history the vice chairman has been an engineering technologist, a finance man, a staff administrator, or simply the guy who ran for the chair and was given the consolation prize (Howard Kehrl got it as a consolation prize, 1981-86, and Don Atwood, the present incumbent, has made it into the high-tech czar's domain). Staff operations—personnel, economics, public relations, etc.—is normally headed up by the vice chairman, but not always. In mid-1987, Roger added his chief lawyer, Elmer Johnson, to the executive committee and gave him all of the staff functions.

The executive committee is supposed to decide in a more-or-less democratic fashion on the broadest policies and directions for the corporation. Yet with the overall lack of communication on the 14th floor, that seldom works. When Roger decided to redirect the corporation to appease Wall Street, he received open opposition from the executive committee. Yet there were four rifts, or factions, in all. There was the traditional operating side, best represented by Jim McDonald, who believed in technology and human relations, a primary commitment to the auto and truck market, and decentralized management. There were the Bill Hoglunds, the totally people-centered managers, who saw high technology as a misdirection. There was a lesser faction, represented by Don Atwood, which was entirely high-tech and believed in strong centralized control. And there was finance, who after a long period of fringe existence, saw themselves in the spotlight with "cost-first" consideration. Roger, by his actions and not his words, was leaning not toward the high-tech, centralized vision of the future, but toward the "cost-first" reality of the immediate situation. Yet there was no substantive communication among these factions; not one of them felt in January of 1987 that they had the inside track or even understood where Roger wanted to go next. Confusion reigned.

There was a second split between virtually all of the manufacturing and engineering side and the financial side on one point—giving up on market share. It was clear the decision had been made by Roger, under direction from the financial analysts and fund managers. Roger's $10 billion action plan, for example, anticipated going from a 44.6 percent market share in '84 to 37 percent in 1990 (by mid-1987, GM was at a 36 percent share). As for the truck share, the most vital and growing market segment, GM's portion was predicted to decline from 34.5 percent in '84 to 32 percent in 1990. Jim McDonald spoke for the car people when he said, "No way can we live with those numbers." And F. Alan Smith represented the opposite view when he told a group of us around a conference table that "those are ambitious expectations." Again, the fundamental question was not whether GM should attempt to maintain a 45 percent or better market share at all costs, but whether there should be communication and consensus among executives and explanation or participation with the employees, when such a major shift in corporate direction is indicated. The direction may not be as important—since there are many roads to success—as the team understanding and commitment to march in the same direction.

Roger would not, of course, acknowledge a split in the ranks, and my own suspicion is that he was largely unaware of the factions. His executives were functioning as a team, as he perceived it, and the Executive Management Conference in February had come off largely the way he had wanted it to. He made it clear to all executives that cost reduction was the only significant game now. "They say that 1987 is the year the Chinese know as 'the Year of the Rabbit,' " Roger said. "Well, for GM executives it's going to be known as 'the Year of the Cost Reduction.' I intend that the largest portion of bonus this year will be allocated solely on measured effective cost reduction, and this is going to apply right across the board to all subsidiaries, all divisions, and all staffs."

At this point, however, Roger felt he was ready to impress the financial community. He had a $10 billion cost-cutting plan, some gee-whiz new technology, and a couple of new products to show. And the annual stockholders' meeting, with the threat therein, was a month away. Kekst suggested that now was the time to put on a dog-and-pony show for the auto security analysts. This powerful cadre of investment analysts was still smarting from last year when Roger had put it through a few hours of dull meetings and had not shared any knowledge it could not have gleaned from the daily papers.

Roger ordered the entire organization to concentrate on ways to impress the analysts. They decided on an extravaganza, a two-day affair of wining, dining, and a full-day tour of the Linden, New Jersey, plant, one of the two new high-tech plants that were building the Corsica and Beretta. Roger ordered every one of the top people to attend. That meant the seven-man executive committee, plus 11 group vice presidents, 16 operational vice presidents, three corporate officers, and a full complement of supporting directors. In all, 46 top GM people would attend, plus another 50 support troops behind the scenes. And there were a few carefully screened hourly employees to present the "cooperation" angle.

To me it appeared to be the most blatant case of oversell I had ever seen. I told Jack McNulty that at a time when our sales were down by 15 percent over last year's less-than-sterling performance and with the Corsica and Beretta not selling anywhere near the launch projections, the analysts would not be impressed by such a big-tent event. After all, earnings are the big news for investors, and GM's for the first three months of 1987 were down to a projected $1.90 from $3.52 a share the previous first quarter. Our story, from a car maker's perspective, didn't look good. We could boast that Roger's diversification efforts were growing, that the combined GMAC, EDS, and GM Hughes Electronics income was up by 55 percent during the first quarter of '87, but vehicle-making business was down an estimated 72 percent. Since the thriving subsidiaries amounted to 10 percent of General Motors, bragging on a healthy tail of a sick dog didn't make much sense. The total company's net income for the first quarter had slipped by 23 percent, and after-tax operating profits, which combined vehicles, EDS, and Hughes, were down 50 percent. It wasn't a pretty story to try to pass off to professional analysts.

Worse, such an all-out show looked to me like an open admission that GM was, indeed, running scared. I fully expected someone to ask "Who is running the store?" in Detroit for the two days. I had a friend in personnel estimate the cost of the two days in salaries alone. It came to about $1 million and some change—not a day at Disneyland, but close. Surely someone in the analyst crowd would calculate the cost and diagnose the paranoia.

Kekst knew his audience better than I. They loved it. Analyst statements after the event were overwhelmingly glowing, and GM stock went up on the New York Stock Exchange by $2.75 the next day, even though the Dow Jones Industrial Average was flat that day. The event started an upward climb of GM stock from $86 a share the day before to $92 a share three weeks later—its highest level in 15 years. Multiply that $6-a-share rise by 319 million shares, and the effort was the biggest profit-making event GM had mustered during Roger's tenure. (And GM benefited handsomely, for it had recently bought back $1.1 million worth of shares of GM common stock under the buyback plan.) But then I should have been able to predict the outcome once I saw the scripts for the analysts' meeting, for Roger and the executives were saying everything the analysts had wanted to hear for three years.

"GM is now in a strong position to provide maximum profitability," Roger told them. "Profitability will be the principal bellwether of our performance. Maximum profitability may be best achieved at less production capacity than we currently have. That simply means a leaner, more productive work force operating in fewer but more modern and flexible manufacturing facilities." And the payoff would begin immediately, he implied: "First-quarter earnings will exceed the consensus of analyst forecasts."

Everything was promise. Capital outlays would drop to an average of less than $6.5 billion compared to the $10 billion a year Roger had been spending for the past couple of years. The stock buyback, Treasurer Leon Krain promised, would come out of '87 cash flow, which he estimated would allow 10 million shares to be repurchased (facilitated largely through a $900 million federal tax refund and a $1 billion dividend that GM would draw out of General Motors Acceptance Corporation). Even GM overseas operations, which had been a financial drain for a decade and lost $550 million in '86, were going to be profitable in '87, Overseas Operations promised. And, Roger assured them, GM was done buying market share with expensive incentive programs. And the biggest promise of all—by 1990 General Motors would be operating on a 15.98 percent return on stockholders' equity.

Roger made it clear that he would be working for the investors in the future. "I intend to give the investment community greater access to key executives," Roger said, "to make more people available to answer your questions and to encourage you to visit as many of our facilities as you'd like."

"I've never seen a large company lay itself open the way this one did," said Donald De Scenza, a Nomura Securities International analyst. "If there was any arrogance, any complacency in GM, it's gone now." Even a more cautious observer like Scott Merlis of Morgan Stanley said, "The worst is over for GM."

Shortly after the analyst blitz, nine judges in Washington, D.C., made even the outside chance of a GM takeover seem more unlikely. The Supreme Court upheld a lower court decision on a tough Indiana state law that all but barred hostile takeover bids. Under that law, a company would have a full 50 days to hold a stockholders' meeting to consider the voting rights on a takeover bid. Most important, the law said that buying 20 percent or more of a company's shares would not give one an equivalent vote unless it was approved by the majority of all nonexecutive shareholders, a nearly impossible task for a company the size of General Motors. Following the Supreme Court decision, many states, including Maryland where GM had been incorporated, immediately began considering duplicate laws. Investors who felt that takeovers were a positive threat against poor corporate management called the decision "the entrenched-management relief program." And the *Wall Street Journal*, after surveying merger professionals, concluded that "hostile bids will become considerably riskier, more expensive, and more mired in lawsuits."

Roger's stockholder blitz—letters, campaign trail, and big-top event—plus the Supreme Court's reassurance that the courts were backing the status quo, placed Roger in a remarkably solid position of control going into the Annual Stockholders' Meeting. It was, however, like the old story of the boy who came home with one *C*-minus and four *F*s on his report card, saying, "That's what I get for putting all my effort on one subject." Roger had thrown everything into impressing the investors, while his other vital constituencies were suffering.

The auto market received little attention. Roger was committing to no major sales incentives, and the few promotional items that were being handed out to the regions were paltry indeed. With modest marketing efforts Ford was up nearly 22 percent in sales for the quarter. Eighty-five-day supplies of many GM car lines were becoming the norm in the dealer network (a 60-day supply is considered healthy). Production cutbacks to reduce inventories were not well planned and were generally too small. GM trimmed 49,000 vehicles from the production schedule, while the auto experts were saying that 100,000 would have been more like it. "As usual," said Ronald Glantz of Montgomery Securities, "GM's eyes are bigger than its stomach."

Morale inside of GM had never been lower, especially among salaried employees who had just been told that Roger had upped the head-count ante by 17,000, which meant that well over 42,000 people—one of every four salaried workers—would be forced out in a two-year period. The idea was to get all of these people to voluntarily take modest buyout payments or early retirement at drastically reduced benefit rates. To resort to a mass layoff meant far too many expensive lawsuits would follow. The "golden handshakes," as these buyouts were called, were not that precious or gripping. On the first and second offers, the vast majority of employees offered buyouts were not extending their hands. A lot of gimmicks were used. A rumor was started that the golden handshakes were not going to be offered for long; soon Roger would start firing outright. Managers were coached on how to broach the subject and how important the employee's sacrifices could be to the survival of their corporation. C-P-C group hired two outside firms, Bray and Associates and Drake, Beam, and Morin, to set up "persuasion shops." Individuals whom C-P-C wanted to get rid of were sent to their shops, where they received pep talks, brainwashing, and a lot of blue sky talk about exciting new careers.

In yoking executive bonuses to cost cutting, Roger had set up a contest among his executives to see how quickly, and how deeply, they could cut into their budgets and staffs. "The way it's set up," Roger explained, "if you meet and exceed your goals this year and the other fellow doesn't, you'll get not only your bonus but his bonus, too." With such incentives, some rather harsh actions were taking place. One director I knew at the Tech Center, for example, had only two years left before his retirement. He wanted a significant final bonus in the worst way, so he eliminated an entire communications department overnight (which made his budget look great), then hired an outside company to do the internal publications (which was easier to hide in the budget). Others I had heard of were eliminating vital ongoing programs, sending back equipment that had been ordered during last year's boom, and pushing many responsibilities from their area to anyone else's.

The new game plan was to do whatever it took to get work outside the door and eliminate head-counts. Pontiac Truck and Bus Group, in fact, went on strike because employees were being placed in different jobs without the proper compensations and laid off when those tasks were turned over to outside contractors. Truck sales were one of the few still bright spots on the market horizon, so the corporation decided to settle quickly, awarding $1.5 million to six hundred laid-off workers who had been admittedly mishandled in the rush to outsource jobs.

The worst excesses, however, were against salaried individuals who would not take the golden handshakes. Managers anxious to show results were resorting to clumsy and crude pressure tactics, such as loading the uncooperative individuals down with the dirtiest tasks they could find and openly humiliating them in front of fellow workers. The *Wall Street Journal* found an instance where groups of individuals were placed in rooms without phones or secretaries and given nothing to do for months as punishment for not leaving on cue. In another instance a manager placed the stubborn employee's desk in the hallway in front of his office where he could "keep an eye on him."

One victim of the purge was a man I knew well from my freelance speech writing with the outer divisions. His name was Joe, a down-to-earth guy who was fiercely loyal to his division, AC Spark Plug, and his company. Joe was told he would have to take early retirement "or else." But he couldn't afford it with two boys in college and his youngest about to enter that fall. The golden handshake would have provided only about half of the income he would receive by staying another five years. With 21 years at GM, he decided to tough it out. "Where is a 57-year-old automotive engineer going to start over in Michigan?" he asked. I talked to Joe several times during this period. I listened to his complaints about the subtle insults he was enduring, and I saw Joe change into an angry, vindictive man. "You know, I didn't talk to my own brother for a month once because he bought a Honda instead of a Chevy?" Joe said. "God, I was a damn fool. To think this company cared about anything but the quick buck was stupid as hell. I guess that's the part that gets me most—being played for such a sucker and breaking my butt for all those years for nothing." A five-minute phone conversation with Joe was enough to ruin my day, and after a while I started avoiding his calls.

Those who were in no immediate danger of being forced out were alienated by Roger's insensitivity. For example, the very week Roger announced the $5 billion stock buyback to appease the shareholders, he also announced that performance awards would be limited to 3.5 percent or less and given out in one lump sum so as not to increase any benefits. And at the Executive Management Conference, Roger did his traditional morale-buster routine by saying:

"There's no doubt in my mind that our salaried people, a lot of them, when we look at the spread, even allowing for the excellence of our people, are overpaid. We can't afford excess costs in salary any more than we can afford excess costs in paint."

Then, when fielding a question about bonuses, Roger added:

"Like all corporations, we must compete for executive talent in the market. And the employees [read senior executives] who contribute to the success of the business should participate in that success. . . . Omitting an earned bonus or a performance achievement award would not be considered a sign of strength, but of weakness."

The word spread quickly through the corporate ranks that Roger felt they were overpaid, while he and his top people had to receive massive rewards for their contributions. It was just one more downer in what had become an endless stream of negative news and implied insults from the chairman's office. The reaction was predictable. Talented young people openly discussed résumés and opportunities away from GM. Some of the best left, including Hulki Aldikacti, the creative engineer who had fathered the space-frame Fiero. Some seemed to become sluggish and disinterested under the stress, while others spent their time modifying old jokes for relief. "What's the most beautiful sight in the world? A bus of 14th-floor executives going over the cliff. What's the saddest sight? Roger Smith missing that bus." A common bit of billboard art was a toilet, with an arrow pointing into the bowl with the words: "You are here." A significant part of each day has been spent in a buddy's office or on the phone to co-workers, commiserating. One researcher at GMR labs told me, "Not a hell of a lot is getting done with so many people upset about wages, cuts, and rumors of worse to come."

About this time I was to do a Jim McDonald speech for an upcoming quality conference. The dramatic improvement in quality audits that had shown up after Jim's "I'm disappointed" talk was slipping away. At least one quality manager blamed the slippage on overall morale and on the fits of production starts and stops from an inconsistent manufacturing program. I decided that the issue of morale was the only subject worth addressing and wrote a note to Jim to that effect. It read in part:

> This is a critical juncture for quality. We've made a lot of progress, but quality numbers have begun to slip again in the past month. This could get worse if we don't deal with the issue of morale now. Morale is faltering and will logically drag quality and efficiency under with it. The sources of the devastation are many:
>
> - Executive bonuses at a time with no profit sharing.
> - Elimination of COLA for salaried people in place of "superior" reward system called Merit. Then Merit elimination.
> - RBS [Roger] statement at management conference that salaried ranks are overpaid, but we can't pay our senior executives enough.
> - Changes, and eliminations, of overtime pay.
> - Stock buyback, which is perceived as benefiting senior executives.
> - Threat of termination for 40,000 salaried people.
> - Plant closings with realization that quality-production plants are not exempt.
> - Constant media attention to GM's failures compared to Ford and Chrysler successes.

- New performance evaluation system that grades on a departmental curve.
- Visible fixation on the financial community, making it appear as if cost is, once again, GM's number-one operating priority.

Jim's response to my thematic suggestion was "I'm not the one to address that right now." He was only a few months from mandatory retirement age, and there was a strong rumor circulating that Roger had asked him about that time to leave early, but Jim had refused for fear the corporation's problems would then be blamed on him. As it was, his replacement would be named four months ahead of schedule "to facilitate a smooth transition." I sent a similar note of alarm over morale problems to Jack McNulty, a direct pipeline to Roger. There was no response.

A Detroit auto editor, recounting a few of these points to Roger in an interview that week, asked: "Do you [Roger] recognize this as at least an acknowledgment on the part of many people who once had faith in you that they don't have faith in you anymore or faith in your management style?" Roger dodged the question.

Going into the Annual Stockholders' Meeting in May, Roger was feeling supremely confident. He had the analysts in his camp, and GM stock was rising despite lackluster performance. The Perot buyout, as far as the people he was most concerned about were concerned, was a memory. He could shrug off internal problems by saying, "When you make changes, nobody likes it." And he could tell his executives, "We all would like to have moved further and faster, but I'm overall satisfied with where we are today."

The stockholders' meeting was held, as always, in the elegant Fisher Theatre across Grand Boulevard from the GM Building. There were picketers out front, mostly Flint factory workers demanding that GM be the 1987 strike target. One held a sign that said, "Hire Ross, Fire Roger." A small army of GM public relations people inside checked invitations and guided them through the palatial vestibule and to their seats. Roger came up the aisle with a rapid, let's-get-to-it gait. The massive two-minute clocks were illuminated to keep comments to Roger's limits. He spoke of sales and new products briefly, then opened up the mikes for comments.

The first stockholder was a young, suited man from a Washington, D.C., consumer group. He wasted no time saying: "Mr. Chairman, we respectfully request that when Ross Perot resigns that you resign with him." The applause was loud and sustained.

Roger had a rebuttal. "I get a lot of calls from people who believe in what we're doing," he said. "I got a call just the other day from a man who said, 'Roger, I hope you will keep going with the improvements. You know we live in an immediate gratification society, and everyone wants everything "right now."' But the caller said, 'I understand what you are doing, Roger, and I'm completely behind you.' That fellow who called, by the way, had three million shares in his proxy."

The next shareholder to speak was a GM skilled tradesman from Kansas City. He drew the same level of applause when he said, "We want you out of the job as chairman." When Roger tried to tell the man how many benefits he had working for General Motors, the tradesman said: "That's not something you gave us—it's something we took with a strong union." More applause.

Evelyn Y. Davis, the flamboyant corporate gadfly who attended numerous corporation meetings, a wiry little woman with a voice even higher and more offensive than Roger's, spoke next. She waved a greenmail envelope in the air, which she said contained $2 for Ross Perot. "That's all the money we should give him," she yelled. "I understand that he carried his own bags at airports to keep from paying a porter. That's how cheap he is," Ms. Davis screeched.

"That's not true," Roger snapped back, clearly irritated. "Ross Perot is a very generous man and a nice person. He has a fine record. I don't think it's fair to besmirch his record. I'm not going to allow anything bad to be said about him. He's a fine man."

Two other shareholders spoke after that, asking Roger to resign. He shrugged them off. He couldn't, however, avoid the resolutions to rescind the Perot buyout and change the bylaws to prevent further greenmail. The amendment to ban the Perot buyout received 20.1 percent of the votes cast. Considering that Roger had the proxies for the vast majority of votes represented at the meeting, 20.1 percent against him meant that the vast majority of those in personal attendance voted against him. That was a record in GM annual meeting history for a proposal opposed by management. It was an embarrassment for Roger, but hardly a defeat. He sailed through the meetings unscathed.

To top off the day's event and once again underscore his profit-first commitment, Roger announced the appointment of a new GM president, Robert Stempel. Bob Stempel is a highly qualified executive, a large man with a commanding voice and gentle ways. He was one of three good choices, but he had one aspect to his portfolio that the other competitors for the job lacked. Bob had made his mark in achieving cost efficiencies in the truck group and recently defined a major cost-cutting program, with major personnel reductions, for the European operations. Bob was known as the man who could squeeze costs out of the system, exactly the image Roger needed at the moment.

The new pattern was set for the remainder of the model year. Roger would keep repeating, "We are now in a position for maximum profitability," and GM stock would rise. GM sales, meanwhile, continued to slump, down 33.94 percent in May and a full 22 percent for the first full half of the '87 calendar year. GM's market share was down to 36 percent. Yet in perfect orchestration, the profits from the GM subsidiaries were announced as rising some 24.5 percent in the second quarter. GMAC led the pack with a 37.9 percent rise in profits. In every case of gains, business outside of the auto industry was the deciding factor. The auto plants, most of which had flexible technology to change over to new products in a matter of days, were shut down for extended summer model changeovers. Yet dealer inventories coming up on the end of the model year were at well over a million. Something had to be done. Roger approved 1.9 percent low-interest car loans or cash rebates on the slower-moving models.

The 1.9 percent was not a capitulation of Roger's commitment not to buy market share. The low interest rate was offered only on two-year sales contracts. The vast majority of buyers could not afford the monthly payments on two-year deals (on a $12,000 car they would top $550 a month). "It's a come-on," a Buick salesman explained. "It brings people into the dealership, but once they realize what's going on, they don't buy." The 1.9 deal had only a marginal impact on end-of-year sales, and GM went into the fall selling season with uncomfortably high stocks. Roger, however, stuck to his promise to let the market determine GM's market share, no matter what the consequences.

In Detroit, the news was beginning to shift to the grand center stage of union-auto contract talks, and Roger seemed to be backing out of the spotlight, at last. Ford and General Motors were both up for contracts, and the big guessing game in Detroit was which one of these companies the UAW would take on first and name as its strike target. The strategy traditionally was to pick the company that seemed as if it would be most cooperative, get a solid contract, then attempt to carry the same concessions to the non-strike target. All logic pointed at Ford as the strike target. Ford was in far better financial shape, had a far greater need to keep the factories open during a stable sales period, and Ford's leadership had been more than conciliatory in its opening remarks, emphasizing leadership's desire to negotiate an equitable agreement for all concerned. The problem, however, was that the rank-and-file union members wanted to strike GM.

"It doesn't matter which company is picked as the official strike target," Stan Marshall, UAW director, Flint, said. "GM is going to be the real target. Our people are mad, and they want revenge. No one is up there [on the 14th floor] worrying about the worker. Roger's doing everything for the stockholder now. So job security is the only issue. They're telling me, 'I don't care how long the strike takes; we must have security,' and they want it in writing. They're not going to trust Roger again."

As a gesture of resolve, on the first day of GM-UAW talks, 20 busloads of union workers showed up to picket the GM Building. As they marched peacefully around the square-block building, they vented their anger by chanting over and over: "One-two-three-four. Shove Roger off the 14th floor."

Roger, of course, was not helping matters. While Ford was making "Let's work this thing out" noises, Roger was making incredible new demands. He offered to freeze all UAW wages, but proposed a 2 percent lump-sum yearly payment, to eliminate COLA at noncompetitive component plants at the corporation's election, and to force all employees into health maintenance organizations that were far cheaper than Blue Cross and far less complete in their coverage. The contract proposal was so absurd that even GM's labor relations people did not want to distribute it to the press. "I understand their reluctance," Ephlin said. "There are penalties for passing out material that tends to incite people to riot."

Don Ephlin, who had been Roger's greatest ally, was both alienated and angered. He had done everything he could to establish cooperation, then was placed in an untenable position at the bargaining table. Despite Ephlin's pleas after that to make GM the strike target, the union decision went to Ford because, a union official said, Ford was willing to work with the union to resolve the job security issue. Ford workers, who had averaged $2,100 in 1986 in profit sharing and stood to make more in '87 if a strike was averted, were ready to negotiate. The GM workers, on the other hand, were angry. Ephlin expressed that GM-wide anger in saying, "We're not going to solve the problems by expecting the hourly work force to be scapegoats and pay the penalties for all the problems, which they did not create."

Feelings within GM were running high, and they were certain to influence the direction of the negotiations. It was the consensus among union people I talked to that striking back at Roger would be more a matter of personal dignity than of rational negotiation. The union leadership was playing back that concern, but with an offer, of sorts, to help. Don Ephlin was saying "I see our task [the UAW's] here at General Motors as trying to save General Motors for General Motors workers." Union president Owen Bieber opened with a frontal assault on Roger's "overpaid workers" argument. If GM was to survive,

Bieber said, the union would have to help manage the company. "Poor management, not excessive hourly pay, is the root of General Motors Corp.'s competitive problems."

Reason prevailed, and a cooperative Ford Motor Company was named as the first negotiations target. Ford and the UAW worked out a truly historic contract that shifted the traditional focus entirely from immediate rewards to long-term job security. Under the new contract, Ford could not arbitrarily eliminate its employees, and for every two employees retired or permanently laid off one would have to be rehired. That allowed downscaling, yet it also required, for the first time, that the company view the employees as fixed, permanent investments. Recognizing the cyclical nature of sales, the union agreed that plant closings during downturns were necessary and acceptable, provided the company brought back its people after the market recovered. While the contracts were historic for the American auto industry, the Japanese automakers yawned. Guaranteed employment was fundamental to their system, where it was regarded as the only way to enlist the workers' commitment to the achievement of common goals.

Roger's initial reaction to the Ford agreement was predictable. "GM cannot guarantee work in any real, meaningful amount because we are a cyclical industry. . . . If you want to guarantee 10 jobs, that's no problem. What good does that do anybody? If you're talking about a reasonable number of jobs, you've got to see where you are in your cycle." Roger chose to stick with the worker-commodity equation.

After the Ford ratification, however, it was clear GM had little choice but to follow suit. GM's third-quarter earnings were already predicted to be down 60 percent from the low third quarter of the previous year. GM was experiencing a larger proportionate drop in sales for the year than any other car maker, and modest incentives were not improving the picture. For GM to take on a prolonged strike would be devastating. The *Detroit Free Press* reported that about this time Don Ephlin met with Roger and reassured him that the Ford contract did have enough flexibility in it to be the model. Ephlin recognized that the Ford agreement alone would not be enough. The GM workers were angry, and Roger would have to stop publicly flogging the employees for all of GM's problems. Shortly thereafter, Roger changed his tune, saying the Ford pattern was a positive step and job guarantees would be acceptable.

In the end, GM ratified fundamentally the same contract negotiated with Ford. The difference was again one of perception. Ford leadership had begun negotiations in an atmosphere of cooperation and concern over the issue of job security, while Roger's posturing statements and late change of heart reaffirmed GM's hard line. At GM, the old adversarial relationship was apparent. It reminded me of the Flint worker at the annual meeting, who, when Roger told him of all the benefits GM had given workers, responded:

"You gave us nothing. Our union had to fight for everything we got."

11
The Reckoning

"Just judge me by the results; that will be good enough for me."

Roger Smith

Teh Saginaw Vanguard Plant was not of my experience. I had worked in factories for three years while in college and had visited dozens more as an auto and science writer. I knew what they were supposed to be like. This wasn't it. Everything was there—the presses and milling machines, the smell of scorched oil, the metal-bending cacophony. But it conjured an eerie image of an amusement park with the rides whirling and clanking but without the squeals and laughter. In place of the men and women at the machines, headless robots bobbed in and out of the breeches. In the aisles there were no reckless hi-lo jockeys to dodge, only odd driverless vehicles sliding effortlessly, emitting an intermittent high-pitched beep to warn people who were not there to hear. Everything was clean. Sterile. Where are the people?

Up in the glassed-in computer room the plant manager of the peopleless plant, Bob Zeilinger, explains: "All machines, robots, and AGVs are coordinated by the mainframe here." Zeilinger is young, lean, and intense, almost a stereotype of the precise research engineer that he is. "The assembly robots will have vision, but with accurate placement of parts in trays we don't need vision on the machining processes. Two system attendants [humans] load the trays at the dock, and from there they go into the plant and through the entire build without any human contact.

"The plant builds one complete trans-axle a minute, 1,440 a day," he says. "Not all the same trans-axle, either. The system can make five, ten, or a hundred of one kind, then change over to a different configuration in 10 minutes or less. All via the computer."

I ask if Saginaw is a "lights out" plant. He laughs. "I don't know who came up with the notion in the first place," Zeilinger says. "There're always going to be one or two people in the plant when it's operating, so we aren't going to turn out the lights and have them groping around in the dark. But calling it 'lights out' does get across the idea that the plant can operate unassisted."

You mean, without people? The ultimate factory of the future?

"No, not without people. Not completely. When we started this demonstration project in '82," Zeilinger says, "it was technology, technology, technology. Now the pendulum has swung the other way. We know we can't just clone this technology and put it into assembly plants or engine plants. It's not that easy. Most of this is maybe ten years out or more. Some suppliers who are working with us say it's 20 years into the future."

The graduating class of the year 2000 started kindergarten in the fall of 1987. The 21st-century corporation, with its factories of the future, is within sight.

"If we fall behind on this technological basis," Roger says, "the rest of the world is going to automate and go by us. That's why we built the Saginaw 'factory of the future.' If you don't have a computer working for you, there aren't any jobs. And I mean that. I'm absolutely convinced that if you don't stay on the front edge of technology you're going to get rolled over."

Roger has not swung the other way from "technology, technology, technology." He remains firmly committed to his 21st-century corporation and to a high-tech future for General Motors and American manufacturing. He has held to his vision and is driving GM further, faster in electronic technologies than any other major manufacturer in the world. But the question remains: At what price and with what profit?

It should be a relatively easy question to answer. Certainly, no industrialist in recent history has had such a well-defined goal or more favorable conditions to achieve it. "Ten years is certainly the factor," Roger said at his ascension in 1980. "I won't be able to look around and see anyone who came before me. After 10 years, everything I see will be mine." Besides a full decade to accomplish his singular goal, Roger was blessed with a rising economy after his first year in office—the longest period of uninterrupted economic growth since the 1960s. Thanks to a pro-industry administration in Washington, D.C., Roger had the advantage of a deregulated economy that encouraged capital formation, low interest rates, and minimal rate of inflation (so devastating to large-ticket items). Even Roger's primary competitors, the Japanese, cooperated by limiting their imports and acquiescing to the devaluation of the dollar. And Roger started with the full resources of the largest, and most consistently profitable, corporation in the automotive world—with more than twice the engineering and scientific talents of any other manufacturing company. Nor was this CEO shackled with a powerful and imposing board of directors. With billions of dollars in the GM Treasury Roger could determine his own course of action far less encumbered than any auto CEO since the free-wheeling 1950s. He had the time, the money, the people, and the power. Few quests have had as many advantages as Roger's.

The question, of course, is what Roger's leadership has done to—or for—General Motors. Where will GM's 21st-century corporation be after Roger's departure in 1990? There is no way to answer these questions with certainty until well after Roger leaves office. As Winston Churchill said, "It is a mistake to look too far ahead. The chain of destiny can only be grasped one link at a time." Yet Roger says the links to his 21st-century corporation are in place and that his plan has gone largely as he had anticipated. GM has virtually all-new assembly and stamping plants and new products moving out the door. The factory of the future is open and operational, and Roger's plans call for a quieter, yet decisive march in the direction of high technology. GM is more of a conglomerate than ever before, with profitable subsidiaries in finance, mortgages, aerospace, robotics, and computer services. If GM has given up entirely on both U.S. economy-car production and the heavy-truck industry, the company's continuing loss of market share is now part of the strategic plan for more profit from less production. Roger still has, in his own words, "the most complete plan for the future of any company around."

The temper of Roger's links to the future will be tested soon. Foreign companies are building new assembly facilities in the United States at unprecedented rates. There will be more than 60 assembly plants in America by 1990, and even with a booming economy it is abundantly clear that there will be major overcapacity. General Motors is already operating well below its current capacity of 5.5 million vehicles. Obviously, some companies are going to lose out in the ensuing competitive shuffle. And most economists say a recession is overdue. A typical recession—with the amplitude and duration equal to postwar averages—will cut another three million vehicle sales a year and could devastate the least-popular company products. There is no question with the overcapacity, even with good times, that some companies will falter. Roger says GM is prepared. Insiders say General Motors has never been as ill-prepared.

For in terms of leadership—defined by the Fortune Group of management consultants as "the skill of attaining predetermined objectives with and through the voluntary cooperation and effort of other people"—Roger's tenure has been a tragic era in General Motors history. No GM chairman has disrupted as many lives without commensurate rewards, has spent as much money without returns, or has alienated so many along the way. An endless string of public relations and internal relations insensitivities has confused his organization and complicated the attainment of its goals. Few employees believe that Roger is in the least concerned with their well-being, and even fewer below executive row anticipate any measure of respect, or reward, for their contributions. No GM chief executive's motives have ever been as universally questioned or his decisions as thoroughly mistrusted. Management, as Roger has said, "is not a popularity contest," but it is a performance contest that cannot be won without popular support.

Buying a Stradivarius does not make one an Isaac Stern. That is the lesson Roger has yet to learn. It is not a new lesson. In fact, it should have been learned once before, with an earlier GM factory of the future. In 1973, when the Arab oil embargo turned the auto industry upside down, General Motors was in the midst of a great experiment to become world competitive with the Japanese. It created a high-tech plant complex called Lordstown (Ohio) and installed the most advanced robotics of the time. It was building the "ultimate import fighter," the Chevrolet Vega. The vehicles, however, were poorly designed. The technology was so balky that an electrician had to be stationed next to each operating robot to fix it as it went down. Worse, the workers perceived robots as a threat to their jobs. They did not trust General Motors, and they had justification. Although car sales plummeted and massive layoffs were everywhere, GM's senior executives gave themselves handsome bonuses. The result was a full-scale worker revolt at Lordstown, with wildcat strikes, unprecedented absenteeism, as many grievances as employees, and acts of sabotage, including purposely set plant fires. Lordstown was a failure. The robots were removed, and the 100-cars-per-hour goal was reduced to 60 an hour.

Roger has often lamented the Lordstown experience. "One of the great regrets I have is that years ago," he says, "when we started Lordstown, we should not have given up on 100 cars an hour down there. . . . Now I know the software wasn't as reliable, but just think, if we had hung tough there, and gotten the plant to work right, we'd have been a lot more ahead of the game."

To Roger, the lesson of Lordstown was the failure of management in not adhering to the high-tech game plan—not "hanging tough." To many others, the lesson of Lordstown had very little to do with machines. It was about people. Lordstown was a failure in human relations. It was about leadership's insensitivity to a young, independent work force faced with an authoritarian management. The Third Wave of advanced electronics technology had begun, and Lordstown was the earliest auto industry example of leadership's failure to grasp the significance of the change.

The assumption that capital investments could directly replace labor costs was, at best, naive. The real lesson of the Third Wave of advanced electronics is that each individual's contribution is more important simply because the tools he or she is using require additional thinking and sophisticated skill levels. The average factory worker can no longer be trained on his job in five minutes. He must be able to monitor computers and robotics, keep statistical historiographs to chart performance and maintain quality, and have an understanding of both electronics and mechanics that would have been considered skilled-trades level not many years ago. The ever-increasing influx of new technologies also requires that the worker be more of a decision maker, both to maintain the fast-moving system and to suggest ways to refine it.

The major productivity improvements in virtually any technology come not with the initial invention, but through the process of continuous refinement. That nurturing has to come from the individual at the operational level, the person most directly involved with the day-in-and-day-out operation of the technology.

Alvin Toffler in *The Third Wave* suggests the outcome of the new age. "Democracy," he says, "burst forth only when the decision load suddenly swelled beyond the capacity of the old elite to handle it." In other words, a dramatically increased decision-making load brought on by advanced electronics will logically lead to a broadening of the decision-making base. The implication, Toffler suggests, is that "we may well be on the edge of another great democratic leap forward." Such a leap has already taken place in the industrial world with democratization of the workplace or, in auto industry jargon, "participatory management."

Small team concepts using continuous improvement methods have been demonstrated to improve performance as much as 50 percent beyond conventional authoritarian approaches. That improvement factor is far greater than any prediction of productivity gains through robotics technologies alone. The technology is needed, but it is only the tool in the hands of the workman. As Haruo Shimada, a Japanese labor expert, puts it: "Only people give wisdom to the machines."

Roger, however, remains convinced that capital can be substituted for labor in a direct improvement equation. This notion has absolutely fixated his gaze throughout his tenure. Yet Ford and Chrysler have higher labor rates (Ford at $27.12 per hour, Chrysler at $25.44 and GM at $24.00), and they have been able to vastly improve productivity without the level of technology GM has sought. Labor accounts for only about 35 percent of the cost of manufacturing a car, and with the benefit of participatory management these costs are being greatly offset in many companies with productivity gains.

It is simply wrong to say that American labor cannot compete in the world market. There are numerous examples of companies that are successfully competing even in markets that are saturated with foreign products. The Harley Davidson motorcycle company is one of the best examples. An entirely American-made product, it is successful against the Japanese cycle makers such as Honda, Kawasaki, Yamaha, and Suzuki. And Harley Davidson is a sought-after motorcycle even in Japan. I had the pleasure of meeting Vaughn L. Beals, chairman and CEO of Harley Davidson, at an international trade conference. He discounted the lower wage structure of the Japanese and Koreans entirely. In his speech he said:

"What it is is management—no more; no less," Beals says. "They [the Japanese] are outstanding professional managers who understand the business. . . . If we had the same labor rates as Japanese manufacturers, we still would be grossly noncompetitive if we failed to manage as well as they do," Beals said.

"Your workers can better solve their production problems than your engineers, and unless every employee is fully using his mind as well as his machine, it won't work. . . . But if you fully adopt their methods of operation, it will work. It will work in Detroit, Milwaukee, and Cleveland as well as it works in Tokyo, Japan."

Roger has been mouthing similar words—I wrote some of

them for him—yet they are not attached to any understanding of what it takes to relate to people. "What you have to do is get out and talk with them," Roger says. "All you have to do is explain things, and they'll understand." Roger appears to have as little understanding of the complexity of human relations as he had about technology readiness. Roger does not see any fundamental contradictions in the way he has related to the employees. Everything he has done, in Roger's perception, has been completely honest and within the rules of the game as he understands them. There is nothing wrong with taking benefits away from the lower-ranking employees while increasing those that go to the upper echelons. There is nothing wrong with transferring thousands of people out of the company and reducing their benefits without consulting them. There is nothing wrong with threatening people with loss of employment while asking them to "commit to the team."

To build the kind of trust that will be necessary for true team effort will require a couple of essentials. First, management has to make the initial moves. It must give before it can expect the employees to do the same. When workers make major pay and work concessions, as they did at GM in 1982, then see that added margin used to diversify into other businesses and for executive bonuses and perks ("braid for the general's caps," as Ross Perot would say), there is no reason to trust the glib offers of management-worker partnership. When management makes lowball offers to workers to see if management can get off cheaply, as GM did with the first compensation offers to GMISCA transferees, there is no reason for workers to believe that management is in any way paternal. Far from making the initial moves toward a trusting relationship, Roger has proven time and again that the them-against-us adversarial relationship remains firmly fixed in the GM corporate mind. Secondly, the trust must be built slowly over an extended period. *Kaizen*—continuous improvement cultures—take five years before enough trust is established for them to pay off. Trust is a radically new idea for the embattled auto workers. And, as Charles "Boss" Kettering, the former inventive genius of General Motors, used to say: "Ideas grow very much like plants. You have to sow the seed. Then, when the shoots first come through the ground, they are quite tender and vulnerable. The proper care of the plant in this state is very important, if it is to live and grow." During Roger's tenure, each time the shoots of cooperation began to break the surface and trust started to grow, Roger would make another colossally harsh statement or reduce a few benefits, thus stomping the frail seedling underfoot.

Yet, the seedlings are already implanted in GM soil. There are many super-perceptive leaders—in both management and labor—who could fairly rapidly turn the confrontation back toward cooperation. Whether that happens or not will depend on whom Roger backs as his successor.

Yet as Roger nears retirement in 1990, his corporate clout may wane. At least two board members have hinted that Roger may not have a free hand at championing his successor and that a shift to operating-side leadership is possible. If that happens, and the GM board exerts its responsibility of corporate governance, GM would make a significant step into the 21st century.

Roger has lost all credibility with his people. Until he steps down, there is little chance that genuine cooperation, based on trust and mutual respect, can take root in General Motors. The lesson of his leadership has been one that all American industry needs to note. High technology, without leadership, is actually counterproductive. Harley Shaikin, an MIT expert in labor and technology, has said it best:

"Success or failure is dependent not so much on the overall technological fireworks," Shaikin says, "as on the day-to-day operating decisions . . . the worst danger would be to combine the technology of the future with the industrial relations of the past."

That worst danger has been realized in Roger's chairmanship, and General Motors may struggle to the 21st century to overcome the experience.

Part of the failure has been Roger's inconsistent, and underwhelming, public image. "Roger will never look like a leader," an executive committee member told me, and certainly his appearance has worked against him. Roger is short, puffy-faced, with an unfortunate blotched complexion that telecasts his every mood and a high-pitched rasping voice that can be described in no other way but as annoying. Yet appearances alone do not explain his leadership failure, for a charismatic leader like Ross Perot certainly would not win any beauty contests. In a highly visual media society, appearance is a factor, but hardly a deciding leadership factor.

In a media-centered society, the role of public relations becomes a vital aspect of any corporate strategy. Sloan, however, created a culture in which the leaders were picked specifically for their lack of charisma, which, he felt, would get in the way of a committee policy making. Traditionally, GM has tended to ignore public opinion. Small heed was paid to the chairman's role as corporate spokesman, and even less, since Roger's ascension, to the public relations impact of each decision. As Bill Hoglund said, "We've had the worst kind of PR that any company could hope to have, questioning everything we've been doing. That just can't create the kind of teamwork we need to get ourselves out of this."

A financial background certainly worked against his leadership image. Even though Roger was as pro-technology as any graduate engineer, the perception of him as "the accountant" was an image he was not able to shake. And a certain measure of criticism for putting a financial man over a manufacturing and merchandising organization is justifiable. Roger's financial background and lack of any significant experience in a production setting left him ill-equipped to critically evaluate the high-tech projects laid out for his decision. He did not have new product start-up experience, for example, that would have told him that every new feature, machine, or untried process is a guarantee of additional delays and costs.

Roger's financial background had kept him away from working with ordinary people. He was raised and trained in the rarefied atmosphere of A-type personalities. Based on his narrow band of experience, he assumed that others were like him. Roger was one of the rare breed of individuals who thrive on constant change and can handle any number of unfamiliar tasks simultaneously. He did not—and does not—understand that the vast majority of people look for stability and consistency in their lives. If most aspects of life are stable, then the stability-oriented person can tackle new tasks, but throw too much at him, and you get a stress-point overload. Enough stress points and the average person buckles under, displaying performance loss and any number of stress-related ailments, from hives to heart attacks. In tearing up everything within GM at the same time, Roger all but paralyzed the majority of his people.

In Roger's favorite book, *An Inquiry into the Nature and Causes of the Wealth of Nations*, Adam Smith said that he felt the success of commerce came about because of the division of labor. Once individuals developed separate specialties, efficiencies and professionalism could increase productivity. Roger, however, was raised in an environment in which a select group of financial whiz kids were treated like Renaissance men, given brief assignments in every office and aspect of the business. Consequently, Roger believes that a solid financial man can do anything. There is no need for a marketing expert to run marketing, a public relations pro to oversee images, or an engineer to run the plant. An incursion of financial people into areas where they were clearly out of their element has hurt the corporation, and Roger's internal credibility as well.

All of these factors, however, pale against one inescapable fact. Roger is an elitist in an era of democratization in the workplace. His family upbringing and Sloan's rigorous succession process fostered a mind-set that placed him apart and above the hoi polloi. Decision after decision has demonstrated his unquestioned belief that success is dependent on the few and not the many. There are only two aspects of corporate life worth having—decision making and money. Roger has been unwilling to share either with the common worker. It is part of his management prerogative to unilaterally make decisions that affect tens of thousands, yet he is uncomfortable with the egalitarian premise that the man on the line should be allowed to decide on the best way to do his own job. Roger's $2 million a year is, in his perception, modest, while the $30,000 earned by a factory worker is unconscionable. He cannot truly believe, as Ross Perot so often says, that "the history of America's greatness is of common people accomplishing uncommon things."

If an individual feels good about himself or herself, and about the contribution made, then productivity will rise. Roger continues to dwell on the fact that GM loses $1 billion a year because of absenteeism. At NUMMI and under enlightened management systems, the absentee problem does not exist. People come to work because they want to come to work. They contribute because they are a part of something meaningful and rewarding.

Roger's stress on "overpaid workers" is both elitist and incredibly uninformed. For the unfortunate truth is that the good life in America is not nearly as good as it once was for most workers. While the typical worker has received a 7 percent increase in wages in this decade, that has been entirely counteracted by inflation. In reality, the worker is taking ever-increasing pay cuts. Real wages—as defined by buying power—in 1986 were back to 1969 levels. Today, the combined take-home pay of a husband and wife working is about what each of their respective fathers alone earned at a similar age. What is needed is not leaders who would rise higher by pressing their people lower, but enlightened management that respects, and rewards, ever-increasing individual contributions.

Roger's vision of the 21st-century corporation was half of a very good idea. Technology is the future; the Saginaw factory of the future is inevitable. But the other half of the equation— by far the more significant half—is the individual. A Stradivarius is only wood and catgut; the music is in the mind and hands of the performer. Getting three million people to perform in harmony is GM's ultimate task. When that happens, it will truly be a cultural revolution. But that will happen only when a leader arises within the corporation who can establish trust and inspire commitment. As Alvin Toffler said in *The Third Wave*:

"Elites, no matter how enlightened, cannot by themselves make a new civilization. The energies of whole peoples will be required."

Epilogue

On January 5, 1988, General Motors invited 14,000 guests to the Waldorf Astoria in New York to see an exhibit called "GM Teamwork and Technology, Today and Tomorrow."

The three-day exhibit, ordered by Roger Smith in late October and prepared in feverish haste by GM's design and public relations people at a cost of $20 million was intended to impress Wall Street financial analysts, GM dealers, suppliers, employees, and stockholders. A select group of journalists were allowed entry. The public was not invited.

One entire wall of the Waldorf's elegant ballroom was covered by a computer-choreographed display of 240 television screens. "It's really spectacular," said John McNulty, vice president for public relations. "In one corner you'll have 40 screens of a guy's head talking. All around him will be shots of workers getting retraining . . . It's very high-tech, very avant-garde."

But the main attraction was a series of concept cars, hand built by the design department to show off future trends in styling and GM's commitment to high technology.

A car called the Cadillac Voyage, a foot longer and wider than the current Seville, was crammed with high-tech electronic accessories such as a TV camera in the trunk and cathode ray tube in the dash replacing the simple rearview mirror. Another screen displayed an inertial navigation system fed by a satellite in outer space which continuously tracked the car's position on a moving map.

The Chevrolet Venture, a $15,000 car for the mid-1990s, featured a voice-recognition system that enabled the owner to operate a radio or cellular phone without touching any buttons.

Even more futuristic was the SRV-I, a fantasy concept from the design studio that had no steering wheel. Instead, a pair of joysticks similar to those in a helicopter would activate electric motors to steer the wheels.

Reactions were not enthusiastic. *Detroit Free Press* columnist Paul Lienert said, "it was almost as if Smith—the Motor City's answer to Rodney Dangerfield—was begging for respect." In the *Chicago Tribune*, Jim Mateja wrote that Roger looked like General Custer surveying the horizon then saying "What Indians?" GM dealers complained of loss of competitive position and asked for price concessions to meet the thrust of Ford and Chrysler.

But it was Roger Smith who provided the most memorable quote. At a news conference for 300 reporters, he was asked what GM had to compete against Chrysler's Dodge Aries and Plymouth Reliant cars, priced at $6,995.

"Our best competition in General Motors right now happens to be a two-year-old Buick," Roger responded.

Appendix

PROFIT MARGINS
Net Income as a Percentage of Sales and Revenues

	1981	1982	1983	1984	1985	1986	1987*
GM	0.5	1.6	5.0	5.4	4.1	2.9	3.6
Ford	−2.8	−1.8	4.2	5.6	4.8	5.4	7.0
Chrysler	−4.8	1.7	5.3	12.2	7.7	6.2	5.1

*First Three Quarters

GM MARKET SHARE
U.S. Passenger Car/Sales

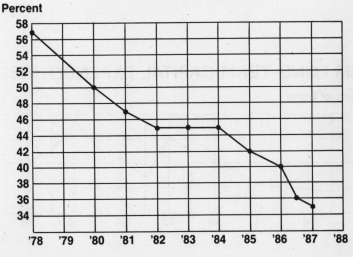

SHAREHOLDER EARNINGS
One Share of Common Stock

	1981	1982	1983	1984	1985	1986
GM	1.07	3.09	11.84	14.27	12.28	8.21
Ford	−3.91	−2.43	6.86	10.53	9.09	11.65
Chrysler	−4.79	1.23	3.86	12.59	9.38	9.47

COMMON STOCK PRICES
End of Year Figures

	1981	1982	1983	1984	1985	1986	1987
GM	39.75	61.00	74.18	77.63	70.88	66.88	61.50
Ford	7.67	16.89	28.25	29.75	38.33	57.63	76.50
Chrysler	2.50	10.58	18.58	20.92	30.58	37.75	22.12

GM LONG-TERM CAPITAL EXPENDITURES

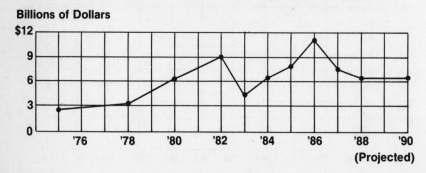

COMBINED U.S. SALES FOR CARS AND TRUCKS
January–November 1987

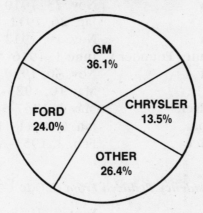

General Motors Chairmen

(No chairman from founding in 1908 to restructuring in 1912)

Thomas Neal	Nov. 19, 1912–Nov. 16, 1915
Pierre S. duPont	Nov. 16, 1915–Feb. 7, 1929
Lammot duPont	Feb. 7, 1929–May 3, 1937
Alfred P. Sloan, Jr.	May 3, 1937–April 2, 1956
Albert Bradley	April 2, 1956–Aug. 31, 1958

Chairmen/CEOs

Frederic G. Donner	Sept. 1, 1958–Oct. 31, 1967
James M. Roche	Nov. 1, 1967–Dec. 31, 1971
Richard C. Gerstenberg	Jan. 1, 1972–Nov. 30, 1974
Thomas A. Murphy	Dec. 1, 1974–Dec. 31, 1980
Roger B. Smith	Jan. 1, 1981–

GM Presidents

George E. Daniels	Sept. 22, 1908-Oct. 20, 1908
William M. Eaton	Oct. 20, 1908-Nov. 23, 1910
James J. Storrow	Nov. 23, 1910-Jan. 26, 1911
Thomas Neal	Jan. 26, 1911-Nov. 19, 1912
Charles W. Nash	Nov. 19, 1912-June 1, 1916
William C. Durant (Founder)	June 1, 1916-Nov. 30, 1920
Pierre S. duPont	Nov. 30, 1920-May 10, 1923
Alfred P. Sloan, Jr.	May 10, 1923-May 3, 1937
William S. Knudsen	May 3, 1937-Sept. 3, 1940
Charles E. Wilson	Jan. 6, 1941-Jan. 26, 1953
Harlow H. Curtice	Feb. 2, 1953-Aug. 31, 1958

Presidency Reduced From CEO to COO

John F. Gordon	Sept. 1, 1958-May 31, 1965
James M. Roche	June 1, 1965-Oct. 31, 1967
Edward N. Cole	Nov. 1, 1967-Sept. 30, 1974
Elliott M. Estes	Oct. 1, 1974-Jan. 31, 1981
F. James McDonald	Feb. 1, 1981-Aug. 31, 1987
Robert Stempel	Sept. 1, 1987-

A Short History of General Motors

General Motors is the largest vehicle manufacturing corporation in the world, accounting for 21 percent of all world car sales and approximately 38 percent of all American passenger car sales.

William "Billy" Durant founded General Motors. A self-made man and super salesman, Durant had created the largest carriage manufacturing company in the United States, Durant-Dort, and was asked to take over management of the faltering Buick Motor Company in Flint, Michigan. Within four years he made Buick the largest-selling nameplate in America, then went on to foster a consolidation of auto manufacturers.

Using Buick as the base, Durant incorporated General Motors Company on Sept. 16, 1908. Within months, Durant purchased Oldsmobile Motor Vehicle Co., Cadillac Automobile

Co., and Oakland Motor Car Co. (later renamed Pontiac Motor Division), thus quickly assembling all of the current GM car divisions except Chevrolet and Saturn Corp. Durant also negotiated to buy Ford Motor Company in 1908, but at the last moment Henry Ford backed out of the deal. Shortly thereafter, Durant bought now extinct car companies with the names of Rapid, Welch, Ewing, Elmore, Rainier, Reliance, Marquette, and Cartercar. While unable to buy the Champion Spark Plug Company, Durant persuaded Albert Champion to join General Motors and start AC Spark Plug Division. Within two years of GM's founding, Durant had purchased a dozen vehicle manufacturing companies and two dozen parts supplier firms.

In 1910, Durant's rapid expansion caused a financial crisis within the corporation. A group of eastern bankers headed by James Storrow of the Lee-Higgenson investment house agreed to refinance General Motors, but only if Durant resigned. Storrow became a caretaker president. Without Durant, General Motors quickly reorganized. Two respected auto men were placed in charge of the Detroit operations, Charles Nash as president, and Walter P. Chrysler in charge of production (both men would later establish companies in their own names). The less profitable car lines such as Cartercar, Elmore, Marquette, and Welch were dropped, leaving only the four largest divisions. The corporation began making significant profits and returning all bank loans well ahead of schedule.

Durant was not through yet. He fostered a new consortium of companies by either purchasing them or founding them, which included the Mason Motor Company, Little, Republic, Monroe, and finally Chevrolet. The last was the most successful, and with Chevrolet stock and his own fortunes, Durant bought GM stock until he had controlling interest in the corporation. He was aided in his takeover by a new investor, Pierre duPont of the wealthy chemical empire. By 1916 Durant was again in control of General Motors. He fired Charles Nash, reorganized GM as a corporation, and went on another expansion binge. He bought Dayton Engineering Laboratories, bringing Charles F. "Boss" Kettering's inventive genius into GM. He then bought the Scripps-Booth and Sheridan car com-

panies, Fisher Body, and companies in other fields including
Frigidaire, Dayton-Wright Airplane, and Sieve-Gril Tractor,
makers of the Samson farm tractor. In 1919, Durant also
started construction of the largest office building in the world
at the time, the General Motors Building in Detroit.

Samson Tractor failed, and a post-World War I recession
again placed General Motors in financial difficulties in 1920.
GM stock was falling, and Durant bought all of the stock on
margin to save the corporation. Bankers again entered to save
the organization. This time, however, all of Durant's fortunes
were consumed by selling out his interest to the bankers, and
he was ousted for the last time.

Pierre duPont took charge and brought in Donaldson Brown
to handle the corporation's finances. Brown did much to establish a financial philosophy at General Motors, including the
"standard volume" approach to pricing—a system based on
annual production figures plus a 20 percent return on investment. Disinterested in auto making, duPont backed out of
daily operation in 1923 yet remained a major stockholder and
board of directors' chairman. duPont placed an engineer,
Alfred P. Sloan, Jr., a former executive of a supplier company
Durant had bought, as president and chief executive officer of
the corporation.

Sloan served first as president, then later as chairman of the
board from 1923 through 1956. He is considered the one
individual who most developed the GM approach and philosophy. He first assumed a leadership role in 1921, the first year
that GM reported a loss. Unable to compete on price alone
against Ford Motor Company, Sloan established the strategy of
selling cars at the top of each price range, competing in quality against less expensive cars and in price against cars slightly
above GM's. "A car for every purse and purpose" became the
GM slogan.

Sloan's management philosophy, borrowed largely from the
German army, consisted of decentralized operations and responsibilities with coordinated controls. Each division re-
tained a high degree of autonomy, with the central GM board
setting guidelines and policies. This became known as the
"GM Management System" and has been widely copied in the

corporate world and held up as the standard in academic circles.

Annual model changes, later called *planned obsolescence*, was another Sloan innovation. He felt changing models each year would make a car "out of date within four to five years, thus creating a market for repeat sales. The annual changes not only worked to sell cars but also helped eliminate competition among smaller companies unable to afford the near-constant redevelopment and retooling costs.

In pursuing his philosophy of tightly bracketed markets for each car line, Sloan inspired a number of new lines. In the mid-twenties, each division was ordered to come out with a companion line that would fill in the price gaps. Thus were fostered Buick's Marquette, Cadillac's LaSalle, Oldsmobile's Viking, and Oakland's Pontiac. Of these, only Pontiac was successful and survived even its parent division in the Great Depression. Until Saturn cars are sold, Pontiac remains the only current car company ever created by General Motors.

By the end of the 1920s General Motors was taking the lead in the auto industry. General Motors sold more cars from 1928 onward than any other company. Ford Motor Company, having held on to the Model T design for too long, lost its dominance. General Motors reached a high point in 1929, selling more than 3.8 million cars.

The Great Depression did not overwhelm General Motors. Able to cut back production every year except 1932, and with nonautomotive profits offsetting vehicle sales losses, the corporation closed even 1932 in black ink. Also, by maintaining profits during the difficult Depression years, General Motors was able to buy into numerous industries and diversify itself for even greater security. GM entered the heavy diesel engine field by buying Winton Engine Company in 1930 and through it became the largest manufacturer of railroad locomotive engines. And GM became a leader in aviation through its acquisition of Allison Engineering in 1929. Also, GM bought 24 percent of Bendix Aviation Corp. and 40 percent of Fokker Aircraft Corp. of America in 1929.

Always conservative, General Motors' car divisions were not noted for tremendous innovations in the 1930s. More innovation came in the 1940s first with the Hydra-matic transmission introduced on Oldsmobile 1940 models (the first completely automatic shift transmission). High-compression V-8 engines, a GM innovation in 1948, were possible thanks to an earlier Charles Kettering invention, leaded gasoline. Also to influence the 1950s was GM's styling chief Harley Earl's creation of the tailfin look for the 1948 Cadillac, which fostered the fin craze (considered by many to be the ultimate example of automotive opulence and design absurdity).

In the mid-1950s an all-out price war among the big three— GM, Ford, and Chrysler—eliminated the last vestiges of broad-based competition. Companies merged, such as Kaiser-Frazer and Willys-Overland, Packard with Studebaker, and Hudson with Nash. All but one, the Hudson-Nash merger, which created American Motors Corporation, soon disappeared. American Motors limped on for another twenty years before selling out to Renault of France, then to Chrysler Corporation in 1987. From this massive industry shake-out, General Motors benefited most in sales and earnings. In 1955 GM became the first corporation in the world to earn more than $1 billion in a single year. On that high point, Sloan would retire from the chairmanship in April 1956.

Producing more than 60 percent of all U.S. cars in the late 1950s, GM became the center of federal government attention. There was much talk about antitrust action to break up the giant corporation. Partly in response to this, General Motors began a twenty-year process of corporate integration. Divisions lost their separate status, becoming manufacturing operations for parts used in all divisions and marketing organizations for nameplates the car divisions had little control in designing.

While GM escaped disassembly, it was affected by the turbulence of the 1960s as consumer groups invaded stockholder meetings to protest exorbitant profits and the federal government began regulating the automakers on safety, emissions, worker health standards, and later on fuel economy.

During this period there was a growing economy-car market that General Motors largely ignored, except for the 1960 Corvair compact and the 1971 Vega. Instead, GM emphasized the full-sized cars that grew much larger with each model year. In 1973 the large-car market received a death blow. The Arab oil embargo cut off fuel supplies to the United States for months, making oil prices rise at an alarming rate. The government warned of dependency on foreign oil as both an economic and a military danger and launched regulations to achieve energy independence.

Under Gerstenberg's and Murphy's chairmanships, General Motors proved that it could be responsive, if not bold. GM led the auto industry in downsizing its mass-volume cars, while the other U.S. automakers resisted the new direction, holding tenaciously to their big-car strategies for as long as possible. GM began by downsizing its full-sized cars in 1977, a move that achieved the industry's highest percentage improvement in fuel economy averages but hurt the corporation in the marketplace. The demand for economy cars dwindled in 1978 as the price of fuel stabilized. Then, in 1979, Iran led another oil boycott, turning the market back to the economical models and rewarding GM for its efforts. Tom Murphy, GM chairman at the time, referred to 1979 as "the year the shah left town." The disruption in the Middle East caught a shaky U.S. economy and plunged it into a major recession, the deepest since the Great Depression. It was at the lowest point in the recession in 1981, with GM recording only its second year of losses in its seventy-three-year history, that Roger Bonham Smith became GM chairman of the board and chief executive officer.

Index

$20.00
338.7   Lee, Albert
Lee   Call me Roger

13 6/90

$20.00
338.7   Lee, Albert
Lee   Call me Roger

JUL 18   44438

Cranford Public Library
224 Walnut Ave.
Cranford, N. J.
Tel. 276-1826